Psychology Revivals

New Developments in Analytical Psychology

Originally published in 1957, *New Developments in Analytical Psychology* built on the work of C.G. Jung. Jung's researches into the unconscious had led him to study the history of religion and the hitherto little understood psychology of alchemy; they had directed him away from child psychology and also, in later years, away from clinical analysis as well. Nonetheless his discoveries and theories have essential relevance in both these spheres.

All the papers in this volume complement and amplify Jung's work. The author made a special study of child analysis and ego development and here publishes his conclusions in a series of papers. The studies of children led to developments in analytic techniques which are worked out in a longer essay on the transference, to the understanding of which analytical psychology has a unique contribution; they have also stimulated a reassessment of the relation between the concept of archetypes and modern theories of heredity, instinct, neurophysiology, and evolution, in which there had been much misunderstanding at the time.

Michael Fordham was the last of the founders of a movement in psychoanalysis, and pioneered the Jungian analysis of children. This significant, early work can now be read and enjoyed in its historical context.

New Developments in Analytical Psychology

Michael Fordham

LONDON AND NEW YORK

First published in 1957
by Routledge and Kegan Paul Ltd

This edition first published in 2013 by Routledge
27 Church Road, Hove, BN3 2FA

Simultaneously published in the USA and Canada
by Routledge
711 Third Avenue, New York, NY 10017

Routledge is an imprint of the Taylor & Francis Group, an informa business

© by Michael Fordham

All rights reserved. No part of this book may be reprinted or reproduced or
utilised in any form or by any electronic, mechanical, or other means, now
known or hereafter invented, including photocopying and recording, or in any
information storage or retrieval system, without permission in writing from the
publishers.

Publisher's Note
The publisher has gone to great lengths to ensure the quality of this reprint but
points out that some imperfections in the original copies may be apparent.

Disclaimer
The publisher has made every effort to trace copyright holders and welcomes
correspondence from those they have been unable to contact.

A Library of Congress record exists under LC control no.: 58000547

ISBN: 978-0-415-83200-7 (hbk)
ISBN: 978-0-203-42808-5 (ebk)

NEW DEVELOPMENTS IN
ANALYTICAL PSYCHOLOGY

By the same author
THE LIFE OF CHILDHOOD

NEW DEVELOPMENTS IN ANALYTICAL PSYCHOLOGY

by
MICHAEL FORDHAM
M.D., M.R.C.P., F.B.Ps.S.

Foreword by
C. G. JUNG

Routledge and Kegan Paul
LONDON

First published 1957
by Routledge and Kegan Paul Ltd.
Broadway House, Carter Lane, E.C.4
Printed in Great Britain
by Western Printing Services Ltd.
Bristol

© *by Michael Fordham*

CONTENTS

Preface	ix
Foreword by C. G. Jung	xi
1. Biological Theory and the Concept of Archetypes	1
2. Reflections on the Archetypes and Synchronicity	35
3. Reflections on Image and Symbol	51
4. Notes on the Transference	62
5. The Origins of the Ego in Childhood	104
6. Some Observations on the Self and the Ego in Childhood	131
7. Child Analysis	155
8. Note on a Significance of Archetypes for the Transference in Childhood	181
9. A Child Guidance Approach to Marriage	188
Index	199

v

LIST OF PLATES

(between pages 144 *and* 145*)*

1. The Golden Rain
2. The Conjunction of Opposites
3. A Developing Mandala
4. The Final Mandala

PREFACE

ORIGINALLY I approached analytical psychology from the biological sciences with a special interest in physiology, neurology and psychiatry. The first chapter in the present work attempts to define the relation between these disciplines and the concept of unconscious archetypes, which often gets formulated so as to violate well-established biological theory. I hope to have gone somewhere towards showing that the separate disciplines need not come into conflict. The subsequent essays show the directions in which my ideas have developed as the result of embarking on studies in analytical psychology.

The title *New Developments in Analytical Psychology* is justified by the fact that a series of observations in child psychology, made many years ago, have led me to something approaching a general view of child analysis and ego development; one consequence has been to emphasize the correctness of Jung's classical concept of individuation as a manifestation of the second half of life. The other significant development has arisen out of the first: I have come to lay far greater emphasis on the transference and its correlate the counter-transference than has been current among analytical psychologists. This emphasis, essential in child analysis, gradually appeared equally important in the analysis of every age group; I have now found it possible to express my views on this topic in the form of notes; a more systematic account of this complex subject continues to defy adequate description. It will be clear that the volume does not aim at covering all the new developments in analytical psychology. Both Jung himself and others are engaged in fundamental research work and an increasing number are applying his concepts in many different fields. The new developments refer only to those in which I have taken a special part.

ix

FOREWORD

by C. G. Jung

IT is not easy to write a foreword to a book consisting of a collection of essays, especially when each essay requires one to take up an attitude or stimulates the reader into discursive comments. But this is just what Dr. Fordham's papers do: every single one of them is so carefully thought out that the reader can hardly avoid holding a conversation with it. I do not mean in a polemical sense, but rather in the sense of affirmation and in the desire to carry the objective discussion a stage further and collaborate on the solution of the problems involved. Opportunities for such enjoyable dialogues are unfortunately rather rare, so that one feels it as a distinct loss when one has to forgo them. A foreword ought not to make remarks to the author and, so to speak, buttonhole him for a private conversation. It ought, rather, to convey to the reader something of the impressions which the writer of the foreword received when reading the manuscript. If I may be forgiven a somewhat frivolous expression, the foreword should be content with the role of an intellectual apéritif.

Thus I can confess myself grateful for the stimulation the book has brought me, and salute the author's collaboration in the field of psychotherapy and analytical psychology. For in this territory questions arise of a practical and theoretical kind, which are so pifficult to answer that they will continue to exercise our minds for a long time to come. Above all I would like to draw attention to Dr. Fordham's discussion of the problem of synchronicity, first mooted by me and now dealt with by him in a masterly manner. I must rate his achievement all the higher because it demands not only understanding, but courage too, not to let oneself be prevented from going more deeply into this problem by the prejudices of our intellectual compeers. Also I must acknowledge that the

FOREWORD

author has in no wise succumbed to the very understandable temptation to underestimate the problem, to pass off one's own lack of comprehension as the stupidity of others, to substitute other terms for the concepts I have proposed and to think that something new has been said. Here Dr. Fordham's feeling for essentials is confirmed in the finest way.

The paper on the transference merits attentive reading. Dr. Fordham guides his reader through the multifarious aspects of this 'problem with horns'—to use an expression of Nietzsche's—with circumspection, insight, and caution, as befits this in every respect delicate theme. The problem of the transference occupies a central position in the dialectical process of analytical psychology and therefore merits quite special interest. It makes the highest demands not only on the doctor's knowledge and skill but also on his moral responsibility. Here the truth of the old alchemical dictum is proved yet again: 'ars totum requirit hominem' (the art requires the total man). The author takes full account of the overriding importance of this phenomenon and accordingly devotes to it a particularly attentive and careful exposition. The practising psychologist would be very wrong if he thought he could dismiss general considerations of this kind based on broader principles, and dispense with all deeper reflection. Even if psychotherapy admits of numerous provisional and superficial solutions in practice, the practising analyst will nevertheless come up against cases from time to time that challenge him as a man and a personality in a way that may be decisive. The usual interim solutions and other banal expedients, such as appeals to collective precepts, which are invariably constructed with 'must' or 'ought', then have a habit of breaking down, and the question of ultimate principles, or of the ultimate meaning of the individual, arises. This is the moment when dogmatic tenets and pragmatic rules of thumb must make way for a creative solution issuing from the total man, if his therapeutic endeavours are not to get miserably silted up and stuck. In such cases he will need reflection and will be thankful to those who have been far-sighted enough to struggle for an all-round understanding.

For it is not only a routine performance that is expected of the analyst, but also a readiness and ability to master unusual situations. This is particularly true of psychotherapy, where in the last analysis we are concerned with the whole of the human person-

FOREWORD

ality and not merely with life in its partial aspects. Routine cases can be disposed of in a variety of ways—with good advice, with suggestion, with a bit of training, with confession of sin, with any more or less plausible system of views and methods. It is the uncommon cases that set us the master test, by forcing us into fundamental reflections and demanding decisions of principle. From this vantage point we shall then discover that even in ordinary cases there is adumbrated a line that leads to the central theme, namely the individuation process with its problem of opposites.

This level of insight cannot be reached without the dialectical discussion between two individuals. Here the phenomenon of the transference forcibly brings about a dialogue that can only be continued if both patient and analyst acknowledge themselves as partners in a common process of approximation and differentiation. For, in so far as the patient frees himself from his infantile state of unconsciousness and its restrictive handicaps, or from its opposite, namely unbounded egocentricity, the analyst will see himself obliged to diminish the distance between them (hitherto necessary for reasons of professional authority), to the degree that it does not prevent him from displaying that measure of humanity which the patient needs in order to assure himself of his right to exist as an individual. Just as it is the duty of parents and educators not to keep children on the infantile level but to lead them beyond it, so it is incumbent on the analyst not to treat patients as chronic invalids but to recognize them, in accordance with their spiritual development and insight, as more or less equal partners in the dialogue, with the same rights as himself. An authority that deems itself superior, or a personality that remains *hors concours*, only increases the patient's feeling of inferiority and of being excluded. An analyst who cannot risk his authority will be sure to lose it. In order to maintain his prestige he will be in danger of wrapping himself in the protective mantle of a doctrine. But life cannot be mastered with theories, and just as the cure of neurosis is not, ultimately, a mere question of therapeutic skill, but is a moral achievement, so too is the solution of problems thrown up by the transference. No theory can give us any information about the ultimate requirements of individuation, nor are there any recipes that can be applied in a routine manner. The treatment of the transference reveals in a

FOREWORD

pitiless light what the healing agent really is: it is the degree to which the analyst himself can cope with his own psychic problems. The higher levels of therapy involve his own reality and are the acid test of his superiority.

I hope Dr. Fordham's book, which is distinguished for its farsightedness, carefulness, and clarity of style, will meet with the interest it so much deserves.

June 1957   C. G. JUNG

I

BIOLOGICAL THEORY AND THE CONCEPT OF ARCHETYPES[1]

INTRODUCTION

JUNG is commonly numbered among those who, by postulating a psychic basis for their researches, have broken loose from their biological foundations. It is therefore significant that in a recent publication he writes:[2]

The fact that all the psychic processes accessible to our observation and experience are somehow bound to an organic substrate indicates that they are articulated with the life of the organism as a whole and therefore partake of its dynamism—in other words, they must have a share in its instincts or be in a certain sense the result of the action of those instincts.

The relation of the archetypes to instinct and indeed to biological theory as a whole is usually considered a dull subject owing to the gap between biological and analytical concepts. But even if this be so, and even if the gap between the two disciplines seems wide, there is every reason to review its extent from time to time. Before going on to see where biological studies seem to reach out towards the study of archetypes it is first desirable to define what is meant by the term.

[1] Part of this paper was read at a symposium on 'Archetypes and Internal Objects' at the Medical Section of the British Psychological Society. It was published as 'The Reality of Archetypes' in the *British Journal of Medical Psychology*, Vol. XXII, Parts 1 and 2, 1949, pp. 3–7.

[2] 'The Spirit of Psychology' in *Spirit and Nature*, New York, 1954; London, 1955, pp. 391–2.

B

BIOLOGICAL THEORY AND CONCEPT OF ARCHETYPES

Definition of Archetypes and Collective Unconscious

In 1936 Jung published a paper[3] presenting his developed argument on the existence of archetypes, and the ideas he there elaborated form a convenient point of departure, since he sets out his argument concisely. It is interesting to study the form of presentation, which will be followed here, though other material and arguments will be added as occasion demands. He begins by defining his conception of the collective unconscious. Its phenomena are, unlike repressed personal material, transpersonal; unlike repressed contents, which have once been conscious, they have never been conscious before but emerge *de novo* from the collective unconscious to be represented there as archetypal images. Jung remarks in justification of his view that 'The hypothesis of a collective unconscious is, therefore, just about as daring as the assumption that there are instincts.'[4] These are likewise unconscious in their functioning and transcend personal consideration.

The theory of the collective unconscious and so of its organs, the archetypes, is based upon the notion that the fundamental structure of the psyche is uniform and that in the last resort, if we could eliminate the conscious, there would be little or no difference between one human being and another. There is therefore an 'X', psychic[5] but unconscious in its nature, out of which consciousness grows. This 'X' is the precursor of dream and fantasy. When it appears in imagery, it seems to be the expression in consciousness of instinct; but it always adds something else which is not, and never has been, exactly defined, and which is, and always has been, referred to in such terms as 'spirit', 'pneuma', or 'numinosum'.

With the distinction between the personal and collective unconscious in mind, Jung proceeds to criticize Freud's discussion of Leonardo da Vinci's picture 'St. Anne with Mary and the Christ Child'. Freud explains the picture on the basis that

---

[3] 'The Concept of the Collective Unconscious', *St. Bartholomew's Hospital Journal*, Vol. XLIV, No. 3, 1936, pp. 46–9. Jung also includes heredity in his definition. For reasons which will appear later I have omitted it.

[4] Ibid., p. 47.

[5] Jung later questioned its psychic nature and referred to the 'psychoid archetype'. Cf. 'The Spirit of Psychology', *Spirit and Nature*, New York, 1954; London, 1955.

BIOLOGICAL THEORY AND CONCEPT OF ARCHETYPES

Leonardo actually had two mothers; Jung refutes this by asserting that the dual mother theme is widespread[6] and embraces the motif of rebirth, the dual descent or the twice born, in which the culture hero has a double birth, one human and the other divine. In his paper Jung gives as examples of this widespread belief, the figures of Heracles, the Pharaohs and Jesus, and underlines it by recording that the rebirth ritual was used as a magical means of healing at the 'first beginning of medicine'; it is also found in mysticism, in the infantile fantasy of today, and is the central idea of mediaeval occult philosophy. Consequently '. . . it is absolutely out of the question that all the individuals who believe in the dual descent have in reality always had two mothers . . .'.[7]

Next Jung turns to the neuroses where the same theme, which the patient appears to believe is the cause of the disorder, is found. On Freud's theory it would be necessary to assume that the patient is right in his delusion of having two mothers though in fact he had only one. If, however, fantasy stems from archetypal activity, not only does it begin to make sense, but it follows that the neurosis under review is not a personal but a collective manifestation.

The importance Jung gives to this argument is well known, since it is repeated again and again in his work. Its significance not only stems from the distinction between subjective, or personal, and collective, objective, or transpersonal notions and experiences, but also because it ran counter to scientific philosophy.

Freud had been studying the phenomena of the unconscious in terms of his theory of repression. He studied the products historically and personalistically, and in doing so fell into line with the current view of the mind as an ontogenetic phenomenon, acquired in the course of personal and individual development, the product of nurture and not of nature. This concept ran through the scientific philosophy of the nineteenth century and, though such an eminent neurologist as Hughlings Jackson rejected it, only in recent years has it become generally questioned. Jung was therefore putting forward a revolutionary idea which cut right across this 'scientific' assumption of the period in which

[6] Cf. 'The Dual Mother', *Symbols of Transformation* (Collected Works, Vol. V), London and New York, 1956.

[7] 'The Concept of the Collective Unconscious', op. cit., pp. 47–8.

3

BIOLOGICAL THEORY AND CONCEPT OF ARCHETYPES

he was living. Jung rebuts the 'scientific' criticism by appealing to the facts. He has always been an empiricist, and therefore, in his paper, he next considers what clinical material is worth investigating for archetypal contents. He selects the following:

(a) *The contents of consciousness.*

These, it is evident, contain mythological products from the unconscious which intrude themselves from time to time, but '. . . language and education provide consciousness with a mass of mythological motives which, however, by no means prove their previous unconscious existence'.[8] Consequently the contents of consciousness can be discarded as unprofitable for the · purpose.

(b) *Dream material.*

Dreams contain firstly material known to the dreamer; secondly, material which could be known: for instance, images which were previously conscious but for one reason or another have passed out of the conscious field; lastly, contents for which no conscious origin can be found. These are likely to refer to archetypes.

(c) *Active imagination.*

Active imagination is a process resulting from the successful relaxation of the conscious mind. As a consequence of this the unconscious can express itself actively in images and myths. This 'method' was found by Jung to be of special value in revealing unconscious archetypal activity.[9]

(d) *The imaginative activity of children.*[10]

(e) *The dreams and hallucinations or delusions of psychotic patients.*

One of the most profitable, but not the only[11] way of examining these phenomena is to study them in series, since certain clearly delineated images can be seen to repeat themselves and to behave typically. Jung examined some 400 dreams in which the theme of the mandala appeared regularly; some of them he published in *Psychology and Alchemy*. Clearly if a particular image

---

[8] Ibid., Vol. XLIV, No. 4, p. 64.

[9] Perhaps the best description of it is to be found in 'The Spirit of Psychology', op. cit., p. 412.

[10] For evidence of the archetypal content of play and fantasy cf. Fordham, *The Life of Childhood*, London, 1944.

[11] Single examples can also be used; cf. *infra*.

BIOLOGICAL THEORY AND CONCEPT OF ARCHETYPES

recurs and functions (behaves) in a characteristic way, we have evidence on which to postulate the activity of an archetype, without however arriving at a conclusion. Obviously the fact of repetition is inconclusive in itself, for a pathological complex repeats but does not behave archetypally.

By way of illustration the following sequence in which active imagination is followed by a number of dreams is here used to postulate archetypal activity. It concerns a woman in the early forties.

The phenomena began with an anxiety attack accompanied by the fantasy of a huge wave threatening to inundate her Soon after this she started to make models of the wave, which gradually turned into a male figure enveloping a small woman. As the analysis proceeded, the figure changed its character, and the following five dreams which occurred within the space of one month show this.

Dream 1. 'Looking through a window, together with a man, I see a fish floating in the air above the sea. It gradually begins to drop down and we both race down to the sea's edge and get there in time to find it in the sea and swimming inland, now a dangerous, bewhiskered creature. The man wades into the surf to catch it and bring it on shore.'

Dream 2. 'Walking along a country road with a man who is making love to me. He is irritated by the interruption of the cars passing along the road and he decides to move to a quieter spot. We move into a small house but are disturbed by sounds of moving upstairs, and looking up the stairs we see the feet and legs of an unknown man standing there listening. We move into an inner room and there at last feel we are safe. Intercourse with continuous orgasm.'

Dream 3. 'Walking along a country road between a man and a woman. The man and I are on easy friendly terms with each other.'

Dream 4. 'Driving in a lorry with a man. We are on a secret and dangerous mission, we are delivering goods to a high walled-in place. It might be a fortress or a prison. The things we are delivering are chemicals of some kind, perhaps ammunition. They are taken in at the gate and the gate is then hastily shut in our faces. My companion is suspicious. He says he believes they are hiding something important. Perhaps treasure, gold. He tells

BIOLOGICAL THEORY AND CONCEPT OF ARCHETYPES

me to wait outside whilst he climbs over the high wall and goes inside to find out what it is all about. I sit outside in the lorry in the dark, waiting for him, with a sense of desperate adventure and danger about the whole business.'

Dream 5. 'I am in a great empty temple. At one end is a gigantic statue of the god. There is a tall priest in robes with me. The atmosphere is Egyptian or Chinese. We walk over the immense empty floor towards the statue at the end. Every few steps I fall on my face and the priest calls out to the god that I am coming as a penitent and he makes confession for me aloud. Our progress is slow and solemn, but in my own thoughts I am very sceptical about it all. I think this is a queer kind of ritual and that the god over there is only a stone statue. We finally come to it. On each side of it there are steps and we go up these and so behind the altar. Once there and before leaving the temple I turn round and look again at the statue, and as I look it slowly turns round and looks at me. I find myself falling on my face in real awe and devotion at last, for it really is the presence of a god with absolution and grace pouring in on me. Somebody says: "It's all a trick, there is a machine to turn the statue round." But I feel passionately that it may be a trick to turn a stone statue round, but all the same it is also a god and I have experienced him. I leave the place with a sense of being illuminated and humbled and glad.'

In each of these dreams there is a man who behaves characteristically: in each he is related to the dreamer as a kind of companion. In dreams 1, 2, and 4 the same phrase is used, 'with a man'; in dream 3 'The man and I are on easy friendly terms'; in dream 5 it is stated 'a tall priest in robes is with me'. Further than this the figure has a tendency to take the initiative; the protective role is combined with it in dream 1, when the 'bewhiskered creature' appears and the man 'wades into the surf to catch it and bring it to shore'; this is followed on in dream 2 where he has 'intercourse with continuous orgasm', and dream 4 where he gets suspicious, tells the subject ('me') to wait and 'climbs over the high wall and goes inside to find what it is all about'. Here he begins to take the role of initiator which clearly shows in dream 5. There '... the priest calls out to the god that I am coming as a penitent and he makes confession for me aloud'.

BIOLOGICAL THEORY AND CONCEPT OF ARCHETYPES

This brief analysis of the 'natural history'[12] of a symbolic image in an individual must suffice for our present purpose, which is to illustrate the procedure.

AMPLIFICATION

The general significance of a symbol is established by collecting material from other sources.

(1) From other patients. For instance, the male figure in my patient's dream can be shown to occur in any thorough analysis of a woman and is called the animus, which is said to mediate between the ego and the unconscious.[13]

(2) From myths, folklore and religious observances, as we have seen Jung doing above. These phenomena are collective beliefs held by groups and are therefore rough 'statistical' phenomena. They are assumed to represent their common psychic structure and way of functioning. They are, with few exceptions, much more perfect than the individual product from which they are derived because it has been worked over and so changed by those who retail the experience eliminating individual differences in the process.

In order to establish a parallel from either source clear criteria must be observed if any scientific validity is to be given it. It is inadequate simply to compare the images alone without reference to their functional properties; that is why we studied the behaviour as well as the form of the animus figure. It is insufficient to say that any image is archetypal without observing whether it functions in a typical fashion.

We may here briefly consider another aspect of the comparative method because it is not just a method of generalizing, it can also be used to throw themes into relief and to penetrate further into their essential core.

It will have been noticed that in the last dream of my patient the animus leads her to the experience of the god which overcame the intellectual resistance of her conscious mind. This intellectual attitude has stood there as a guard, a protection throughout her

---

[12] Cf. 'Psychology and Religion', *Psychology and Religion* (Collected Works, Vol. XI), London and New York, 1957.

[13] Cf. *Two Essays on Analytical Psychology* (Collected Works, Vol. VII), London and New York, 1953.

BIOLOGICAL THEORY AND CONCEPT OF ARCHETYPES

analysis, until she was able to grasp the essential numinous experience of the religious archetypal image.

The whole atmosphere of the dream is religious, impressive and ritualistic, and many of the features are oriental, not only on the statement of the patient but also as seen in her acts, for instance falling on her face as she proceeds. On the other hand the idea of penitence is derived from Christianity as well as oriental sources, whilst the ideas of absolution and grace can be derived from her Christian education alone. All this is part of an educated woman's, and so of my patient's, consciousness.

An obscure point in the dream is why, when my patient has passed the statue and the initiation is over, the stone figure becomes animated. The parallel that at once springs to my mind is the fetish, which shows a similar variability in its effective content. The fetish is an object used to produce magical effects, and if a surprising or untoward event occurs in reality, the fetish is taken from its usual position and is recharged by a suitable ritual carried out by one who believes in the process; in other words, the 'fetish' is not a fetish until it contains libido—that means, it depends upon the subject whether it is effective or not.

In my patient's dream the stone figure would therefore appear to be charged by the animus but the charge is not effective until the ego is off its guard, the scepticism keeps it in check. This consideration increases the evidence for the general significance of the dream.

It also illustrates the principle of the method which is used with great elaboration in Jung's works. By collecting numerous parallels of the kind here described the collective elements in the material can be thrown into relief and amplified.

The vast amount of material collected not only by Jung and his followers but by independent researches undertaken by others trained in different disciplines is sufficient to establish beyond reasonable doubt the existence of archetypal forms which must have an origin in the unconscious psyche. This evidence is far too full to summarize here, only the principles upon which it is based can be reviewed.

THE HEREDITY OF ARCHETYPES

In establishing the generality of the primordial images and postulating the unconscious archetype as their source Jung

BIOLOGICAL THEORY AND CONCEPT OF ARCHETYPES

defined a field of study which has occupied him for the rest of his life. There is no necessity for him to investigate their origin but it would strengthen his position if he did so.

Since he rejects the developmental hypothesis as the only source of the images, he logically seeks for evidence of their being hereditary units. But the complexity of the human psyche is such that positive proof is not yet possible. All that can be done is to prove that an archetypal theme in an individual could not have been in his consciousness before it emerged from the unconscious, i.e., it could not have been the consequence of nurture.

In 1906 Jung was struck by the delusion of an insane patient which he recorded, having at the time no idea of its meaning or significance. Some years later he discovered a parallel to it which was first published in 1910. The time lapse excludes the possibility of suggestion on Jung's part and also the possibility of the patient having derived his delusion from an external source. The patient was a case of paranoid schizophrenia with the delusion of being God and Christ at once. One day he approached Jung in a benevolent and friendly way, saying that he would show him something very interesting. 'When I [Jung] asked him what he saw, he was surprised that I myself saw nothing, and said, "Surely you see the solar penis—when I shake my head, it also shakes, and that is the origin of the wind."'[14] The Dieterich text, that published in 1910, with an extract from Jung's comments, runs as follows:[15]

Draw breath from the rays, draw in three times as strongly as you can and you will feel yourself raised up and walking towards the height and you will seem to be in the middle of the aerial region. . . . The path of the visible gods will appear through the sun, the God, my Father; *similarly will become visible also the so-called tube, the origin of the serving winds.*[16] For you will see from the disc of the sun like a dangling tube; and this is in the region toward the west, endless as eastwind; when the destination towards the regions of the east belongs to the other, you will similarly [see] in the regions of that *the reversal of the visions.*[16]

Jung continues:

The text shows the intention of the author to enable the reader himself to experience this vision, which the author has had or which, at

[14] 'The Concept of the Collective Unconscious', op. cit., p. 65.
[15] Ibid.
[16] My italics.

BIOLOGICAL THEORY AND CONCEPT OF ARCHETYPES

least, he believes in. The reader is to be initiated into the inner experience of the author or—what seems more likely—into one of those mystical communities then existing, of which *Philo Judaeus* gives contemporary evidence. . . .

Our patient was about ten years older than I. He was a megalomaniac, being God and Christ in one. His attitude towards me was benevolent— he liked me, as the only person with any sympathy for his abstruse ideas. His delusions were mainly of a religious nature, and when he invited me to blink into the sun like himself and to wag my head, he apparently intended to let me partake of his vision. He played the *rôle* of the mystic sage and I was the pupil. He was even the sun-god himself, creating the wind by shaking his head.

This example, one amongst many, together with a mass of more circumstantial evidence makes it worth while trying to relate the theory of heredity with the concept of hereditary archetypes.

Biologists have related the concept of heredity to the mathematical laws first discovered by Mendel who was the first to postulate discrete units, called genes, in the germ plasm causing particular physical characteristics to appear in the animal or plant. These units have been located by microscopic and chemical methods.

Linked up with the theory of genes is Weismann's theory of the continuity of the germ plasm. This theory states that the body is a by-product of the germ plasm brought into being through union of the male and female cells. In consequence, nothing that is acquired during a lifetime, nothing that happens to the body, no injuries or diseases from which it suffers, no skills or talents it develops, nothing it thinks or imagines or in any way experiences, has any effect whatever upon the germ plasm; therefore all these acquired characteristics die for ever with the body. Thus any heritable changes in the body structure and also in psychic organization orginate in variable combinations of genes or through mutations in their structure.[17]

At first it was naively assumed that visible characteristics in the organism were the direct consequence of the action of the genes, which become distributed by fission of the cells throughout the whole organism. It was therefore thought that

---

[17] This well-established theory is the most potent instrument with which to demolish the notion that archetypes are the deposit of racial experience.

BIOLOGICAL THEORY AND CONCEPT OF ARCHETYPES

characteristics were inherited. More careful analysis showed, however, that the problem could be stated more exactly, for it is clear that the environment makes a very considerable contribution to the appearance of any physical characteristic. Indeed, if a favourable environment is not provided no characteristic will form itself at all. This proposition is self-evident, for if a fertilized mammalian ovum be removed from the body of the female, it will die, and further, if the intra-uterine environment is seriously disturbed anomalies in development will result. Therefore the only factors which are inherited are those contained within the fertilized ovum; everything else is a product of the inherited factors *and* the environment. It is only owing to the relative stability of the environment that it is permissible, if inexact, to speak of physical characteristics as hereditary. The truth is that the hereditary influence is greatest given a relatively stable environment.

It follows that when it is said that the archetypes are hereditary functions what is meant is that they must be somehow represented in the germ cells and that therefore any archetypal image recorded by the conscious mind likewise contains within it the effect of genetic factors. This consideration raises the whole complex problem of the nature of the images under consideration. Their analysis can be best undertaken in connection with their development in childhood (cf. pp. 120 f.), and so will not need consideration here.

INSTINCTS

On numerous occasions Jung has related the concept of archetypes to that of instincts. His latest view[18] is that if instincts be taken as innate patterns of behaviour then the archetypal images show a comparable pattern. In this he reaffirms his earlier idea[19] that the archetypal images are the representatives in consciousness of the instincts themselves.

The study of innate patterns of behaviour has long fascinated biologists, and though they have never been able to define the

[18] 'The Spirit of Psychology', *Spirit and Nature*, New York, 1954; London, 1955.
[19] 'Instinct and the Unconscious', *Contributions to Analytical Psychology*, London, 1928.

BIOLOGICAL THEORY AND CONCEPT OF ARCHETYPES

boundaries of this concept they have none the less found it useful as a working hypothesis. Many of the studies on this topic have been behaviouristic. The most recent and most fascinating of them have been beautifully described by Lorenz, and to these reference will be made later on. Latterly experimental studies upon the physiological mechanisms of undoubted instinctive behaviour have been undertaken as well and have produced some highly significant results. The techniques used are relatively simple.

Obviously animal biologists are in a much better position to decide whether a particular behaviour is innate or no. Not only can they study very young animals with more rigour than we can study babies, but they can isolate the animal and ensure that it could not have learnt, say, mating behaviour till the mating impulses appear. In the human being there is, on humanitarian grounds, no possibility of isolating the child and in consequence we have to be content with less rigorous criteria. But this does not mean that the discoveries made with animals cannot usefully be applied to man, as has happened in other departments of science.

Recent experimental research has been summarized by Tinbergen,[20] from whose book the following conclusions are derived. The first line of investigation was to work out what stimuli were needed to produce instinctive behaviour. These stimuli are specific and exact, as the following example shows: directly after birth a baby gull takes up a position immediately below the mother's beak and receives its first feed from her; it is the red spot on the mother gull's beak which evokes the response. Further analysis proves that the red colour is the most important factor. Specific stimuli of this type are called 'sign stimuli'. There are usually more than one of them, and in long and complex reactions they occur in chains; when one stimulus has been exhausted, another takes over, and so on.

The study of sign stimuli leads to the conclusion that the pattern of behaviour is initiated by a stable perceptual system within the animal, called the 'innate release mechanism' (I.R.M.). This selects the suitable stimuli from the perceptual field, and releases the instinctual response which is more than a reflex mechanism in being a functional system within the animal which determines the whole behaviour pattern.

The instinctual activities are related to:

[20] *The Study of Instinct*, Oxford, 1951.

BIOLOGICAL THEORY AND CONCEPT OF ARCHETYPES

(1) *The endocrine system.*

Most of the work on this influence has been done on reproductive behaviour, a field of study likely to be fruitful, since ovarian and testicular hormones have been isolated, and so controlled experiments can be undertaken. The method adopted combines the application of sign stimuli under different concentrations of hormones introduced into the animal. In this way it has been proved experimentally that hormones influence all the essential features of mating behaviour. The same procedure has been applied to other behaviour using different hormones.

(2) *The central nervous system.*

Apart from the reflexes which are accepted as innate it has been proved that spontaneous rhythmic activities of the brain, spinal cord and autonomic nervous system, take an essential part in the instinctive response.

The proof is simple in principle. All sensory stimuli can be cut off by severing the afferent nerves, and the behaviour of the animal can be observed under these conditions. Alternatively, the activity of the nervous system can be studied electrically by inserting an electrode into a particular area and recording the current produced by the activity of the neuronic system. Suitable steps to isolate the area anatomically can then be taken by making sections through the nerve tissue. By these and other means it has been shown that the central nervous system contributes special movements, particularly those of a rhythmic kind, and further that these, far from being stimulated, are released from an inhibitory influence by the sign stimuli acting through the innate release mechanism.

By far the most significant feature of this work is the discovery by experimental means of an innate neuro-endocrine system lying at the basis of instinctive behaviour. This puts the earlier theory of the reflex origin of instinct which had gained ground through the discovery of conditioned reflexes, in a different perspective. Not only are reflexes innate, but also, it seems almost certain, the neural pattern of instinctive behaviour.

Tinbergen adds an interesting concept, which also has bearing on our subject, that of the hierarchical nature of the instinctive patterns. This is of importance because the concept is also found in neurophysiology. It has been elaborated, for example, in England by Sherrington and Hughlings Jackson.

BIOLOGICAL THEORY AND CONCEPT OF ARCHETYPES

ARCHETYPES AND NERVOUS ACTION

Of all the organs of the body, the brain is the most psychic. As it is now established that in any instinctive behaviour the nervous system, its receptors, its central structure and function, and its effective motor units play the major part, it appears likely that the study of the brain, its structure and function, will assist most in bridging the gap between body and psyche.

Furthermore the concept of instinct leads inevitably to the study of neurophysiology and its psychical equivalents, for instincts involve on the one hand the sensory motor reflex apparatus and on the other innate neural patterns of energy discharge.

Inasmuch as archetypes are perceived in terms of acts and images the organization and function of the brain must show some very close relation to the organization and function of archetypes.

In man and the higher animals the instinctive pattern of behaviour is highly complex, much too complex to give a point of departure for the study of the nervous system. For this a simpler dynamic unit, the reflex arc, has proved more useful, and forms a basis for analysing the nervous system in terms of sensory and motor components. The reflex arc can be studied by simplifying the total structure in various surgical ways, i.e. by making sections at various levels from the peripheral nerves to the spinal cord and upwards. In man disease performs a comparable role, though less precise, to the knife in animals; it produces disturbances in the functioning of the nervous system, sometimes of great complexity but sometimes, as in the case of traumata, localized haemorrhages, and thromboses of the artery, of a fairly simple kind.

By far the most useful concept in neurology, apart from the reflex, is that of the hierarchy of the nervous system. For purposes of description the nervous system can be considered as a sensori-motor system, each part being analysed separately but each having a hierarchical structure of its own.

The sensory system comprises at least three levels. A stimulus passes first from the sense organs to the posterior horn of the spinal column; from thence it is relayed up the spinal cord to the thalamus and other centres of a similar kind such as the amygdaloid nucleus, to be relayed again to the cerebral cortex where the

BIOLOGICAL THEORY AND CONCEPT OF ARCHETYPES

area stimulated, say the sole of the foot, is 'represented'. This means that if the area representing the sole of the foot is extirpated by disease, touch there cannot be felt; if on the other hand the intact convolution be suitably stimulated, the subject will feel a touch on the sole of the foot even though no touch has actually taken place. By this dual method, i.e. studying on the one hand the negative effect of disease, and on the other the positive effect of stimulation, it has become known that perceptions of the body can be located topographically on the cortex, indeed a map of body areas can be sketched out on the surface of the brain.

Similarly the motor system can be envisaged as hierarchical: starting from the motor nerve which innervates small muscle groups, then segments of muscles, to become progressively organized until in the cortex movements of particular muscle groups are 'localized' in the motor area.

The concept of localization has undergone many vicissitudes, and it has even been held that in every perception and in every act the whole brain is brought into a state of activity, and always acts as a whole. This extreme position is not in agreement with the evidence, but rigid localization of functions has had to be discarded for all higher operations. Consideration of the body image will make this clear. This image is implied in any process of localization of sense perception on the body surface. If it is recorded that the left big toe has been touched, then immediately the left foot must be envisaged, and likewise a right one, as well as the location of both in relation to the body as a whole. The same principle applies to any discrete perception since all physical sensations are automatically localized. Therefore it must be assumed that in any perceptual act the whole sensory system is in some sense brought into play as the consequence of activity in one particular localized area.

It will be apparent that the localization of a sensory stimulus does not involve consciousness of the body image as a whole, though upon analysis it is apparent that it is implied. The importance of this for the relation of analytic concepts to neurophysiology can scarcely be overrated.[21]

[21] Cf. Scott, who has related this concept to those of analytical psychology in his 'Notes on the Body Image and Schema', *Journal of Analytical Psychology*, Vol. I, No. 2, 1956.

BIOLOGICAL THEORY AND CONCEPT OF ARCHETYPES

Neurologists have constantly operated with the concepts of a neurophysiological substrate on the one hand and consciousness on the other; they have never taken into account unconscious psychic activity at all. In this concept of the body image they are bound to perceive that it is usually unconscious. This has indeed recently been taken up by several neurologists who have gone even further, postulating an unconscious body schema as a necessary and essentially unconscious principle for understanding speech disorders.[22]

These researches and many others have necessitated new concepts of cerebral activity, concentrated upon the idea that the cortex, and the subcortical ganglia and network of association fibres[23] acts as a whole where higher more psychic activities are considered. The whole brain, particularly in cybernetics, has, till recently, been conceived as a kind of elaborate telephone exchange, the incoming impulses being distributed to their appropriate destination by the ganglia and grey matter which functions after the manner of a telephone operator. Lately, however, the concept has become more dynamic and 'purposive', and is expressed in terms of 'reverberating circuits, negative feed-back, scansion and oscillation'.[24]

[22] Cf. W. Russell Brain, 'The Concept of the Schema in Neurology and Psychiatry', *Perspectives in Neuropsychiatry* (ed. D. Richter), London, 1950.

[23] Recently the reticular formation has been subjected to concentrated research. Cf. *Brain Mechanisms and Consciousness* (ed. Delafreshaye), Oxford, 1954.

[24] I cannot do better here than quote Professor Meyer (*Recent Progress in Psychiatry*, Vol. II, 1950, pp. 285 f.) 'The deepening penetration of *electronic principles* into neurophysiology has led to radically new concepts of brain function. These have found their most complete expression so far in the book on *Cybernetics* by Wiener (1948), the constructor of one of the great electronic computing machines. In a historical chapter Wiener gives an outline of the developments which led up to the introduction into neurophysiology of well-known electronic concepts, such as reverberating circuits, negative feed-back, scansion and oscillation. (See also the reviews of the book by Cobb, 1949; Ashby, 1949, and Brazier, 1950.) The essence of reverberating circuits is that a closed chain of neurones can be set in action by a single incoming impulse, and the impulse continues to pass round the circuit as long as metabolism supports it or until other incoming impulses change it. Feed-back implies a mechanism by which the activity of a dynamic system is modified by the return of some fraction of the output of the systems as input; in a servo-mechanism the feed-back is so arranged that it maintains the whole system in a state

BIOLOGICAL THEORY AND CONCEPT OF ARCHETYPES

This formulation therefore recognizes purpose which, however, it explains as a consequence of extremely complex mechanisms. In spite of this there is a parallel with analytic concepts, for it falls into line with that of the unconscious as a dynamic unit which functions as a whole and is yet made up of operative centres (perceived, in consciousness, as archetypal images). The parallel has greater force if the concept of relative localization be compared with that of the archetypes, for in each case the functions are relatively transferable and yet have an apparent specificity. When it comes to the nature of the nuclei, the psychic and neurophysiological concepts diverge in that the one is finalistic and purposive and the other mechanistic.

In the past there has been a trend in neurophysiology towards dividing off that discipline from psychology, but in recent years the division has rapidly begun to break down.[25] Yet we have to go back to Hughlings Jackson to find the kind of concept Jung employs. Long ago Jackson[26] wrote that he '. . . accepted Herbert Spencer's doctrine of the inheritance of organized experiences' and further that '. . . it is reasonable to infer that their physical bases are given with them'. He goes on to say that '. . . they have been slowly evolved organismically and racially; they are inherited imperfectly and are rapidly perfected after birth'. Since he wrote this the development of knowledge has been very considerable. It is no longer necessary to postulate the 'inheritance of organized experiences', and we can speak of organized predispositions, the archetypes, or of organized schemata.

of dynamic equilibrium; in a homeostat this arrangement is found automatically by the machine itself. Scansion is a term derived from television and means a rhythmic sweep of impulses in non-specific afferents (perpendicularly or otherwise) through the cortex. It has been suggested that the alpha rhythm is the 'smoke' of the rhythmic sweep, energized perhaps, from the thalamus. Oscillation is a common phenomenon in servomechanisms, due to faulty feed-back. Simple excessive negative feed-back can produce excessive stability, i.e. rigidity or fixity, rather than oscillation.

'Not only has extrapyramidal function and dysfunction been given a new explanation, but, what is more important to psychiatrists, a physiological interpretation has been suggested for psychological processes, such as perception of universals, memory and purpose.'

[25] Cf. also Sherrington, *Man on his Nature*, Cambridge, 1940; or Russell Brain, *Mind, Perception and Science*, Oxford, 1951.

[26] Cf. *Selected Writings of John Hughlings Jackson* (ed. James Taylor), Vol. II.

BIOLOGICAL THEORY AND CONCEPT OF ARCHETYPES

In spite of these modifications the essence of the statement stands, especially the idea of their being 'rapidly perfected' after birth, as Piaget has shown very beautifully in his series of monographs.[27]

It has already been observed that the theory of instincts leads to the concept of a nervous system containing innate patterns of energy and not only reflexes.

The attempt to analyse the whole nervous system in terms of reflex mechanisms has now indeed become untenable, particularly since the introduction of electrical methods for analysing nerve cell activity. As a result physiologists have introduced the concept of 'spontaneous'[28] rhythmic activity of the brain cells.

These postulates have inevitably led to a change in the theory of reflex mechanisms in nervous activity of the 'spontaneous' type; no longer do hypothetical reflex units explain the whole of nervous activity because of the complexity of nervous structure which we are unable to describe in sufficient detail.

Bringing these conclusions into relation with instinct theory the nervous system can be conceived as a system in which positive 'spontaneous' rhythmic and other energies play an essential part. It is possible to correlate this view with phenomena observed by psychologists, for rhythm is an essential component of the infant's earliest sucking and other pleasurable activities such as arm and leg movements. It is further manifest that many highly differentiated cultural occupations—music, dancing, sport, to give three examples—are all based upon the element of rhythm. The interrelations between these various different manifestations are highly complex, but strikingly enough had long ago been made the subject of a research by Jung, who embodied his conclusions in a masterly and erudite chapter called 'The Transformation of the Libido' in *Symbols of Transformation*.[29] In these studies there is thus a visible closing of the gap between analytical psychology and neurophysiology.

---

[27] Cf. particularly *Play, Dreams, and Imitation in Childhood*, London, 1951; and *The Origin of Intelligence in the Child*, London, 1953.

[28] Sherrington says of this term: 'The physiologist uses "spontaneous" here just as he uses it of the heart, which beats "of itself", i.e. is self-activated.' *Man on His Nature*, Cambridge, 1940, p. 230.

[29] Cf. Collected Works, Vol. V, London and New York, 1956, pars. 204 ff.

BIOLOGICAL THEORY AND CONCEPT OF ARCHETYPES

EVOLUTION

The concept of archetypes inevitably needs relating to that of evolution. This has not escaped Jung's attention. Two problems have presented themselves to analytical psychologists: first that of the origin of, and second, whether a discernable evolutionary change has occurred in the archetypes themselves. Since there appears to be some uncertainty about the states of these problems often posed as a consequence of a somewhat sketchy knowledge of biological theory, the concepts from which the psychological ideas are derived may be briefly outlined.

Towards the end of the eighteenth century Lamarck put forward the notion that the hierarchical arrangement of species already defined by such authorities as Linnaeus and Buffon was the result of a natural process of evolution. It was he who first held that evolution was caused by the inheritance of acquired characteristics, a concept whose consequences have already been considered in the discussion of heredity. This idea, however, ran up against the religious belief that the animals and plants had come into being once and for all by a series of separate creative acts of God. There was no adequate evidence to support the time dimension presupposed in the theory, since all the species studied existed at the same time, i.e. the present, and so the theory failed to find general acceptance or application.

When Darwin began his massive collection of material, however, the position was very different: palaeontology had made considerable progress and he could point to the evidence of fossil remains which had collected material demonstrating the arrangements of the species in time. It could be shown that species had come into being, become extinct, and been replaced by other species of a more developed kind, the evidence supported the notion that one species had evolved into another. Darwin was therefore in a far stronger position than previous evolutionists.

It was not only this, however, that appealed to the biologist, it was also his ability to put forward an attractive idea of how the process came about. This idea was the hypothesis of natural selection, through which variants of a species were fostered if favourable to adaptation and weeded out if unfavourable. This hypothesis, together with the evidence of palaeontology, Darwin's massive accumulation of data and capacity to marshal and

BIOLOGICAL THEORY AND CONCEPT OF ARCHETYPES

present them was what won the day; but even so it would not have had its overwhelming effect had not T. H. Huxley taken up the cudgels on its behalf and overcome clerical objections, particularly when the origin of man came under survey.

Darwin did not succeed in discovering how the structural variations in the species came into being; he only considered it probable that natural selection acted upon small changes. It acted so that favourable alterations accumulated, unfavourable ones were eliminated. The problem of the origin of variations was and still is unsolved but it turned at that time on the nature of inheritance, about which much more is known today.

Jung has not paid much attention to the origin of archetypes, though he has once suggested that '. . . their origin can only be explained by assuming them to be deposits of the constantly repeated experiences of humanity'.[30] It is clear that these experiences cannot be inherited if we adhere to biological concepts. If archetypes are inherited they are, as far as present knowledge goes, not the result of experience, but the manner of experiencing the world must somehow be the result of changes in the germ cells. I can see no objection to aligning Jung's concepts with biological theory here, for there does not seem any difficulty in saying that primitive man experienced the world in terms of archetypal images as a consequence of the activity of archetypes in the unconscious. This statement aligns the phenomena with what is known of heredity.

Once established in biology evolution was applied to every field of human endeavour, and to anthropology and archaeology in particular, and as a result it has been possible to reconstruct in outline a probable view of how man evolved from ape-like mammals and what sort of development has occurred since then.

It appears that certain apes gave up their arboreal existence, assumed an upright posture and so freed the arms and particularly the hands from taking part in the process of locomotion. The opposable thumb made these hands of particular use, and they became serviceable units, making possible the refined movements necessary in the construction of tools, pots, etc.

These early men apparently started to form small inbreeding

[30] *Two Essays on Analytical Psychology* (Collected Works, Vol. VII), London and New York, 1953, p. 68.

BIOLOGICAL THEORY AND CONCEPT OF ARCHETYPES

groups or clans, which lived by hunting. They roved over the land and developed primitive weapons, existing thus for thousands of years.

Once the idea of evolution is applied to man, an important new factor stares us in the face; this is the enormous development of consciousness, in which he differs most from all other animals in whom evolution takes place more or less blindly: transmissible variants are produced in the genes, and express themselves in new anatomical changes, physiological processes, and so in instinctual patterns. Favourable variants survive, unfavourable ones are weeded out by natural selection; the whole process is quasi-mechanical, and each individual starts from its genetic constitution. Very little is learnt and there is little or no education, there being nothing to teach because behaviour is almost entirely instinctive; even where it is acquired it is, comparatively speaking, on a very elementary level.

The importance of tradition and non-inheritable transmitted learning is manifest in man, and reaches its peak in his schools and universities, which have behind them something unknown to animals, namely consciousness of history. The emphasis on transmissible knowledge has given rise to theories about the development of culture which attempt to eliminate developments not dependent on learning. Elliot Smith, for instance, postulated that the essentials of all civilization began in Egypt and were spread thence throughout the world. This idea is in principle the one put forward by the diffusionist school of anthropology, which sets out to trace the ways in which culture diffused outwards from a single centre. An obvious recent example of this is the diffusion of Western scientific knowledge all over the world, though it can only be thoroughly grasped by a relatively small number of sufficiently gifted people, the majority merely experiencing the consequence of their discoveries.

There are two limits to this theory. Firstly, it takes no account of the origin of discovery, and secondly, diffusion depends upon the consciousness of the people in any particular area, country, or continent, being developed enough to make use of the advance coming from a centre of more advanced civilization, and this in turn depends on education, in which we again meet the problem: learning depends on individual capacity and age, as well as on what is to be learnt. Just as we cannot teach children

BIOLOGICAL THEORY AND CONCEPT OF ARCHETYPES

until they are ready to be taught, so a cultural group, whether large or small, cannot acquire a new product of culture until it is ready to do so.[31] The soil turns out to be as vital as the seeds of knowledge planted in it.

A familiar example of the pitfalls of the diffusion theory is the spread of Christianity which, though it has been the official religion of nearly all European countries for centuries, has never, so far as is known, percolated into the psyche of the mass of the people. Coulton, in his *Five Centuries of Religion*, elaborates this thesis for the Middle Ages and asserts that there were really two religions in Europe: the religion of the Church and the religion of the people; these would seem to have run, as they manifestly do today, side by side.

The essential failure of the diffusion concept as an explanation of civilization is that it takes no account of how the assimilation of a new concept of whatever kind takes place, and it is just here that psychological studies are necessary. If we identify the development of culture with the emergence of consciousness, then a new and revealing line of approach is opened up.[32] It redefines the whole problem as follows: the conscious originates in the unconscious, its first expression is in the form of images, inspirations, dreams, etc. Amongst these the archetypal images take the main place; only later do they become systematized as knowledge. Science is not only the most recent but also the best example to take for the illumination of the problem, since never before the 'scientific age' has consciousness increased so rapidly.

Jung has given striking examples of how scientific theories can be based upon primitive quasi-mystical experiences,[33] and Pauli has discussed the problem at length in a recent essay.[34] Starting from the problem of how to find a bridge between sense perception and concepts which logic is '. . . fundamentally incapable

[31] Cf. V. G. Childe, *Social Evolution*, London, 1951.
[32] A recent volume by Neumann, *The Origins and History of Consciousness*, London, 1954, elaborates this subject at length.
[33] Cf. *Two Essays on Analytical Psychology*, in which he discusses Robert Mayer's description of how he discovered the law of the conservation of energy.
[34] W. Pauli, 'The Influence of Archetypal Ideas on the Scientific Theories on Kepler', in *The Interpretation of Nature and the Psyche*, London and New York, 1955.

BIOLOGICAL THEORY AND CONCEPT OF ARCHETYPES

of constructing . . .',[35] Pauli says, 'The process of understanding nature . . . seems to be based on a correspondence, a "matching" of inner images pre-existent in the human psyche with external objects and their behaviour.'[36]

Thus the process of scientific discovery is a particular example of unconscious activity coming into relation with the conscious. If this thesis be true it demolishes the rationalistic basis of science, though obviously it does not demolish reason and logic as part of scientific discovery.

We may now turn to the question whether archetypes evolve. In embarking on this topic it must be born in mind that if the archetypes are inherited there is little to interest zoologists or anthropologists in it since evolution at this level is known to require much longer periods to manifest itself than the comparatively brief historical period covering part of man's sojourn on earth. The question has, however, been implicitly raised by Neumann[37] and is a current topic of discussion in analytic circles; it therefore requires consideration. Since, however, the concept of evolution is essentially biological it follows that if psychologists transfer it into their discipline they will have to bring forward very strong evidence in its favour.

Let us now turn to science as the most recent manifest development in the evolution of consciousness. It is in this process of scientific discovery that we may expect to find changes in the archetypes, for by comparing the images evoked in the process with others in the past we might expect the most marked alterations in them. But no evidence of change has been recorded, indeed Jung points out that the concept of the conservation of energy is based on age-old archetypal forms and Pauli shows how Kepler's scientific discoveries are linked up with symbolical religious doctrines of great antiquity. Therefore at the root of discovery lies an archetypal form which does not change; what does change is the form which it is given. It makes all the difference if the consciousness of man is ready and has been prepared to '. . . dream *the myth onwards* and give it a modern dress'.[38]

---

[35] Op. cit., p. 152.   [36] Ibid.

[37] *The Origins and History of Consciousness.*

[38] Jung, 'The Psychology of the Child Archetype', *Introduction to a Science of Mythology*, London, 1951, p. 109; or *Essays on a Science of Mythology*, New York, 1951.

BIOLOGICAL THEORY AND CONCEPT OF ARCHETYPES

Mysticism is overtly most remote from instinct, but since mystics spend much of their time studying and experiencing archetypal images here surely is another source for radical changes to be found. If, however, mystical material be studied, though there is a great variety of forms, amplification of them does not reveal any fundamental change in the archetype itself; even in the highest forms the instinctive basis can usually be discerned, and where it cannot it may very well be because too little is known about instinct. This caution is founded on analytic experiences and upon the study of mystical texts. So as to show how easy it is to overlook an instinctive content, a text from a collection of the writings of Mechthild of Magdeburg[39] will now be considered and compared with some behaviour of wolves, described by Lorenz. It was only when his book *King Solomon's Ring*[40] came into my hands in 1954 that I noticed the analogy, though the text had interested me for quite other reasons.

Of a woman who was gladly at Court and of her devil who brought her seven evils[41]

A certain woman had dedicated herself
And yet wished to serve at Court.
I prayed for her with all my might,
Both day and night,
For I saw the evil coming to her to be so great
That if it went on she would soon rank
As a friend of the devil.
She loved authority too much
And lived not to the glory of God;
But rather followed the futile practices of the Court,
And had ever before her eyes
The rank of her lords and ladies.

Then a great devil, fiery, bleeding, black, with claws and horns and glass eyes, came and stood before me. I was not afraid of him but I crossed myself before I went to sleep. He floated over me like a skin full of water and troubled me so much that I asked our Lord for mercy. Then a white angel came to my aid; it came from the fourth choir of angels and was the guardian of the woman. I asked who this fiend was and what he wanted of me; 'Ah!' said the lovely angel in a heavenly

[39] L. Menzies (Trans.) *The Revelations of Mechthild of Magdeburg*, London, New York and Toronto, 1953.
[40] London, 1952.
[41] Menzies, op. cit., p. 111.

BIOLOGICAL THEORY AND CONCEPT OF ARCHETYPES

voice, 'he is the worst devil Hell can send; his mission is to bind together in hurtful love the hearts of those who desire to live well. He torments you because you would drive him away from this woman.' 'Alas! will he torment me for long?' 'Nay! God will show his mercy.' After that the devil came and shot me through with fiery rays which gave me pains of Hell in body and soul. I said to him, 'Do whatsoever God allows thee to do!' Then he became weak and said, 'Because thou givest thy soul meekly to torment, I lose all my power.' Then the soul spoke: 'I command thee by the living God that thou tell me thy name and what thy mission is to this woman!' 'My name?' he said. 'That will I not tell thee for it might do me much harm. Thou must ask it on the last day. I foster in that woman bitter pride, flighty cleverness and powerful desire. I am wrathful rage and I disturb the hearts of spiritual people.'

This mystical experience contains all the ideas and reactions of a Christian and could not possibly have occurred without extensive religious instruction. Its form is typical of its period in which all the reforming members of the monasteries were combating the ravages of the devil, whose power penetrated to every corner of the Catholic world. Mechthild was one of those in whom these beliefs came to life through visions. The doctrines account for the form in almost every respect, but they do not account for their dynamic content which is assumed to be due to her spiritual gifts. So far there are little or no grounds to see anything instinctive in the episode.

Mechthild has an intuition of evil for a 'certain woman'—she is seen to be vulnerable to the devil because of excessive love of authority, power, flighty cleverness, pride and desire. Mechthild therefore prayed for her soul with all her might, and as a result of this activity two independent images became active. First it is the devil and then an angel who gives information and reassures Mechthild of the happy outcome of her torments. Mechthild manifestly takes up the right attitude: she ceases to resist and says to the devil 'Do whatsoever God allows thee to do.' Then he loses his power. The salvation is brought about by withdrawing from the conflict and leaving it to the interaction of the devil and God upon her person. This attitude seems to be based upon the principle of turning the other cheek, but it is not quite exact, for she was informed beforehand that the outcome would be satisfactory, and this is not in the Bible.

BIOLOGICAL THEORY AND CONCEPT OF ARCHETYPES

The following is a description by Lorenz[42] of an episode in a right of possession conflict between two wolves.

An enormous old timber wolf and a rather weaker, obviously younger one are the opposing champions and they are moving in circles round each other, exhibiting admirable 'footwork'. At the same time, the bared fangs flash in such a rapid exchange of snaps that the eye can scarcely follow them. So far, nothing has really happened. The jaws of one wolf close on the gleaming white teeth of the other, who is on the alert and wards off the attack. Only the lips have received one or two minor injuries. The younger wolf is gradually being forced backwards. It dawns upon us that the older one is purposely manoeuvring him towards the fence. We wait with breathless anticipation what will happen when he 'goes to the wall'. Now he strikes the wire netting, stumbles . . . and the old one is upon him. And now the incredible happens, just the opposite of what you would expect. The furious whirling of the grey bodies has come to a sudden standstill. Shoulder to shoulder they stand, pressed against each other in a stiff and strained attitude, both heads now facing in the same direction. Both wolves are growling angrily, the elder in a deep bass, the younger in higher tones, suggestive of the fear that underlies his threat. But notice carefully the position of the two opponents; the older wolf has his muzzle close, very close against the neck of the younger, and the latter holds away his head, offering unprotected to his enemy the bend of his neck, the most vulnerable part of his whole body! Less than an inch from the tensed neck-muscles, where the jugular vein lies immediately beneath the skin, gleam the fangs of his antagonist from beneath the wickedly retracted lips. Whereas, during the thick of the fight, both wolves were intent on keeping only their teeth, the one invulnerable part of the body, in opposition to each other, it now appears that the discomfited fighter *proffers intentionally that part of his anatomy to which a bite must assuredly prove fatal.* Appearances are notoriously deceptive, but in his case, surprisingly, they are not!

This was not a piece of inartistic narrative on my part, since the strained situation may continue for a great length of time which is minutes to the observer but very probably seems hours to the losing wolf. Every second you expect violence and await with bated breath the moment when the winner's teeth will rip the jugular vein of the loser. But your fears are groundless, for it will not happen. In this particular situation, *the victor will definitely not close on his less fortunate rival. You can see that he would like to, but he just cannot! A dog or wolf that offers its neck to its adversary in this way will never be bitten seriously.* The other growls and grumbles, snaps with his teeth in the empty air

[42] Op. cit., pp. 186 f.

BIOLOGICAL THEORY AND CONCEPT OF ARCHETYPES

and even carries out, without delivering so much as a bite, the movement of shaking something to death in the empty air. However, the strange inhibition from biting only persists so long as the defeated dog or wolf maintains his attitude of humility. Since the fight is stopped so suddenly by this action, the victor frequently finds himself straddling his vanquished foe in anything but a comfortable position. So to remain, with his muzzle applied to the neck of the 'under-dog', soon becomes tedious for the champion, and seeing that he cannot bite anyway he soon withdraws. Upon this, the under-dog may hastily attempt to put distance between himself and his superior. But he is not usually successful in this, for, as soon as he abandons his rigid attitude of submission, the other again falls upon him like a thunderbolt and the victim must again freeze into his former position. It seems as if the victor is only waiting for the moment when the other will relinquish his submissive attitude, thereby enabling him to give vent to his urgent desire to bite. But, luckily for the 'under-dog', the top-dog at the close of the fight is overcome by the pressing need to leave his trade-mark on the battle-field, to designate it as his personal property—in other words, he must lift his leg against the nearest upright object. This right-of-possession ceremony is usually taken advantage of by the under-dog to make himself scarce.

The common features of these two accounts are:

(1) In each case the conflict is one of possession; in the case of Mechthild it is for possession of a soul, in the case of the wolves it is for possession of a piece of land.

(2) There is a battle; in the case of Mechthild, it is between herself (the weaker) and the devil (the stronger), in the case of the wolves between a younger, weaker wolf and an older, stronger one.

(3) There is a crisis. In spite of making the sign of the cross Mechthild finds it intolerable. This corresponds to the weaker wolf being pressed still fighting, but he 'goes to the wall'.

(4) In each case the weaker submits and is not only saved from disaster but escapes unscathed.

(5) In each case the attacker wants to attack but just cannot.

In Mechthild's experience the angel appears and tells her she is going to be saved from torment; she thus has foreknowledge of the end. In the case of the weaker wolf it is only as if he knew this, it appears to be an instinctive law.

The differences between the two experiences are enormous, but so are the differences in consciousness between a mediaeval

BIOLOGICAL THEORY AND CONCEPT OF ARCHETYPES

Christian mystic and a timber wolf. Therefore it is not beyond the bounds of possibility that in each case there is a common instinct operating.

The behaviour of the wolves is not isolated; the instinctive pattern is found in many animals. The fight is only pressed home if the weaker animal persists in the fight. Is it not a perception of this instinct in man that gave rise to the doctrine of turning the other cheek?[43] This cannot be proved but it is conceivable that it could be, and if instinctive behaviour can have such a striking similarity to such exalted mysticism, who would dare to affirm with any conviction that archetypes change in the course of history?

But are all the differences due to nurture? This cannot be asserted either, indeed it is most improbable. Nurture would merely give a flat account of the whole experience; it accounts for much of the form of the experience, but it would not give the 'numen', it would not give it its dynamism. Is this given by the dynamism of instinct? The answer of analytical psychology is Yes and No; it is derived from instinct and spirit combined in a single unconscious unity which we call the archetype.

THE BIOGENETIC LAW

The fact that students of embryology have shown that the development of the bodily organs does not follow the simplest route but a devious one analogous to the course of evolution has given rise to the concept that the life-history of the individual organism (ontogeny) recapitulates the evolutionary history of the species (phylogeny).

This concept has attracted psychologists who have transplanted it from the organic to the psychic field, because children produce fantasies which are strikingly similar to myths. Neumann has devoted a chapter of his recent volume *The Origins and History of Consciousness* to a theoretical statement in support of the theory without, however, presenting any evidence to support it.

[43] Lorenz, ibid., p. 197, at least thinks so, for he says: 'I at least have extracted from it a new and deeper understanding of a wonderful and often misunderstood saying from the Gospel which hitherto had only awakened in me feelings of strong opposition: "And unto him that smiteth thee on the one cheek offer also the other." (St. Luke vi. 26).'

BIOLOGICAL THEORY AND CONCEPT OF ARCHETYPES

He says (p. xvi): '. . . the individual has, in his own life, to follow the road that humanity trod before him'. And again: '. . . in the course of ontogenetic development, the individual consciousness has to pass through the same archetypal stages which determine the evolution of consciousness in the life of humanity'. He thus speaks as though the biogenetic law were established.

In my book *The Life of Childhood* I recorded some analogies between children's dreams, play and pictures and mythological themes, but refrained from discussing them in relation to the biogenetic law as I thought any such discussion premature, and also because in biology the theory had fallen under a cloud for the following reasons:

(*a*) Though at first the comparisons between ontological and phylogenetic development were striking, closer examination showed that they were sketchy, and it was constantly found necessary to introduce hypothetical stages in evolution in order to make the ontological development fit with phylogeny. It was hoped at one time that the discoveries of embryology would throw light on the course of evolution, but this hope has not been fulfilled and the theories of evolution derived from ontology have in the main failed to get placed on an evidential basis.

(*b*) It was soon realized that the development of a number of each species occurs in a radically different environment from its phylogenetic equivalent and the organs reveal differences in structure and organization adapted to the different requirements. Though this consideration sometimes led to further support of the hypothesis the differences were often so great that the recapitulation could only be inferred by the addition of a plentiful admixture of speculative hypotheses which could not be substantiated.

(*c*) Finally it was realized that as a whole the organic development of the member of a species is remarkably specific—the organism is itself and no other.

Drawing conclusions from a comparative study of phylogeny with ontogeny is thus full of pitfalls, some of which may be made clearer by a simple example. The law under discussion would assert that the gill-clefts of the mammalian embryo recapitulate a stage in evolution corresponding to fish as we know them today. But the embryo of a mammal is never a fish, and its gill-clefts are structurally different and serve quite a different purpose:

BIOLOGICAL THEORY AND CONCEPT OF ARCHETYPES

in the fish the gills are the organs of respiration, but in the mammalian embryo they are organs which appear either to disappear or to form the basis of new organs as development proceeds. In the fish they are adapted and useful organs essential to the life of the fully grown animal, in the mammal they are short-lived, vestigial organs serving the purpose of development.

Before considering ways of translating the law from the physical to the psychological field, there are further difficulties. Not only are the psychic units to be handled essentially different from the physical, but further the biological theory is based upon that of heredity and presupposes genetically determined units. We can, it is true, postulate that genetic factors contribute to archetypal forms, but there is far less justification for supposing that consciousness is genetically determined in anything but the broadest outline. These considerations mean that the whole theory of recapitulation has to be throughly re-established on a different basis. But this has never been attempted; instead it is not infrequent for analogies to be taken to substantiate a theory whose foundations are insecure. The use of the analogy is, as we have seen, to help in detecting archetypes; that children express archetypes is only to be expected, but that their consciousness recapitulates that of the race is far less inherently probable than that organic ontogeny recapitulates phylogeny.

If in the more exact studies of biology the recapitulation is difficult enough to unravel to make many biologists doubt the usefulness of the hypothesis, how much more must this be so in the much less stable and transforming spheres of psychological imagery which lack the stability of bodily organs and are subject to complicated progessions and regressions often exceedingly difficult to trace, let alone evaluate.

We are on much surer ground if we consider that children develop towards the culture pattern of their parents of which the myth is a part. A myth is a cultural form, as Jung formulates when he says:[44]

The first attempts at myth-making can, of course, be observed in children, whose games of make-believe often contain historical echoes. But one must certainly put a large question-mark after the assertion that myths spring from the 'infantile' psychic life of the race. They

[44] *Symbols of Transformation* (Collected Works, Vol. V), London and New York, 1956, pp. 24–5.

BIOLOGICAL THEORY AND CONCEPT OF ARCHETYPES

are on the contrary the most mature product of that young humanity. Just as those first fish-like ancestors of man, with the gill-slits, were not embryos, but fully-developed creatures, so *the myth-making and myth-inhabiting man was a grown-up reality and not a four-year-old child.*[45] Myth is certainly not an infantile phantasm, but one of the most important requisites of primitive life.

Now let us examine how far mythological imagery can be used to support the hypothesis that the consciousness of the individual recapitulates that of humanity. If we compare myths of the origin of the cosmos, assuming that they reveal how consciousness began, with manifestations of the corresponding period in child development, the onset of consciousness in childhood, it is necessary to take the following into account, if we are to avoid serious errors:

(1) Myths are all composed by adult people who are using complex functions undeveloped by the child. Adults can use words easily, combine them to make sentences and combine these together into coherent stories; infants can only make sounds. Such simple facts are regularly overlooked with disastrous consequences. To consider the cosmic myths: the investigator is led to look for mythological forms of expression from elder children imagining that these register the onset of consciousness. The infant's first consciousness is expressed in quite a different medium, it is in terms of the bodily objects that are most important to them. These form the basis of the affective processes which lack even approximately the coherence of form and structure to be found in all myths. If fantasies are investigated in childhood with a view to determining when consciousness originates, a valid conclusion is impossible: it will be far too late.

(2) Myths are part of the social structure. For example: matriarchal myths in which there is no father refer to a culture pattern, and all the persons in that culture had already known grown-up men who lay down a pattern of behaviour for the children and towards which they will develop. In this respect they are 'fathers' even though their sexual role is not recognized and their cultural status is quite different from that maintaining in a patriarchal society.

The states of consciousness in an infant in which there is no

[45] Italics mine.

BIOLOGICAL THEORY AND CONCEPT OF ARCHETYPES

known father at all but only a mother, differ essentially from the adult state of mind to which the matriarchal myth refers.

(3) Any individual differences in development are important. So as to illustrate further the problems which arise when comparing children's material with myths we may consider an example from Neumann's work. He says:[46]

Before the comprehensive human *figure* of the Great Mother appeared, innumerable symbols belonging to her still unformed image arose spontaneously. These symbols—particularly nature symbols from every realm of nature—are in a sense signed with the image of the Great Mother, which, whether they be stone or tree, pool, fruit or animal, lives in them and is identified with them. Gradually, they become linked with the figure of the Great Mother as attributes and form the wreath of symbols that surrounds the archetypal figure and manifests itself in rite and myth.

These symbols appear early in the archetypal stages enunciated by Neumann in his concept of an evolving consciousness, but not one of them is a symbolic form which appears early on in the development of a child's consciousness. It is necessary to look not at archetypal forms, but to the pattern underlying them if any comparison is to be made. Then it becomes clear that both infant and early man have this in common: the images started from part objects, and evolved into a whole object. Just as the infant first experiences parts of his mother's body in numerous images which gradually coalesce into a single one of her whole body, so early man, according to Neumann, formed many spontaneous nature symbols referring to the 'still unformed image' of the Great Mother which later came into being.

But this does not mean that ontogeny has recapitulated phylogeny, for if this had happened it would be necessary to assume that the infants of 'early man' formed no image of their womenfolk at all till after the myth had established its pattern in history![47] There is every reason to assume that the children of 'early man' formed the mother imago in much the same way as our infants and children do today, and just as with our children the

[46] *The Great Mother*, p. 12.

[47] This is the direct consequence of the theory, for according to it the organs are developed first through evolution and then repeated in their evolutionary sequence by each individual embryo. No development of the embryo is possible until the historical process has already occurred.

32

BIOLOGICAL THEORY AND CONCEPT OF ARCHETYPES

complex, organized, mythological forms appeared in consciousness comparatively late in the development of the ego, the early development proceeding on the same basic patterns as that of the later development.

From the point of view of a child psychologist, the origins of social consciousness can and have been regarded as a recapitulation of the earlier stages in the growth of consciousness in childhood. Thus the biogenetic law is reversed, for the adult man is recapitulating the infant's discovery of how a whole mother imago forms when he discovers the 'innumerable symbols' belonging to the Great Mother whose whole image forms out of or through them. This thesis leaves out of account the completely different level and intensity of consciousness and the functional difference between imagination in childhood and adult man.

Both of these hypotheses can be rejected. There is no recapitulation in the sense postulated by the biogenetic law or its reverse, rather there is the same basic pattern, the archetypal entity expressing itself in a different sphere and adapted to a different purpose in consequence of a different orientation of the ego.

From the angle of ego development there is all the difference in the world between an infant and a still greater difference between a child and an adult, as Jung has frequently insisted.[48] The difference is even important in the realm of relatively complex images of the imagination as I have stated elsewhere, by contrasting imaginative activity, which is characteristic of children, and active imagination, which is characteristic of mature humanity.[49]

CONCLUSION

Much of what has been said on the relation of biology to the theory of archetypes is vague. This is intentional; it is justified by the consideration that the relation of body to psyche is still obscure. In drawing analogies I have two considerations in mind: firstly I seek to define fields in which further investigation is

[48] Cf. for example Jung, 'Psychotherapy Today', *The Practice of Psychotherapy*, pp. 95 ff.

[49] Cf. Fordham, 'Active Imagination and Imaginative Activity', *Journal of Analytical Psychology*, Vol. I, No. 2, 1956, pp. 207 ff.

BIOLOGICAL THEORY AND CONCEPT OF ARCHETYPES

likely to prove fruitful, and secondly I am leaving the door open to the possibility that the relation between body and psyche is based not on causal connections but upon synchronicity. Where I have gone further and become precise it is because analytical psychologists have sometimes violated biological theory in a manner which I believe to be unnecessary.

II

REFLECTIONS ON THE ARCHETYPES AND SYNCHRONICITY[1]

JUNG defines synchronicity as meaningful coincidence and in his latest elaboration of his thesis[2] relates it to the theory of scientific knowldge.

Scientists aim on the one hand at establishing facts, on the other at developing coherent, organic theories. The theory is said to be true or false according to whether it fits the facts or not. This assertion does not, however, cover the whole subject, for facts which help in the development of the theoretical structure are, by and large, much more acceptable than awkward ones which threaten it. Scientists are, however, bound to accept all facts if they can be substantiated, but the awkward ones will have to run the gauntlet of a much more virulent critical estimation than the others. There is thus a close relation between facts and theories and they are often considered as belonging to the same class of phenomena.[3] If natural scientists can consider them thus, psychology, in which theories and observable facts are interchangeable, ceases to become such a dubious science.

The supposed phenomena of parapsychology and so of synchronicity have always been suspect because the theory regarding what happens is very weak. There is indeed scarcely any adequate definition of the problems the phenomena present. The

---

[1] A revised version of a paper read to the Analytical Psychology Club, London, which was published with a few alterations in their journal *Harvest*, Summer, 1955.

[2] 'Synchronicity, An Acausal Connecting Principle', *The Interpretation of Nature and the Psyche*, London and New York, 1955.

[3] Cf. Pauli: 'The Influence of Archetypal Ideas on the Scientific Theories of Kepler', ibid.

35

REFLECTIONS ON ARCHETYPES AND SYNCHRONICITY

concept of synchronicity does not fill this gap since it hardly rises to the status of a theory; it is rather an attempt at further definition of the problem

By and large the success of the physical, experimental sciences, which are the most 'scientific' of all the sciences, has depended upon the application of mechanistic concepts. Causality ranks highest amongst them because it makes prediction profitable. But causes do not always produce a predicted effect, they do so only under sufficiently stable conditions, and these are not always forthcoming. Thus I may predict that if I turn on the electrical circuit of my car and press the starter the engine will work. But this does not always happen, and when it does not I look for the cause that has upset the prediction in my mind when I pressed the starter. On the whole, I am glad to say, what is predicted happens!

The phrase 'on the whole' introduces a statistical concept, and a kind of mathematical thinking which has gradually become increasingly important in science. Statistics distinguish between two sets of phenomena: those which are sufficiently ordered to indicate causal connections and to which the notion of prediction can be applied with considerable success, and those whose action is random and which as such obey the laws of chance where the notion of prediction is of little use.

Now Jung has defined synchronicity as an 'acausal connecting principle' manifesting itself in meaningful coincidence: it is random and unpredictable. He therefore makes it clear that synchronicity and chance are related very closely indeed. His general thesis is that in nature there is a class of phenomena manifesting the characteristics of freedom, meaningfulness, acausality. Considered statistically they will appear as chance, but they will not be due to chance; i.e. he cuts right across the duality chance-cause axiom on which statistics are based. As a consequence his use of statistics is, as we shall see, highly original and peculiarly his own.

In order to get to grips with Jung's procedure it is essential to be clear about what it means numerically if we say that events are chance occurrences. Take a large box covered so that nobody can look in; put ninety-nine white billiards balls in it and one which is black. Let somebody put a hand in; lo and behold he picks out the black one. He returns it, shakes up the box vigorously, puts his hand in a second time—it is the black one

REFLECTIONS ON ARCHETYPES AND SYNCHRONICITY

again. This can happen, and it can be by chance; further it can be chance if he does it a number of times and each time draws out the black ball, but it becomes increasingly improbable on each occasion. The overall improbability increases progressively, even though each time he puts in his hand the probability of drawing out the black ball is the same, i.e. $\frac{1}{100}$. Because the matter is not always so simple, mathematicians have invented a whole set of equations to help in deciding whether groups of events of this kind are 'significant' or not. The term 'significant' has a technical meaning, namely that the phenomena under scrutiny are not likely to be due to chance because they are so improbable on the chance hypothesis (Null hypothesis) that the hypothesis can be questioned. It will be noted that this leaves room for extraordinary events, i.e. events that are very improbable on a Null hypothesis and for which no cause is conceivable. Thus 'significant' events can be due to chance, but it is unusual for them to be so. With this consideration in mind Jung conducted an experiment in which he used statistics (see below). He found that none of his results were significant in the technical sense, i.e. they do not disprove a Null hypothesis. His use of statistics, therefore, had an aim exactly the reverse to the usual one. He used them to define the region in which synchronistic phenomena are most likely. This is one of his ingenious uses of statistics; though it has been criticized, it is original and clearly relevant from his standpoint.

Chance and the idea of probability are closely connected. It has already been necessary to use the concepts together, so further consideration of the latter is called for. Probability can be a numerical concept. To start from our billiard balls: it is improbable that anybody will pick out the black ball two consecutive times so long as the balls are indistinguishable in other respects than their colour, which cannot be seen.

The probability of drawing the black ball twice in succession can be stated mathematically using the multiplication law; it is $(\frac{1}{100})^2$. Thus it is unlikely to be due to chance, but we have to remember that extraordinarily improbable events can occur by chance: for example, it is possible by chance to draw out the black ball ten consecutive times, but it is very improbable indeed, and if it were to occur we should have to be very sure that there was no cause operating. The probability would be $(\frac{1}{100})^{10}$. In

37

REFLECTIONS ON ARCHETYPES AND SYNCHRONICITY

practice nobody would believe that such a run was due to chance.[4]

It is the principle of convergence which makes statistics more satisfactory if large numbers be used. This can be seen by returning to our example.

The empirical probability (p) resulting from our drawing out the black ball twice ($n=2$) in two draws ($N=2$) and then making no more draws is $\frac{2}{2}=1$, or absolute certainty; on 10 draws it is $\frac{10}{10}=1$, again absolute certainty. Both these would suggest that we can be certain of drawing out the black ball every time. However, if N be infinitely large, then the true probabilities are quite different—they are those which are stated above, i.e. $p=(\frac{1}{100})^2$ for drawing the black ball out twice in succession, and $p=(\frac{1}{100})^{10}$ for drawing the black ball out ten times in succession; these are the figures to which p will converge as N becomes infinitely large. It was because of this principle that Jung took a large number of horoscopes (966 in all). The principle of convergence was quite evident in his experiment, for as the figures became larger he converged towards the true probability; this confirms that his observations all fall within the sphere of chance. It thus seems that if one is going to look for synchronicity it is desirable to ignore the true probability and operate with empirical probability using small numbers.

It is thus important that Jung's synchronistic events showed up in the smaller batches—indeed it is quite clear that if we want to observe synchronicity large numbers are undesirable. Thus most of the more outstanding synchronicities are observable only once and are not repeatable.

There are other kinds of probability. When the events under consideration are relatively unknown mathematical logic cannot be used. This is very common in war, when you do not know what the enemy will do, but a general can and does act on an assessment of a large number of more or less unknown factors, at the end of which he has to make up his mind and act on a probability.

[4] A numerical definition of probability runs as follows: 'If we try an event N times and on n occasions we get a "success", then the empirical probability is $p=\frac{n}{N}$. The true probability is the value to which p will *converge* as N becomes infinitely large.'

(For this definition I am indebted to M. J. Moroney, whose excellent *Facts from Figures* (Penguin Books) I have consulted in all this work. For the more philosophical questions of probability theory, cf. Bertrand Russell: *Human Knowledge* (London, 1948)).

REFLECTIONS ON ARCHETYPES AND SYNCHRONICITY

This probability is different from mathematical probability inasmuch as it is much less exact and usually involves intuition in contrast to mathematical logic. For example, Jung may have thought it probable that his patient who dreamt of a scarab (see below, pp. 43 f.) would be upset if he showed her the beetle, and he was correct.

Finally events can be regarded as probable or improbable on completely non-rational grounds. They can be accepted or rejected because of the affects to which they give rise.

Turning to credulity, which is also an affective condition closely associated with probability: if an event is probable it is more credible, and if it is improbable it is less credible. This is a relation between credulity and probability, and a relation which has proved important in connection with synchronicity, for one of the features of synchronicity is its incredibility. Sometimes it is not believed because the phenomena are doubted for a variety of good and bad reasons, sometimes because the interpretation of them cuts across current theories or makes a development of them impossible.

(1) The first two objections against the objective occurrence of the phenomena state them to be falsifications:

(*a*) The events are often reported under affective conditions so that the subject may be in error owing to projection or hallucination. The phenomena are often of a startling kind and on this account can be repressed or distorted. For instance, some people will turn up the *I Ching*[5] when under the influence of an apparently insoluble conflict, and when the text says something relevant will be so shocked that they call it nonsense or reason it away or repress it. This difficulty can be checked by the presence of a second person—an analyst for example.

(*b*) The particular phenomenon cannot be repeated, though phenomena belonging to its class can be observed over and over again. This objection is one of exactness—no phenomena that have occurred can be repeated; once a particular atom has been split it cannot be split again. It is a problem of definition of the class of phenomena under consideration, not of repeatability as such.

[5] The *I Ching* is a Chinese book of wise, more or less paradoxical sayings of great antiquity. It can be and has been used for purposes of divination. Cf. the *I Ching or Book of Changes*, trans. Wilhelm and Baynes, London and New York, 1950.

REFLECTIONS ON ARCHETYPES AND SYNCHRONICITY

(2) The difficulties over the interpretation arise from their arousing scientific scepticism since they cut across current scientific theories, particularly the statistical ones which because of their increasing usefulness are very firmly entrenched.

Jung has occupied himself with events which appear very improbable and on this ground would seem to have a cause. Yet a cause cannot be conceived which is credible. Therefore they seem extraordinary, and this at once leads to strong resistances against their serious consideration and they are either rejected or enthusiastically accepted lock, stock, and barrel. Yet we know that such unresolvable dilemmas belong to a typical mythological theme in which the impossible happens, that is why they evoke archetypal patterns. This gives an insight into why parapsychology leads to theories based on powers and forces of various kinds, and why we get initials like E.S.P., or P.K., which give the appearance of scientific respectability and do not introduce mythology.

Turning to Jung's experiment in synchronicity: he collected a large number of horoscopes of married people and he investigated the conjunctions (δ) and oppositions ($\mathcal{S}$) of sun ($\odot$), moon ($\mathbb{C}$), Mars (δ), Venus ($\female$), Ascendent and Descendent in them. He investigated all the δ and $\mathcal{S}$ of these aspects in the married pairs and set them out in a table. Statistical assessment showed that all the frequencies of the conjunctions and oppositions came within the sphere of chance.

The horoscopes, collected by random sampling, were assembled in three batches and the greatest frequencies in each batch were found to be $\mathbb{C}$ δ $\odot$, $\mathbb{C}$ δ $\mathbb{C}$, $\mathbb{C}$ δ Ascendent. In each case, though occurring as chance phenomena over the whole collection,[6] they were apparently less probable if considered in the small batches. If, however, the three conjunctions be taken as a class, and astrological tradition holds that they can be so regarded, then they become highly improbable, and so it is possible to say that the phenomena are at once chance and yet not chance. Therefore Jung considers that he has defined a set of synchronistic phenomena consisting of three improbable chance events corresponding to the astrological traditions dating from Ptolemy and Cardanus.[7]

[6] Principle of convergence, see above.
[7] The synchronistic basis for astrology has been interestingly developed by Philip Metman in the first volume of *Harvest*.

40

REFLECTIONS ON ARCHETYPES AND SYNCHRONICITY

There is no real difficulty over the essential feature of this experiment once the necessary elements of statistics are understood, and so long as it is realized that Jung has a set of phenomena in mind which do not fit statistical preconceptions. The critic must turn to criticism of the astrological traditions which Jung appears to regard as meaningful because of his concept of archetypes and not because of any belief in astrology, which he points out is irrelevant. It will be noted that it seems as if the chance events had been rendered meaningful because of the archetypes operating in the experiments.

Nowhere is it clearer that Jung uses statistical computation in his own way. By taking the three conjunctions as a class, a mathematician would immediately note that a new element is introduced resulting in a calculation which made chance most unlikely. What would he do? He would at once automatically look for a new hypothesis based on causality. This might lead him to investigate the astrologers' claim to predict, and therefore causality is implied in their calculations. These considerations would open up a new field of investigation into the astrological traditions and their empirical foundations.

Jung is not in the least interested in this, since from his standpoint it is not relevant. He goes with the mathematician so far as to reject the Null hypothesis, but he chooses synchronicity as the alternative, and finding that the phenomena fit his definition of it he has no need to look for incredible causes. Thus it is more clear that Jung's experiment is not statistical in the technical sense. Statisticians base their thinking upon the mutual exclusiveness of the causal laws and the laws of chance, there is no room for synchronicity. If synchronicity influenced the probability theory the basis of their science would have to be completely revised. This they naturally do not want to do without very good reason indeed.

Jung's psychological standpoint, however, makes it much easier for him to remain unmoved by the logic of statistics which is based on the abstraction of opposites which synchronicity transcends because of its symbolic (archetypal) associations.

Rhine's experiments have been useful in drawing attention to the peculiar phenomena under consideration and are particularly interesting here because he has used statistics. They have given rise to much uncritical credulity together with increased scepticism

REFLECTIONS ON ARCHETYPES AND SYNCHRONICITY

as if to balance it. Rhine started from the idea that the phenomena he observed were due to chance (i.e. he started from a Null hypothesis), and then believed he had shown that they could not thus be explained.

He believed that he had shown that certain individuals can predict the random behaviour of cards or dice with a frequency greater than would be expected if the predictions were based upon chance. Rhine further discovered that the number of correct predictions rose if the subject was credulous, and diminished if he was sceptical about the whole proceeding. This means that there is some connection between the psyche of the subject predicting and the turn of the cards or the fall of the dice. The psyche must be important in his experiments since the objects behaved according to chance—Rhine and his co-workers took much care to ensure this—but the prediction by the subject appeared not to do so. Further, he showed that the conscious attitude of the subject was significant and that the experiments were not influenced by changes in space and time. Rhine does not seem to see that this upsets a causal hypothesis and he thinks in terms of perception and energy.[8]

Rhine's experiments in fact open a door for those who want to think that his observations reveal the existence of something more than chance, and they conclude that since chance is most improbable there must be a cause. Jung, however, points out that Rhine's results transcend space and time, therefore they cannot be energic phenomena, and further that causes do not work if space and time are not fixed. Therefore the Rhine results are exceedingly peculiar, i.e. they are predictable but no cause can be conceived; they are meaningful acausal phenomena, or in a word fall into the class of events which Jung calls synchronistic.

So much for the framework of Jung's experimental research and the application of his view to Rhine's experiments. He has not only, however, investigated synchronicity using statistics, for the main bulk of his investigation and indeed the basis for formulating the concept has been derived from clinical observation of individual patients. The investigation of individuals brings about great changes because theory becomes more clearly an object of study and can be evaluated in relation not so much to the general corpus of knowledge as such as to the person as an individual.

[8] Cf. *The Reach of the Mind*, London, 1948.

REFLECTIONS ON ARCHETYPES AND SYNCHRONICITY

For instance, there are patients who think about synchronicity, but these thoughts are now evaluated in terms of the total psyche. From this position it may well be evident that it is desirable for a patient to think about chance, causality and synchronicity rather less because his thinking is defensive, or for another to do so rather more, since all sorts of coincidences get given meanings which are not relevant.

Jung's case of the scarab illustrating synchronicity is extremely significant from the individual position even though it cannot be investigated numerically.

Let us look more carefully at Jung's case.

A young woman I was treating had, at a critical moment, a dream in which she was given a golden scarab. While she was telling me this dream I sat with my back to the closed window. Suddenly I heard a noise behind me, like a gentle tapping. I turned round and saw a flying insect knocking against the window pane from outside. I opened the window and caught the creature in the air as it flew in. It was the nearest analogy to a golden scarab that can be found in our latitudes, a *Scarabaeide*, the 'common rose-chafer' (*Cetonia aurata*), which contrary to its usual habits had evidently felt an urge to get into a dark room at this particular moment. I must admit that nothing like it has ever happened to me before or since, and that the dream of the patient has remained unique in my experience. . . . Up to the time of the dream little or no progress with the case had been made. I should explain that the main reason for this was my patient's animus, which was steeped in Cartesian philosophy and clung so rigidly to its own idea of reality that the efforts of three doctors—I was the third—had not been able to mollify it. Evidently something quite irrational was needed which was beyond my power to produce. The dream alone was enough to disturb ever so slightly the rationalistic attitude of my patient. But when the 'scarab' came flying in through the window her natural being could burst through the armour of her animus possession and the process of transformation could at last begin to move. Any essential change of attitude signifies a psychic renewal which is usually accompanied by symbols of rebirth in the patient's dreams and fantasies. The scarab is a classic example of a rebirth symbol. The ancient Egyptian Book of What Is in the Netherworld describes how the dead sun-god changes himself at the tenth station into Khepera, the scarab, and then, at the twelfth station, mounts the bark which carries the rejuvenated sun-god into the morning sky.

Supposing Jung's example be due to chance, what would it mean? It would mean that he has done something like putting

REFLECTIONS ON ARCHETYPES AND SYNCHRONICITY

his hand in the box and taking out the black ball twice, or rather a black one and another resembling it. The fact that the patient was upset by this is another matter; a statistician might raise his eyebrows, or a sceptical analyst would infer that it was due to her transference to Jung which he was exploiting to impress his patient with the limitation of her outlook. This consideration opens up the problem of transference in the examples of this kind.

The individual analytical method of approach thus has clear advantages over experiments with a large number of units. Firstly, in the individual it is possible to see thinking, or its absence, more accurately in relation to the psychic functions as a whole and to get a sense of the numinosity of a meaningful coincidence which a general statement can only give with great difficulty. Secondly, since it occurs within the transference the matter becomes more 'real' and less abstract. The following case illustrates my meaning.

The man concerned was aged about thirty-one years. He was part owner of two yachts. One was an ocean racer, the other a Norwegian-built vessel—a converted lifeboat. His share in the racer had been given to him by his father, whose ambitions in the sphere of ocean racing, he hoped, would be realized by his son. The money for the Norwegian vessel came from his mother; it was much preferred by the son, who liked the more robust, solid and seaworthy craft.

Each year there is an ocean race, the most famous and arduous of the season, and the father had come to England from his home abroad in the hope of seeing his son win it; this was not to be. It so happened that the son was going through a period of acute conflict with his father, and only after many misgivings did he captain the boat. They started off with a fair breeze, but, opposite the Needles in the Solent, the mast fell overboard for no apparent reason, and put the boat out of the race.

At a loose end, and somewhat shaken by this surprising solution to his conflict, my patient decided to join the other boat which his partner and two girls were sailing down the coast, and he knew they would reach harbour that evening. He arrived to see a boat high and dry with its mast projecting over the top of a cottage close to the jetty; it was his boat which had run aground and could not be refloated.

Here is a meaningful coincidence. It delivered a severe blow to

44

REFLECTIONS ON ARCHETYPES AND SYNCHRONICITY

his racing career and he soon decided to sell his share in the boat.

Jung has stated that these meaningful coincidences are always related to the archetypes of the unconscious, and in this case the whole incident is associated with the son's relation to his father. The conflict between them was a typical archetypal one, but I did not discover its detailed content till a long time afterwards. Further, his whole relation to boats and sailing was pregnant with meaning and some of the experiences while at sea had a cosmic and even mystical character clearly pointing to active archetypes. He would experience a dissolving sense of unity with the universe in which he learnt to orientate himself in various ways, particularly with the aid of a sextant and compass, with which he felt he could not only take his bearings in the material world but also in his psychic one.

In order to illustrate how meaningful this coincidence was, another related phenomenon is worth recording. For months afterwards he looked for and found 'significant coincidences': two people, one after the other, looking at him in the same way in the street, or two people wearing the same type of hat, all these and many others seemed meaningful. There arose, indeed, a sort of system of coincidences as an echo to the real synchronicity. Jung has pointed out that the occurrence of coincidences does not in itself constitute synchronicity—it is its meaningfulness which is important: without this meaningfulness synchronicity cannot be said to have occurred. This case amplifies the proposition and makes it clear that not all coincidences which seem to be meaningful are necessarily synchronistic. There is a psychopathological use of coincidences—it is when a significance belonging to another source is displaced.

To return to the example: the first two events have about them a quality of surprise. There were other surprising events. As the Norwegian boat was sailing into the harbour a woman was looking out of the window of her cottage. She had been housekeeper to my patient and his friend 'H' when they were at a naval collage and she thought as the boat came in, 'That must be "H"'. As if to emphasize the relation between the boat and one of its crew, after the ship ran aground and when the tide ebbed, the mast of the vessel came to point directly over the cottage in which the housekeeper lived.

REFLECTIONS ON ARCHETYPES AND SYNCHRONICITY

This coincidence is significant because the ship was already associated with the patient's mother and the housekeeper clearly stood as a maternal figure to the boys.

In subsequent months I gradually learnt that there were causes of a fairly obvious kind which contributed towards these events. My patient never discovered any cause for the mast falling overboard, though there must have been a mechanical one; he did, however, succeed in finding out at least a likely reason for the second boat running aground: there were two women and 'H' on the boat; 'H' had been having a love affair with one woman but had become attracted to the second; he had, indeed, come to the conclusion during the cruise that he wanted to terminate his affair with the first and marry the second. As the boat came into the harbour he left the tiller to attend to other matters, handing it over to the first woman—the one he was abandoning. It takes only a little knowledge of human nature to realize that she would not be the best person to control the vessel, indeed she had the best of reasons for wrecking the vessel in which she had lost her lover.

This example illustrates the interplay of factors in such a complex series of events which can now be enumerated. The synchronistic events are:

(1) The mast falling overboard and so ending the race, coupled with the second boat running aground.

(2) The housekeeper's intuition and the mast pointing over her cottage.

The analysis of the causal factors in a case cannot and should not be avoided. Not only has Jung stated that synchronicity is acausal, so that all obvious causal factors must be eliminated, but for another more psychological reason.

It will be remembered that Jung's case in which the scarab appeared at a crucial point, resulted in the collapse of his patient's defensive rational consciousness, and presumably as a consequence she was from then on able to allow the images of the unconscious a place in her psychic life.

In the analytic process the relation of the conscious to the unconscious is all important. In my patient's case it was important to take into account his conscious reasoning attitude which did not show itself to be enough in evidence owing to the profusion of dream and fantasy. If he paid attention to

REFLECTIONS ON ARCHETYPES AND SYNCHRONICITY

causes, i.e. the more humdrum aspects of the incidents, it was valuable.

We have now arrived at the position of seeing that synchronicity can be considered in two ways:

(1) From the viewpoint of the conscious.

(2) In relation to the unconscious archetypes.

(1) The various factors contributed towards my patient's conscious attitude. This was one of interest and fascination. The patient had a good intellect. He had begun training as a physicist and was successful in this field, but gave it up in favour of a more 'humane' occupation. He was prepared for the acceptance of acausal happenings, since causality had lost its fascination, partly because of his high intelligence and partly as a result of his studies in his original subject. Further, his intuition smelt out such events, and this somewhat too easily. This accounts for the echo phenomena which I mentioned in passing—I refer to his tendency to presuppose synchronicity in coincidences.

In addition he knew of synchronicity from analytical psychology, though he had not read Jung's papers which had not been published at that time.

We therefore have three elements combining to make up his conscious attitude:

(*a*) his function type;

(*b*) his training and experience as a scientist;

(*c*) his complex and highly ambivalent transference into which came the knowledge that I accepted Jung's observations upon this topic.

Note that (*c*) contributes towards the conscious attitude but contains unconscious elements.

There is a further consideration whilst we are anatomizing the conscious attitude of my patient. Let us consider what would have happened if the *dramatis personae* had been more conscious, by which I mean more able not only to know about what was going on, but at the same time to control it and take action about it. We can see at once that there need not have been any synchronicity if the patient had been able to handle his conflict with his father; he would not have gone on the racing yacht. Suppose a friend had taken the boat on the race and the mast had fallen over, he would have regarded it as an odd event or even rather a joke. If he had not taken part in the race, he would, in all

REFLECTIONS ON ARCHETYPES AND SYNCHRONICITY

likelihood, have gone on the other boat and piloted it safely into harbour, for if he had been conscious he would not have let the girl take the tiller. The only extraordinary event—not particularly meaningful to the patient—was that the housekeeper had an accurate intuition (guess) about 'H'.

But let us suppose that all the events happened exactly as recorded, but my patient's problem was solved. They would not have had meaning; he might have cursed his bad luck and gone his way uninfluenced.

In other words synchronicity depends upon a relatively unconscious state of mind, i.e. an *abaissement du niveau mental*.

(2) Relation of synchronous events to archetypes.

It is to my mind Jung's most useful contribution to have linked up the meaningful coincidences with the activity of archetypes. In this way it is possible to differentiate real synchronicity from what he calls 'runs of chance'.

The case I have described was not connected with the appearance of a manifest archetypal image after the manner of Jung's patient, but the conflict was a typical one and much later on the primordial image revealing the archetype appeared.

My aim in giving such an example was to underline the importance of keeping clearly in mind the unconscious nature of archetypes. The image is one and only one of its manifestations. So much research has been undertaken on the images from the unconscious that it tends to be taken for granted that an archetype is its image. On the contrary, the images which tell us most about it only refer to, but do not reveal, its essential nature which according to Jung is 'psychoid'.[9]

CONCLUDING RUMINATION

My case is half way between Jung's and another one. The other one should be of a person who lives by synchronicity, i.e. who regularly experiences synchronistic phenomena and who in consequence disregards cause and prediction; but that would have to be the subject of another paper. I can, however, say that according to my idea such a person would be very unconscious— using the word in its technical sense—and it would be very hard

[9] Cf. 'The Spirit of Psychology', *Spirit and Nature*, New York, 1954; London, 1955.

REFLECTIONS ON ARCHETYPES AND SYNCHRONICITY

for him to live in our civilization; we may note, however, that Jung asserts that synchronicity lies at the foundations of Chinese culture.

Perhaps I can refer indirectly to the imaginary second patient by a comment on the *I Ching*, which Jung says, and I take it that most analytical psychologists can agree, is based upon synchronicity. The motif for using this remarkable book is important; furthermore the book itself appears to know this, for on one occasion after getting a good answer to an acute problem to which I could get no other solution, I decided to throw the coins again on the same problem with a view to seeing what would happen. On the second throw I got the following:

MENG—YOUTHFUL FOLLY

The Judgement

Youthful folly has success.

It is not I who seek the young fool;

The young fool seeks me.

At the first oracle I inform him.

If he asks two or three times, it is importunity.

If he importunes, I give him no information.

Perseverance furthers.

Only recently I was told by a patient that he had got the same result.

My motive had, at least in consciousness, been scientific. I had acted on the scientific assumption that if it can produce a good answer once it can do it again. I had not expected the same hexagram, but had rather supposed that the ambiguity of the pronouncement would suffice to produce a second good answer. This was apparently wrong; the *I Ching*'s answer was explicit and conclusive, it completely destroyed any possibility of my perpetrating such an experiment again for a long time. The *I Ching* produced such a strong effect that only since I started writing this paper could I conceive myself doing it again. The experience gave me an extraordinary regard for the volumes which I anticipate will continue for the rest of my life. It struck right into the unconscious psyche and mobilized there all the peculiar psychology that is connected with oracular utterances.

This statement introduces a theory of my own[10] which states

[10] I can now disown this theory, for I had overlooked that Jung says almost the same. In his essay 'The Spirit of Psychology', in *Spirit and Nature*,

REFLECTIONS ON ARCHETYPES AND SYNCHRONICITY

that there is a relation between the degree of consciousness and the occurrence of synchronicity. I have already pointed to this, asking the reader to imagine that no synchronicity would have occurred if the members of the drama of the two boats had been more conscious.

It will now be apparent that though I am interested in the general problems presented by synchronicity I believe it is more valuable to consider them under the circumstances of analysis or in relation to the individual. There is one great advantage in this. It is possible to get in far greater detail than would otherwise be possible, the circumstances of the event and the psychological factors and dynamisms involved. Under these circumstances it does not necessarily matter whether the material events are proved to be chance or caused, since the synchronicity occurs in an individual; but *it is important that the individual's belief in a cause be undermined* where this is used in the service of repression.

This advantage appeals to me and outweighs other considerations; firstly that owing to the transference situation the matter needs special handling, and secondly that in analysis the primary concern must be the patient. With regard to the first consideration, if the transference be properly handled it can be valuable because the archetype to which the synchronicity is related can be hidden in it and so come under closer scrutiny than might otherwise be possible.[11] The second consideration applies to all medical science which has a humane objective. For humane reasons it may be necessary to neglect the phenomena altogether, or the patient may be insufficiently concerned with the scientific requirements and so the phenomena be rendered valueless from a research point of view.

In conclusion I would say that I have only tentative reflections to offer upon this difficult, obscure and controversial topic, which unfortunately threatens to become fashionable. This means that credulity makes nonsense of the whole subject.

London and New York, 1954, he says (p. 441): 'When an unconscious content passes over into consciousness its synchronistic manifestation ceases; conversely, synchronistic phenomena can be evoked by putting the subject into an unconscious state (trance).'

[11] The archetypal phenomena related to my patient's experience have not been exhausted for several years after the events he reported.

III

REFLECTIONS ON IMAGE AND SYMBOL[1]

THE nature and content of any particular image, especially if it appears in a dream or product of imagination, inevitably raises complex questions which would seem to be reflected in the protean use of the word symbol. The word, as Stein[2] points out, is derived from

> . . . *sym*, i.e. *syn*, which means 'together, common, simultaneous, with, according to', and *bolon* which means 'that which has been thrown', from *ballo* 'I throw'. 'Symbol' thus means something perceptible as the result of an activity which throws together such things *as have something in common*, and in such a way that one thing somehow accords with another not presented to the senses and is synchronous with it.

In spite of the difficulty of exact definition, the question of whether an image be symbolic or not is an urgent one for any analyst to ask himself. He knows that the answer is significant in terms of psychic life, for symbols live, can be broken up, killed, or turned from good to evil by neglect or malusage. On the other hand those that appear corrupted or evil can be revived or changed for the better, though once dead they cannot be brought back to life in the same form.

Lately the problem of symbolism has been raised in relation to the theory of sense perception and has led to surprising and significant conclusions: the perceptual image, originally unquestioned by the ordinary man but disputed by the philosophers,

---

[1] The original version of this paper was read to a group of interested persons at St. Anne's House, Soho, London, as part of a series of papers discussing symbolism. The original version has been greatly altered and was published in the *Journal of Analytical Psychology*, Vol. II, Part I.

[2] Stein's paper 'What is a Symbol Supposed to be', *Journal of Analytical Psychology*, Vol. II, Part I, pp. 73 ff.

REFLECTIONS ON IMAGE AND SYMBOL

has been broken up by scientific investigation so that the original naïve experience of it as a direct, so to say, photographic image of the object no longer holds.

It has been discovered that the stimulated neurones in the brain form patterns on the cortex unlike the shape of the object under observation. This is almost all that the body is known to contribute to the apparently true conscious image of the external object.[3]

This image is called symbolic by neurophysiologists because it represents the external object closely enough for its existence to be established by inference. This usage is striking and more significant than the defined sense indicates, for in ancient Greece symbols were tallies. They were:

halves of two corresponding pieces of a bone, coin, or other object which two strangers, or any other two parties broke between them in order to have proof of the identity of the presenter of the one part to the other. . . . The symbol, the broken off part, is not a separate element, but carries with it and points to wherever it goes, the whole in which it has participated as well as the situation in which it was broken in half; when it is 'thrown together' and matched with the remaining half the whole has value because the symbol grips the two opposites together and so can convey—not create or apply—this value.[4]

If we are prepared, following Stein, to accept the idea that certain words are rooted in the primitive layers of the psyche, and so mean more than we do consciously, it would seem that the choice of the word symbol is here more significant than its conscious choice would indicate.

Its defined sense corresponds clearly to part of Jung's definition of a symbol, though he is referring only to inner symbolic images when he says:[5] '. . . the symbol always presupposes that the chosen expression is the best possible description, or formula, of a relatively unknown fact; a fact, however, which is none the less recognized or postulated as existing.'

We know next to nothing about the process of inner perception, but it will be agreed that for neurophysiologists to have hit upon such a closely analogous concept is striking.

The comparative study of myths has led to the concept of

[3] Cf. Russell Brain, *Mind Perception and Science*, Oxford, 1951.
[4] Stein, op. cit., p. 77.
[5] Cf. *Psychological Types*, London and New York, 1923, p. 601.

REFLECTIONS ON IMAGE AND SYMBOL

the mythologem, which refers to the core of a single myth or a group or class of myths. Kerenyi, the Hungarian scholar, has grouped together many myths on the basis of this concept; an example is the 'divine child' under which heading he instances Buddha, Krishna, Hermes, Cupid, Dionysus, Kullervo. Tom Thumb, Strong Hans, Jesus, and many others. Here is his definition of a mythologem:[6]

> In a true mythologem . . . meaning is not something that could be expressed just as well and just as fully in a non-mythological way. Mythology is not simply a mode of expression in whose stead another simpler and more readily understandable form might have been chosen. . . . Like music, mythology too can be more appropriate to the times or less. There are times when the greatest 'thoughts' could only have been expressed in music. But in that case the 'greatest' is precisely what can be expressed in music and in no other way. So with mythology. Just as music has a meaning that is satisfying in the sense that every meaningful whole is satisfying, so every true mythologem has its satisfying meaning. This meaning . . . can be fully expressed only in mythological terms.

It will have been noticed that the term symbol does not enter into this definition; why Kerenyi does not use it is, I expect, because of his association with Jung. Nor does he refer to the myth as a perception, though I believe this term is appropriate; his emphasis is upon expression and meaning and he leaves out that these must be perceived. The meaning is contained in the myth and we can be aware (i.e. conscious) of it or not; that is as far as he goes.

In the *Introduction to a Science of Mythology*, Jung fills in the gap and takes up the problem of psychological meaning in his contribution. Here he asserts that it comes from the psychoid archetypes[7] of the unconscious which are expressed indirectly in the consciousness as images, the archetypal images, and these correspond almost exactly to Kerenyi's mythologems. Thus behind the image is an unknown 'X'. We shall see that the symbol necessarily includes the 'X'. The mythologem in this way represents the 'relatively unknown fact'.

[6] Jung and Kerenyi, *Introduction to a Science of Mythology*, London, 1950, p. 4.

[7] Cf. 'The Spirit of Psychology' in *Spirit and Nature,* Essays from the Eranos Yearbooks, New York, 1954.

REFLECTIONS ON IMAGE AND SYMBOL

But Jung appears to think that the archetypal image alone is not the symbol, for he states:[8] 'A symbol is always a creation of an extremely complex nature, since data proceeding from every psychic function have entered into its composition.' He means that both the conscious and the unconscious, i.e. the archetypes, are needed to make a symbol, and therefore the images are an essential part, but not the whole, of symbolic life. What, therefore, is the activity that converts the image into a symbol?

An essential part of Kerenyi's attitude is to regard the image as a true representation. In this he is almost religious, except that he stands outside the myth with an air of impartiality. But he is certainly not religious in the dogmatic sense, though there is something close to a belief in his view that the myth is an expression of an inner process. Here he reaches out towards the type of mysticism of which Blake is a good example, or Catholic religious like St. Teresa of Avila, or Mechthild of Magdeburg. Religion is the subject-matter of Kerenyi's studies, but he is never inside the whole process like the mystic, who believed he was discovering how to perceive a reality of far greater significance than either external or psychic reality.

Kerenyi's attitude is also not so far removed from the naïve view of perception, the more or less sensuous perceptions being replaced by meaningful forms.

By way of comparison here are two attitudes which are not symbolic.

(1) Instead of being accepted, the image is explained. For instance, it is said to be the result of an earlier perception because it is like a picture which was seen earlier, or is a reproduction of some event which took place in the past and has been forgotten, i.e. the image is conceived in terms of more or less clear memory traces.

(2) Where the image does not seem comprehensible in these terms it is said to be in need of analytical dissection before its true significance emerges. The image is not the best possible perception or expression, but a distortion or deception which can be better expressed. Stein wants to call this the *metabole*, for he says:[9]

[8] Cf. *Psychological Types*, Definition 51.
[9] Cf. op. cit., pp. 74f.

54

REFLECTIONS ON IMAGE AND SYMBOL

. . . during the classical Greek period *syn* was used only by poets and by Xenophon, whilst in ordinary language the word *meta* was employed in the sense of 'with, together'.

Just as in fairy tales, dreams, and in discourse with patients we take notice not only of what does happen but also what does *not* happen or is *not* mentioned, so we must be aware that the compound *symbolon* is formed by means of a noble archaic word of the poets, and not by means of the word *meta*. The word *meta* too was used to form a compound with the word *ballo*; *metaballo*, whence *metabole*. But here the original meaning of throwing together has developed into that of 'turn-over, change, conversion, substitution'.

These two general attitudes can be more or less adequate according to the images under consideration.

Religion is the discipline in which the symbolic attitude is most evident and where the correct images are chosen for its application. The validity of mystical experiences may sometimes be doubted, but mystics dwell in the midst of living symbols which continue to live because of their attitude towards them, which gives metaphysical reality to a cosmic system in which God is central, ultimate and incomprehensible. This cosmic system is conceived as a reality just as much as the material object and religion bends its energies towards realizing it in consciousness.

In contrast, and sometimes set in opposition to it, is the scientific attitude, which has indeed forced religious people to review and change their concepts of religious experience in important respects, and is even used in the hands of rationalists to try to demolish religion altogether. In this they ignore the historical affinity between essential elements in both disciplines—an affinity well expressed by Bertrand Russell in *The Scientific Outlook*:[10]

> Until quite recently, men of science have felt themselves the high-priests of a noble cult, namely, the cult of truth; not truth as the religious sects understand it, i.e. as the battleground of a collection of dogmatists, but truth as a quest, a vision faintly appearing and again vanishing, a hoped-for sun to meet the Heraclitean fire in the soul. It is because science was so conceived, that men of science were willing to suffer privations and persecutions, and to be execrated as enemies of established creeds.

Scientists are thus vulnerable in denying the validity of a religious attitude, but the efficiency of abstract thought has

[10] London, 1931, pp. 102–3.

55

REFLECTIONS ON IMAGE AND SYMBOL

undoubtedly led them to overlook the possibility that their abstract theory is the equivalent of mythology and that they may be in a somewhat unusual sense religious without knowing it.

Pauli, the physicist, has indeed suggested something of the kind in a recent essay, 'The Influence of Archetypal Ideas on Kepler's Theories',[11] in which he has set out the following argument. Because scientific theories have developed far beyond the possibility of experience, the question of the nature of the bridge between sense data and concept needs investigation. Pure logic cannot construct the bridge, and therefore he suggests that in the first place the process of scientific discovery is not based upon perception on the one hand, and the elaboration of logical constructions on the other, but primarily upon '. . . a "matching" of inner images pre-existent in the human psyche with external objects and their behaviour'.[12] The inner images he relates to the archetypal images and he considers that the scientific theory is the abstract equivalent of these archetypes: 'As *ordering* operators and image-formers in this world of symbolical image, the archetypes thus function as the sought-for bridge between the sense perceptions and the ideas and are, accordingly, a necessary presupposition even for evolving a scientific theory of nature.'[13]

He explains the failure to observe this step in scientific discovery to rationalism, which has not obliterated it but only kept it unconscious. In order to illustrate his thesis he therefore elucidates the example of Kepler in whom symbolical images of a religious nature ran side by side with abstract scientific concepts.

It is commonly realized that the metaphor is a useful instrument in the process, but already some abstraction has occurred. However, scientists frequently like to dispense with metaphors with more satisfaction than respect, and without realizing the possibility that their abstract theories rest upon an even more despised and rejected parent, the myth. Yet it may very well turn out that the symbolic images have a necessary and even essential, but provisional, status in the process of scientific discovery and therefore science does not differ from an essential feature of religion, since both depend upon symbolic activity in the psyche.

[11] In *The Interpretation of Nature and the Psyche*, London and New York, 1955.
[12] Ibid., p. 152.   [13] Ibid., p. 153.

REFLECTIONS ON IMAGE AND SYMBOL

By now it will be clear that the conscious attitude is important in relation to the symbol, even though it may be repressed, and we can now return to Jung's statement that '. . . data proceeding from every psychic function have entered into its composition'. It is possible to get an idea of what he means in a very precise manner because he has succeeded in constructing a provisional model of the psyche. The model, of which there could be many, is an abstraction derived from innumerable observations and its form corresponds to psychical experiences. Jung's model is as follows: he divides the psyche into two divisions, the conscious and the unconscious. In the centre of the conscious is the ego nucleus; it has a sort of coherent body and is conceived as the centre which organizes and handles the contents of the conscious.

The ego can have two main attitudes; it can face the outer world—when it does this it is extraverted—or it can face the inner world, when it is introverted. It has at its disposal four modes of functioning, two perceptive and irrational, termed sensation and intuition. Sensation perceives facts outwardly or inwardly—it is the reality function; intuition possibilities, and when introverted can evoke inner images which seem to appear from nowhere and for no reason. Then there are two rational functions, thinking and feeling, the latter being the valuing function.

This model is clearly complex, for each of the functions can be directed outwards or inwards and can combine in numerous ways, but taken as a whole the idea is not difficult. Sensation perceives facts, and intuition their possibilities; thinking organizes them, and feeling gives them value.

The unconscious by contrast cannot reach definition in the same way and is an inference from the observation that dream images and images of the imagination seem to collect in clusters or to revolve round a central nucleus which can only be referred to. These unconscious nuclei are the archetypes and they can, up to a point, be classified and enumerated through special images —the mythologems—but these have a tendency to, as it were, dissolve into each other so that they seem at one time to be numerous and at others to be a single entity.

A significant property of the unconscious is its apparent arbitrariness; there is no reason to suppose that it has any sense of space or time, and if images of the archetypes often appear they seem to do so spontaneously, but closer analysis shows that the

REFLECTIONS ON IMAGE AND SYMBOL

conscious always takes an essential part. It is as if an almost timeless, spaceless monster suddenly collided with a bit of the conscious, liked it and let the conscious give it a form.

To illustrate what Jung must mean by his definition of symbol we can use the model and watch symbol formation in an episode reported by a patient in analysis; it illustrates how the unconscious seems to operate and how the four functions engage with it to result in symbol formation.

The man is mature in most respects and is a good thinker, his intuition is also good, and the two functions work in a kind of partnership. His feeling and sensation are inferior, and their activities are often expressed in moods and peculiar states of mind which he has learnt to handle by letting sort of childlike fairy stories develop. His feeling is evidently somewhat infantile, and he is liable to become afraid and ashamed of it, therefore he tends to resist using his introverted intuition which could very well help him to have a guess at what might be in the strange conditions which seem to threaten his conscious style of life. However, on this occasion he succeeded in circumventing his fears and the following experience emerged.

'A large magician was able to reduce the sun and moon to a small enough size to go into the holy mountain, but he could not get them into the maze that lay inside there because his hands were too big. He wanted to get the sun and moon into the centre of the maze because if he did so unlimited energy would be provided. As he was a hermaphrodite, he made out of himself a tiny man who did the trick.'

It is not easy for a rationally minded man to express his mood thus. His ordinary conscious attitude had to be suspended in order to let this rather simple child-like story come alive, for it did become alive and—to continue the drama—'he got very much upset because the little man got so above himself at accomplishing a feat which the magician could not, that he nearly went up in flames'. The excitement went on for several days. The temptation to return to reason was very strong, but by this time he could not do it, he was fascinated and 'began to care desperately what happened to the little man. After some time an old man with a long beard appeared; the little man liked him and climbed into his hair to fall asleep.' Then and only then could my patient return to reason.

REFLECTIONS ON IMAGE AND SYMBOL

But some bit of mood still remained, the solution was unsatisfactory, and he had to go back. 'I confronted the old man, who, I found, was very much enjoying a tickling in his beard caused by the activity of the little man. I reprimanded him for insufficient care of his charge. The old man, however, was stuffily contented, and paid no attention, so I took the little man away from him and gave him to the large magician who had big breasts. The little man turned into a baby and nestled down contented. This really was the end!'

I said earlier that symbols could be killed. At one point the feeling of concern for the little man became so intolerable, that the patient began to think it ridiculous to persist, because it was so irrational and childish. If he had followed this thought he would have destroyed the imagery, or at the least turned it into a negative form. Then again he might have let the little man go on getting excited till he went up in flames. When tempted to let this happen he remembered the fate of Euphorion in *Faust*, who casts himself into the air to meet his death and returns to the mother. 'Leave me not, mother', the soul of Euphorion cries from the depths.

What has happened in terms of the model? Thinking, and so sense, had gone by the board, intuition had found an image to fit a bit of the unconscious, first expressed by the mood and the indescribable condition. Once the image fitted the unconscious it took on the character of reality (sensation) and things began to happen. The events fascinated him, this is the numinous quality of the archetypal image, and his feeling got hold of him (he began to care desperately), only indeed when this was satisfied and its infantile element represented was he released from the spell of the drama.

Now he could return to thought, and he spent considerable time contemplating the episode wondering about the inner meaning of 'atomic energy', and also considering it in terms of what is known of magic and alchemy.

One or two parallels from alchemy must suffice to indicate the trend of his interest.

Hoghelande says:[14] 'They have compared the *prima materia* to everything, to male and female, hermaphroditic monster, to heaven

[14] Cf. *Psychology and Alchemy* (Collected Works, Vol. XII), London and New York, 1953, p. 306.

REFLECTIONS ON IMAGE AND SYMBOL

and earth, to body and spirit, chaos, microcosm and to the mixed mass (*massa confusa*); it contains in itself all colours and potentially all metals; there is nothing more wonderful in the world, for it begets itself, conceives itself and gives birth to itself'.

Of the changeable nature of the *prima materia* Jung says: '. . . it was thought of either as the *materia* itself or as its essence or *anima*, which was designated with the name "Mercurius" and conceived as a paradoxical double being called *monstrum, hermaphroditus*, or *rebis*.'[15]

Out of the *materia prima* (compare the 'magician') is born the son of the philosophers (the 'little man'), who after many vicissitudes, including being eaten by the father (compare the danger to the little man in the old one's beard) and suckled by Earth—also *prima materia* (compare the magician in his later role) and many and various adventures, is saved after the manner of hero myths and a rejuvenation is attained.

This episode is symbolic in Jung's sense. But the definition appears to restrict the term symbol to an unusual extent; in fact, if pushed to its logical conclusion, it limits the term to a single entity, the self or whole man. It may seem strange that I should assert this after saying that a bit of fantasy is symbolic yet it contains all the functions of that man. It is manifestly only a fragment of his whole psychic life, yet the symbolism has many references to the self, particularly the hermaphrodite which in alchemy is a symbol of the completion of the opus as well as the *materia prima*, the union of opposites which psychologically refers to the union of the conscious with the unconscious. Thus the imagery as well as the analysis in terms of functions refers to the whole man.

Jung refers to the transcendent function of the symbol; it binds together incompatible opposites of which man appears, not only psychically but also physically, to be composed. While the ego is simply an observer, a science can be made out of the study of images—this Kerenyi aims at doing. The mythologem and the concept of the archetypes and their images are still observable and can be studied as objects analogous to the physical objects. A kind of natural history can and is being constructed of them.

But a symbol goes further; it prevents this observational and

[15] Ibid., pp. 413–14.

REFLECTIONS ON IMAGE AND SYMBOL

intellectual process, the observer gets drawn into his objects, fascinated and even awe-inspired by them, and they evoke in the end his whole conscious activity till he is eventually 'thrown together' into a unity. This process is long drawn out and only gradually do the symbolical experiences of the wholeness, which revive again and again, become more and more real and abiding. Yet what this wholeness is nobody has much idea; it is only known that it is a symbol, and is related to the child images and childlikeness.

I scarcely think that it would be justifiable to restrict the term symbol to the self alone. Jung never does so, it is only implied in his definition, and he does not confine his use of the term to his definition. None the less this idea certainly lies behind the question the analyst asks himself so frequently, 'Is this material symbolic or not?', for the original root meaning of the term carries in it a reference to the concept of wholeness as an integrate of all those contradictory and incomprehensible elements which, when thrown together, make the whole man.

IV

NOTES ON THE TRANSFERENCE

Part I. Introduction

IN his Foreword to 'Psychology of the Transference' Jung says,[1] 'The reader will not find an account of the clinical phenomena of the transference in this book. It is not intended for the beginner who would first have to be instructed in such matters, but is addressed exclusively to those who have already gained sufficient experience in their own practice.'

It is nothing short of astonishing to find how little has been published in the past about the clinical transference experiences which Jung presupposes in his book. There is no reference to the subject in the index of Baynes' comprehensive series of case studies, *Mythology of the Soul*, nor does Frances G. Wickes make specific reference to it in her book *The Inner World of Man*, while J. Jacobi devotes to it only a cursory discussion in her authoritative work *The Psychology of C. G. Jung*. Recently, however, papers by Adler,[2] Henderson,[3] Moody,[4] Plaut,[5] Stein,[6] and myself[7] have appeared, and these have begun the filling in of

[1] Cf. *The Practice of Psychotherapy* (Collected Works, Vol. XVI), London and New York, 1954, p. 165.

[2] 'On the Archetypal Content of Transference', *Report of the International Congress of Psychotherapy Zurich 1954*, Basel and New York, 1955.

[3] 'Resolution of the Transference in the Light of C. G. Jung's Psychology', ibid., pp. 75 ff.

[4] 'The Relation of Personal and Transpersonal Elements in the Transference', ibid., pp. 531 ff.

[5] 'Research into Transference Phenomena', ibid., pp. 557 ff.; and 'The Transference in Analytical Psychology', *British Journal of Medical Psychology*, Vol. XXIX, Part 1, 1956.

[6] 'The Terminology of the Transference', *Report of the International Congress of Psychotherapy Zurich 1954*, Basel and New York, 1955.

[7] 'Note on a Significance of Archetypes for the Transference', cf. pp. 181 f. below.

NOTES ON THE TRANSFERENCE

Jung's outline, which this essay continues. Here I shall discuss those aspects of the transference which have struck me as especially significant because they have given rise to discussion among trainee analysts and colleagues.[8] I have not attempted to define the term in detail, since this has been done already by Stein,[9] and it is only necessary to state that it will be used here in a wide sense to cover the contents of the analytic relationship.

Jung, in his writings upon the transference, lays special emphasis upon the part played by the personality of the analyst in any analysis.[10] This was first expressed when he was a psychoanalyst; he then proposed that all analysts should undergo a training analysis, and he has since stressed it over and over again. His view appears to have stemmed from the association experiments, for Baynes, who should be in a good position to know, says:[11]

Jung discovered the unavoidable influence of this personal factor when experimenting with word association tests. He found that the personality and sex of the experimenter introduced an incalculable factor of variation. . . . Jung realized that it was quite impossible to exclude the personal equation in any psychological work. He accordingly decided to take it fully into account.

Much of the Jungian analyst's behaviour arises out of this 'discovery': the relatively informal setting, the use of two chairs with the analyst sitting in view of the patient, and the axiom that the analyst is just as much in the analysis as the patient, lead inevitably, in any thorough analysis, to his divesting himself of his persona; he is enjoined to react with his personality as a whole to the patients in analysis. It is manifest that only those with a differentiated personality can do this without making nonsense of the whole procedure, for an analyst's attitude and behaviour need to accord with what he says and, since he will be drawn into the state of primitive identity with his patient, it is essential for

[8] My paper does not aim at giving an account of the transference as a whole, for such an undertaking would virtually mean recording the entire analytic procedure.

[9] Op. cit.

[10] Cf. 'Some Crucial Points in Psycho-analysis', *Collected Papers on Analytical Psychology*, London, 1922, and numerous passages in *The Practice of Psychotherapy*.

[11] 'Freud versus Jung', *Analytical Psychology and the English Mind*, London, 1950, p. 108.

NOTES ON THE TRANSFERENCE

him to be conscious of his primitive reactions. It is this that makes a long and thorough personal analysis an absolute prerequisite for all analytical psychologists who wish to become practising analysts.

It is Jung's thesis that there is a therapeutic content in the analyst's personality. This cannot be just his consciousness, indeed it is the unconscious which is far the most important in this respect, and so his theory of transpersonal archetypes may be expected to orientate us here. With it we can explain why the patient apparently calls out suitable or adapted therapeutic reactions in the analyst which, together with the unadapted ones of the patient, form the main substance of all intense transferences. It is, further, the analyst's archetypal reactions that form the basis of his technique,[12] which without them must lack all true effectiveness. Thus Jung's theory has deepened our understanding of the 'incalculable factor' to which Baynes referred, converting it into a definable class of personal and transpersonal functions whose further investigation is thus made possible.

The distinction between the personal and the transpersonal unconscious, made by Jung in order to demarcate his investigations from those of Freud, is extremely subtle, and it is impossible to agree the setting up of a clear dividing line between the two,[13] for many personal relationships, particularly those of the transference type, express archetypal forms, and *vice versa*. Consequently, though the distinction is useful in other fields of study, I have found it better, in describing the transference, to conceive of a single unity which appears in consciousness in either personal or transpersonal form, or in both. The objective quality of experience, described as part of the numinous archetypal images, cannot be overlooked in any of the transference manifestations, and this is true in whichever form they appear. It is this which makes the study of the analyst-patient relationship so fascinating and rewarding.

From this complex relationship it results that both analyst and patient are laying the foundations of an increase in consciousness of all the innumerable psychic experiences which emerge out of the unconscious within the transference. By analysing them

---

[12] The meaning of this term will be expanded later (p. 90).

[13] Cf. Adler, op. cit., p. 285, who here elaborates the thesis that the two spheres can be clearly enough delineated for them to be subjected to different treatment.

64

NOTES ON THE TRANSFERENCE

all the patient's personal relationships are affected, particularly his capacity to handle interpersonal affects more fruitfully by distinguishing between what is within and what beyond the powers of his ego to control and manipulate.

Those outside the control of the ego comprise the contents of the transpersonal or objective transference which forms the subject-matter of Jung's essay on the transference in the individuation process. Yet even though they may be recognized as transpersonal they frequently, indeed more often than not, are first experienced personally.

The recent renewal of interest in the transference among analytical psychologists has given rise to uncertainty as to its place and importance in the analytical process. This would appear to centre on whether there are psychotherapeutic methods in which it does not occur.

Studying Jung's ideas on this topic makes it clear that he believes the bulk of psychotherapeutic procedures do not involve transference analysis, and in many of his essays the argument does not take the transference much into account. He divides treatment up in various ways and specifies his own contribution in a variety of styles, but he is consistent in holding that methods and techniques such as confession, suggestion, advice, elucidation, and education all aim at making the patient more normal, and he links this up with the needs of the majority of patients and particularly those in the first half of life who, if they need analytic treatment, should be treated by the methods of psycho-analysis, which is classed as a method of elucidation or interpretation of the unconscious process, based on a general theoretical outlook, or individual psychology, essentially an educational procedure aiming to socialize the individual.

But these methods are not valid with the class of patients to whom normality is meaningless and of whom individual development is, so to say, demanded. With these patients all methods must be abandoned 'since individuality . . . is absolutely unique, unpredictable and uninterpretable, in these cases the therapist must abandon all his preconceptions and techniques and confine himself to a purely dialectical procedure, adopting the attitude that shuns all methods'.[14] Then the patient's psychical system be-

[14] *The Practice of Psychotherapy*, pp. 7–8. This attitude corresponds to Jung's definition of 'modern man'.

F
65

NOTES ON THE TRANSFERENCE

comes 'geared to mine [Jung's] and acts upon it; my reaction is the only thing with which I as an individual can confront my patient'.[15]

For a long time Jung found great difficulty in describing what happened when the patient's and the analyst's psyches were geared together. In 1931 he wrote: 'Although I have travelled this path with individual patients many times, I have never yet succeeded in making all the details of the process clear enough for publication. So far this has been fragmentary only.'[16] Later on this gap was filled in to some extent by 'Psychology of the Transference'.

I surmise that Jung's difficulty arose from emphasizing the highly individual nature of the process; indeed if the individuality is 'unique, unpredictable and uninterpretable' it is also indescribable in general terms. When, therefore, Jung wrote an essay on the transference in individuation using the alchemical myths to do so, he must have decided that it was possible to generalize. His decision can only be understood by realizing that as the result of abandoning preconceptions and setting the individual in the centre of consciousness a very general process begins to operate, as indeed the theory of compensation postulates. It is the general processes which he describes.

In various places Jung recognizes that the transference can become a central feature in any analysis, for instance in his qualified agreement with Freud that the transference 'was the alpha and omega of the analytic method',[17] but he came to regard the transference in psycho-analysis as different from that which developed in the individuation process because of the different attitude of the analyst towards the patient.

The value of Jung's differentiation between patients who require treatments which aim at normality, and those who seek individuation is useful, but has its limitations. It could blind us to realizing that in the first class of case individual characteristics cannot be lacking, and that the individuating case not infrequently shows signs of needing to be more normal. My analytic studies of children forced me to see this in a surprising way, for I found that the attitude which Jung defined as correct for patients

[15] Ibid., p. 5.
[16] 'The Aims of Psychotherapy', ibid., p. 51.
[17] 'Psychology of the Transference', ibid., p. 72.

NOTES ON THE TRANSFERENCE

embarking on individuation was just the attitude which led to developments in the ego in children. A direct relation between the analyst and child was indeed essential. This consideration, first based on individual analysis of children, was then supported by an opportunity provided during the last war when hostels were organized for difficult children. There I was fortunate enough to observe the remarkable work of one matron whose capacity for establishing a direct therapeutic relation with the children in her care rendered it possible for her to relax imposed discipline to a far greater extent than would otherwise have been possible. She became a 'fellow passenger in the process of individual development' which occurred in each child.

These observations naturally surprised me, but then I began to see that there was something essentially the same in all my analytic procedure. I had a basic 'belief' in the individual of whatever age, and began to criticize the attitudes described by Jung as methods or techniques of interpretation and education because they seemed to be imposed on patients. I came to consider that it was not necessary to impose adaptation on a younger personality or an unadapted one, because the aim of the young individual or the unadapted person was in any case to do what other people did, i.e. his natural aim was to become normal or adapted.[18]

Later I came to see that the archetypes have a special relation to ego development,[19] and this led me to examine closely the significance of archetypal forms in the interpersonal transference relationship formed by younger people. I soon realized with particular force that archetypal activity in a young patient took on a more personal form than in the second half of life, and that in consequence they were to be found in the transference projected on to the analyst. These projections call forth a response in the analyst which leads to the condition of primitive identity with the patient, out of which a stronger ego can develop.[20] This conclusion led to my giving more emphasis to the value of analysis in the first half of life than is generally current in analytical psychology.

The position would seem to differ where individuation in its

[18] Except, apparently, for psychopathic personalities.
[19] Cf. 'The Origins of the Ego in Childhood', pp. 104 f., below.
[20] Cf. p. 108.

NOTES ON THE TRANSFERENCE

proper sense begins, for this process presupposes that the problem is not one of developing the ego but of differentiating it from and bringing it into relation with the unconscious, out of which the self appears as an experience apart from the ego. It presupposes that the patient has reached the stage at which his vocational aims are satisfied and spiritual problems are pressing to the fore.[21] In these circumstances the transference can take on the more obscure, less intense, more collective, transpersonal, even social form. But even here the reactions of the analyst, while they are different because inevitably orientated in the direction of individuation, are no less important.

It appears to me consistent with Jung's position to state the basis for my own analytic work by asserting that 'I believe in the individual'. This gives me a certain detachment from my belief and makes it possible to develop it into a theory and then proceed to investigate the transference in the light of it. For if my theory be correct, then absence of manifest transference in younger people must be due to insufficient appreciation by the analyst in the first place and later by the patient of what he is doing.

That the transference develops under special circumstances will be generally agreed. In this paper these will be considered first before the content of the relationship between analyst and patient is gone into. Though I recognize that there is no clear line of demarcation between the formal setting of analysis and its content, and that the two interact, yet this distinction is useful. Thus the frequency of interviews, the naturalness or artificiality of the situation, the way in which the patient's libido is deployed (discussed below under the heading 'Energy Distribution') all depend upon the transference of the patient and the reactions of the analyst, to be discussed under the heading of 'Counter-Transference'. None the less I have designed this paper with the contrast in mind, as the reader will find if he follows the headings of the sections into which the text is divided.

[21] Cf. Henderson, op. cit.

68

NOTES ON THE TRANSFERENCE

Part II. *General Considerations*

THE ANALYTIC INTERVIEW

Analytic interviews consist in the regular meeting of two people for an agreed period, it being assumed that one of them, the patient, wants to come enough to repeat his visit, while the other, the analyst, agrees to put himself, his experience, his knowledge, and all his attention at the patient's disposal for this agreed period. The analyst was once himself a patient; he has been analysed as part of his training experience, and through this experience he knows what it is like to be on the other side of the bargain. He also has knowledge, acquired during his training, and techniques[22] which are going to be useful in what follows. It can be assumed that his training will have made it possible for him not to use his techniques to interfere in the 'alchemical' process which will gradually involve patient and analyst more and more. The analyst will know that every single statement he makes is an account of the state of his psyche, whether it be a fragment of understanding, an emotion, or an intellectual insight; all techniques and all learning how to analyse are built on this principle. It is thus part of the analyst's training experience to realize that he is often going to learn, sometimes more, sometimes less, from each patient, and that in consequence he himself is going to change.[23]

The patient's position is in many respects similar to the analyst's, for everything he says will be treated as an expression of his psyche; he also will be using techniques, though less refined ones; he also will be using his understanding and employing his insight, in relation not only to himself but also to his analyst. The essential difference between patient and analyst is to be sought not in these spheres, but in the patient's greater distress, his lesser awareness, and his greater need to increase his consciousness so as to change himself and his way of life. It is not to be

[22] The nature of techniques will be taken up later on when discussing counter-transference (cf. pp. 90 f.).

[23] Jung emphasizes this when he discusses the stage of transformation in 'Problems of Modern Psychotherapy', *The Practice of Psychotherapy*. Other references to this concept will be found in the same volume.

69

NOTES ON THE TRANSFERENCE

sought in the absence of involvement in the process on the part of the analyst. Analytical psychologists all follow Jung in rejecting the idea that the analyst can possibly act only as a projection screen.

Though the analysis starts on a simple basis the interviews soon become filled with the complexities which form the subject of the bulk of this paper. Here it need only be said that the complexity is brought about by the specific aim of investigating the unconscious. This conscious aim has archetypal roots and so has a long historical background, originating in the earliest initiation ceremonies and proceeding through religion, mysticism, and alchemy to their more scientific, analytic equivalent. It is, however, important to keep firmly in mind the simple basis of the interview and to maintain it by such arrangements as keeping the time and frequency of interviews relatively stable. The stable form then becomes an expression of the analyst's reliability when all else is in a state of flux. The simple outline gives a frame of reference to which fantasies, projections, and speculations can be referred.

'NATURALNESS' VERSUS 'ARTIFICIALITY' OF THE TRANSFERENCE

The definable basis of the analytic interview may be seen as embodying the naturalness with which the analyst meets the patient, but the recurrent discussion of whether the transference is natural or artificial covers a wider field. The antithesis could be stated in another way by considering how far the analyst's technique induces the transference and how far it is the inevitable consequence of two people meeting together under the conditions just described. Since the meaning of technique will only appear later the vaguer definition of the issue will here be adhered to.

In the essay already referred to, Jung makes it clear that he regards the transference as a 'natural' phenomenon, by which he means that it is not peculiar to the analytic relationship, but can be clearly observed in all social life.[24] Jung's view is without doubt

[24] One reason for the constant preoccupation of analysts with 'naturalness' undoubtedly springs from the ascetic nature of analysis. Analysts are subject to the reproach of unnaturalness because of the sexual tensions aroused in the patient, who reproaches the analyst for his 'unnatural behaviour'. This reproach, however, usually springs from a projection of incest fantasies which the patient wishes to misunderstand and act out. (For the definition of acting out cf. pp. 77 f.)

70

NOTES ON THE TRANSFERENCE

supported by many observations and by comparison with other relationships all confirming the application of his theory of archetypes to the transference: since archetypes occur within the transference and in many spheres of life so that they are general phenomena, the transference must partake in this general phenomenon. Yet in regarding analysis as the equivalent of these social situations, it must at the same time not be overlooked that in none of them is so much attention given to the psyche of two persons under relatively standard conditions, and in none of them is so much effort expended in undoing resistances. Furthermore, in other personal relations and social situations little effort is devoted to finding out what is going on in them, and so the main bulk of the energy bound up in them remains unconscious. In this sense the word 'artificial' might be appropriate, but only with the qualification that the patient comes because of the distortion of his personality which has been induced by failures in his development. It is this 'artificial' distortion which analysis of the transference seeks to correct, and therefore what is 'artificial' in the analysis is more than matched by what is distorted in the patient, particularly at the beginning of any analysis; but the distortions progressively lessen as the analysis proceeds until at its ideal termination all residues of frustration will be dissolved by the patient leaving his analyst. Then the simple basis of the whole process from which the analysis began can once again be clearly envisaged by the patient.

ANALYSIS AND LIFE

Closely related to the discussion whether the transference is 'natural' or 'artificial' is the question how it is related to something broadly termed 'life', by which is usually meant all the patient's everyday activities other than his analysis which get related to what is 'natural'.

Henderson[25] implies that almost the whole psyche of a patient becomes concentrated in analysis, so that 'life' would theoretically almost cease while the personality is being transformed. Because of this he finds it necessary to posit a post-analysis period in which a new adaptation to life by the new personality is achieved.

[25] Op. cit.

NOTES ON THE TRANSFERENCE

My experience does not accord with this view. It is true that if a satisfactory result is to be achieved, many changes in the life of the individual are inevitable, but these take place step by step during the analysis rather than after it, and life continues but reflecting the changes that are continuously taking place within the analytic transference. The type and degree of change vary according to the subject's character; the outward changes are likely to be greater in younger persons and in the more severely neurotic or psychotic patients, whose aim, as Henderson has pointed out, is vocational rather than spiritual. It is in the patients for whom individuation or the formation of a philosophy of life is the main issue that outward changes tend to be less in evidence.

There are two basic considerations which need to be taken into account in any case.

(1) The patient comes with a presenting symptom for which he seeks a solution. It is the aim of the analyst to elucidate this, and one of the results of this process is the development of a transference in which the energy previously directed into the symptom is now transferred to the person of the analyst.

(2) The problem then is how to handle and ultimately resolve the transference.

From this, as we shall later detail, most of the material revealed in the transference is not of a kind which could lead to satisfactory living, for otherwise it would not have given rise to the symptoms, but rather is made up of just those parts of the personality which are unadapted to life. Therefore when Jacobi states that Jung '. . . holds an "attachment" to a third person, for example in the form of a "love affair" to be quite a suitable basis for the analytical solution of neurosis . . .'[26] she appears to misunderstand the nature and importance of the transference and its relation to 'life'.[27] In general, if a patient is capable of sustaining a satisfying 'love affair', then the libido invested in it is not of the kind that needs development through transference analysis. Over and over again patients come for analysis just because their erotic experiences do not produce a solution of their neuroses, and only when the illusions contained in these 'affairs' are lived through in the transference, and nowhere else, can a solution be found.

[26] *The Psychology of C. G. Jung*, London, 1951, p. 85.
[27] This notion does not seem to appear in any of Jung's own writings.

NOTES ON THE TRANSFERENCE

I have taken up the supposed dichotomy 'life' and analysis because it is current among analysts, but it is only a rough distinction, for one of the essential qualities of the transference is its living dynamism. Here the question arises whether analytic phenomena are induced or released. My contention is that they are released, and upon this view my thinking about transference is largely based.

ENERGY DISTRIBUTIONS

A study of the distribution of manifest energy released by analysis in relation to the interview bears upon such questions as interview frequency, fantasy, and active imagination, all of which are particularly relevant to analytical psychologists, if only because they have no prescribed standard of interview frequency, but rather relate it to the varying needs of patients under different circumstances.

My usual practice is to start with three interviews a week, increasing or reducing the number as occasion requires. Jung has prescribed specific frequencies for his individuating cases, whom he aims at putting in a position to conduct their own analyses under his supervision. This subject will be taken up later, though his definite statement that he aims at reducing interviews in his cases has led me to the following considerations.

Let us now consider two extreme cases, one in which the main bulk of the analysis is conducted in the interview, the other in which the interview is supervisory and the main bulk of the manifest activity is expressed in active imagination and dream analysis outside the interview. Since the duration of an analysis can be important, the comparison is useful in seeing that the time available for study of the imaginative and dream products is vastly greater in the second case, and it might be thought that the analysis would be shortened. Since, however, all the time spent on dream and fantasy may depend upon an unrealized projection upon the analyst, and since this drives the patient to produce enough material to fill the interview with reports of dream and fantasy, the duration of the analysis can easily be considerably increased rather than shortened.[28]

---

[28] I mention this topic here because it is sometimes held that analytical psychologists have discovered methods which shorten the time of analysis; they can also lengthen it!

NOTES ON THE TRANSFERENCE

It is the consideration of these defensive uses of dream and fantasy which makes it useful to distinguish between behaviour in the interview and the reporting of what has gone on outside it; this covers all that the patient tells the analyst about himself, his relation to other people in his environment, his dreams, his inner world as exemplified in fantasy, day-dreaming, or active imagination. Using this distinction it is then easier to perceive when the patient is referring to the analyst in talking about somebody else, or when what he tells is conditioned by his attitude to the analyst, so that sometimes the very reporting of material is conditioned solely by the patient's attitude to the analyst.[29]

A young man who was having difficulties in talking during his interviews reported that between them he could converse easily with an imaginary analyst whom he identified with me. In these conversations he would prepare what he was going to say to me in the interview, but when he attempted to put his plan into operation, the thoughts were replaced by various other interests, or there were no thoughts at all. It would seem that most of what is usually called analysis in its positive sense was, in his case, conducted outside the interview, the whole time in the latter being spent in analysing the resistance which conditioned this state of affairs. Since this was very strong no apparent progress was made for a long time.

This example shows clearly how much more energy can be expanded outside the interviews than in them, but as the analysis of my patient's resistance progressed the situation began to change so that the imaginary figure became a less prominent feature and it became easier for the patient to talk openly to me. He then spent less time conducting his analysis outside the interviews. This I regarded as a favourable development.

Gerhard Adler, in his paper 'On the Archetypal Content of Transference',[30] describes the phenomena in reverse. He cites a woman patient whose relation to him during interviews could be divided into two parts; the first positive, in which she played the role of a good daughter, the second negative, in which she entered into an aggressively toned conflict with him. She then went away

---

[29] The application of this fact to early psychiatric interviews is important. Here the transference operates immediately and reported facts can become, if not falsified, valued in ways which are determined by the attitude of the patient to the interviewer.   [30] Ibid.

NOTES ON THE TRANSFERENCE

into the country, and there painted a picture in which a sado-masochistic pattern was depicted; this led on to an animus figure which revealed a vision of the self as a fantasy of the inner cosmos; all these developed away from the interviews. Adler believes that the transference, which continued between interviews, acted as a container (transcendent transpersonal temenos) inside which these events could happen.

Because Adler was aiming to show how the personal was transcended by the archetypal transference, and because the case was one in which the individuation process had been constellated, there was no necessity to enter into the motives for experiencing fantasies away from the interview. But had an analysis of these been necessary he would have been led to consider the tendency of depressive patients to split their love-hate conflicts so as to internalize the aggressive components which were so manifest in the picture and seemed to have disappeared from the transference. This might very well have proved important in leading to new developments in the transference of his patient had he wished to investigate them.

It can happen that if experiences of this type are not considered, the archetypal contents of the transference can dissolve the personal aspect of it, thus leading to depersonalizing defences. This is particularly liable to happen when the unconscious is active enough to give rise to frequent disturbances in consciousness during the patient's life away from the analytic interview. Probably the most important single consideration in avoiding such defences is for the patient to see that the image of the analyst does not disintegrate, melt away, or otherwise become inaccessible between interviews; none of these things appear to have happened in Adler's case or in my own.

So as to illustrate this depersonalizing defence I may instance a patient who had used active imagination in a previous analysis. She would come to see me with a book in which her dreams and active imaginations were written down, and would read out the experiences she had recorded and the thoughts she had accumulated, thus following a recommendation of Jung's.[31] When I came to make an interpretation I encountered strong defences, and I soon began to suspect that this technique was a means of ensuring that my influence was neutralized. Amongst the figures

[31] Cf. *The Practice of Psychotherapy*, pp. 47 f.

75

NOTES ON THE TRANSFERENCE

with which she conversed was a venerable 'old wise man' who almost invariably supported the patient in her own views and would sometimes tell her that what I had said in the last interview was wrong. It was not this, however, which struck me so much as the nature of the thoughts which 'he' produced; they were in no respect unusual, so that I asked why she could not think them for herself. My question led the patient to reveal that her 'active imagination' had started from a seminar at which she had been present, in which it had been asserted that active imagination was the be-all and end-all of Jungian analysis. As she had always, from childhood onwards, spent part of her life in an inner world, she took to this technique like a duck to water. She had further gained the impression that all Jungians thought better of people who presented their ideas in this form and that it was easier to contradict the analyst if she got an 'old wise man' to do it, as he would then be more impressed. Once this was revealed she was able to be more open with me, to react more immediately to my interpretations, and to spend her time outside the interviews in more useful occupations than making up fantasies with a view to controlling her analyst.

It will now be clear that, when we draw attention to the distribution of energy released by the analysis in relation to an interview, we are doing so with a view to studying the nature of the transference more carefully. The motives for this distribution are only to be brought to light in the end by realizing the nature of the face to face behaviour of analyst and patient in the interview itself; if this be overlooked it is only too easy for an impeccable 'technique' to become a defence against the very aim it was designed to achieve.

The whole trend of my patient's analysis was changed by the revelation of her defensive use of dream and fantasy; it turned into a process of testing what I could love, endure, or hate, while at the same time the trend of her life changed radically and her personal relationships were deepened and extended.

Such experiences have led me to consider all energy distributions and reporting in relation to the transference, and to believe that the omission of motives for telling anything to an analyst may open a rift in the analyst-patient relationship.[32]

---

[32] Clearly this does not mean that the motives are brought to light on principle, but only when the occasion requires it.

NOTES ON THE TRANSFERENCE

'ACTING OUT'

It will now be apparent that the gradual development of an analysis can lead to the analyst's becoming the centre of it, so that the whole patient may become involved in the process of transformation. If, as sometimes happens, this concentration of libido is made into an aim, almost anything, whether adapted or not, which happens outside the transference in the life of the patient is considered undesirable. These supposedly undesirable activities have come to be termed 'acting out', and this term seems to have received greater prominence than its more vivid equivalent of 'living the shadow'.

The term 'acting out' is borrowed from psycho-analysis, in which it is used to cover the acting of unconscious experience in an inappropriate setting; Fenichel[33] says: 'Under the influence of transference, everyone whose infantile conflicts are remobilized by analysis may develop the tendency to repeat past experiences in present reality, or to misunderstand reality as if it were a repetition of the past, rather than to remember the repressed events in their appropriate connection.'

A male patient telephoned to tell me that he was dissatisfied with his analyst and wanted an interview with me for various reasons, which he stated. I replied that I would see him if his analyst agreed. His analyst told me that she was quite prepared for her patient to consult me, but she did not think he really meant what he asked for, because he had not raised the matter with her.

When he arrived at my consulting room he seemed in a somewhat confused state. He repeated what he had said to me over the telephone, and then became relatively incoherent. I gathered, however, that it was his relatives as much as he that wanted the change. So I told him that I thought his relatives had played on some doubts he had about the goodness of his analyst which he really hoped were not true. At this he became coherent and told me that this was indeed the case, so I went on to tell him that I had no intention of suggesting a change, since I thought his doubts were part of his relation to his analyst and needed working through with her. He left my consulting-room, so far as I could

[33] Cf. *The Psychoanalytic Theory of Neurosis*, London and New York, 1945, p. 375.

77

NOTES ON THE TRANSFERENCE

see, completely reassured, and I heard later that he returned to his analyst forthwith. In this example the act was not seriously intended.

If the patient means what he does, then it is not acting out, however socially undesirable his act may seem to the analyst or to those in his environment. It would seem probable that the patient cited by Gerhard Adler was acting out, though nothing undesirable in a social sense occurred. If, however, she was acting out, the fantasy which determined the experience, which occurred during the week-end, did not appear. It is not essentially a question of whether the behaviour occurs in the interview or outside it, for many patients—hysterical ones in particular—dramatize their affects in the analytic hour and thus prevent unconscious fantasies or memories from becoming conscious. Acting out is a special form of defensive behaviour wherever it occurs, and is based, as my example indicates, upon a projection to which neither analyst nor patient has been able to gain access. It will have been observed that the contents of the patient's doubts did not come into consciousness at the time he was interviewed by me.

Acting out in the interview has been described by Stein in his article 'Loathsome Women'.[34] There he found that two of the patients '. . . walked round the analyst's chair in a menacing manner. They described increasingly narrow circles, reminiscent of the "hag track" . . . in order to try and stir him up.' Stein found that they were aiming at getting him to 'man-handle' them. Here he suggests that a primitive drama is being enacted and this is not realized at first, either by him or his patients. They are 'living their shadow' which contains an archetypal image.

In using a psycho-analytic term acting out, it is necessary to realize that it is being altered in the process and at the same time extended, to cover and emphasize the purposive aspect of the act in question, i.e. an attitude which Stein emphasizes in using the phrase 'in order to stir him up'.

In psycho-analysis acting out is a replacement activity and as such needs to be reduced to its source. It is therefore undesirable inasmuch as it is inadequate as a form of expression.

Living the shadow is likewise considered undesirable in analytical psychology, but for the added reason that it is acting

[34] *Journal of Analytical Psychology*, Vol. I, No. 1, pp. 69–70.

NOTES ON THE TRANSFERENCE

in a primitive manner and is undesirable because it is consequently unadapted. For instance, the aim of getting the analyst stirred up with a view, as Stein remarks, to induce him to 'manhandle' the patients will not succeed, and they do not really want this to happen, for they have come to the analyst just because of the failure of their primitive and guilt-ridden activities to produce adequate satisfaction.

A PROJECTION-PERCEPTION SCALE

Though transference can only partly be described in terms of projection,[35] yet this mechanism has the advantage of being easily defined, and furthermore it can be analysed, though not thereby necessarily dissolved.

Alongside projections the patient makes observations which turn out to be objective. Both processes are recognized by repeated tests on the part of the patient, who sometimes as if by revelation, sometimes by slow laborious analysis, comes to realize their nature. As the analysis proceeds the patient may be expected to get an increasingly true view of the analyst, so that a progression can be defined from illusion, due to projection, which may very well be creative, to reality based upon perception of the analyst as what Fairbairn[36] calls a 'differentiated object'.

The patient's perceptions lead, in any thorough analysis, to his becoming aware not only of contents in the analyst of which the analyst may know, but to those of which he is unconscious. If, under these circumstances, the analysis is to proceed it must be recognized that the patient gets into a position from which he can make the analyst aware of a part of his personality which he himself had either not seen or not been able to integrate with his ego. If the analyst can recognize it and benefit from it, all is well. Analysts find it difficult to do this.

But this is not all: an interesting situation arises when the patient makes a true projection on to the analyst, and again he may be conscious or unconscious of the situation. Where the patient's projection corresponds to an unconscious conflict of

[35] I have assumed the reader knows the projection theory of the transference. Those who are unfamiliar with it are referred to Jung's essay, 'Psychology of the Transference'.

[36] *Psycho-Analytic Studies of the Personality*, London, 1952.

NOTES ON THE TRANSFERENCE

the analyst the analysis may terminate if one or the other does not become aware of it in time; it is not necessarily the analyst who is the first to make the discovery. A patient of mine with a particularly strong father fixation told me she had to wait for two years in order to take up her problem because she saw that I was not ready to handle it. On looking over the period I had to admit that her view had substance, even though the subsequent analysis showed that this waiting was an ego-defence on her part. It is one of the advantages of the analyst's sitting in full view of the patient that these difficulties can be more easily handled than if he is out of sight and uses that position to maintain a supposed anonymity.[37]

I mention these limiting problems because it is necessary to understand that the concept of a projection-perception scale has complications, but they do not invalidate the general idea which is of value in considering such problems as the relation of active imagination to transference.

Jung has pointed out that the content of some projections can be dissolved, but that finally the projected archetypal images cannot, but only become detached from the person of the analyst. If there appears to have occurred at the same time an increase in positive perceptual awareness of the analyst, then it may be said that the projection has not only been withdrawn, but has become adequately integrated, inasmuch as the ego of the patient has become strengthened. If on the contrary this does not occur, it is almost certain that either the projection is still active or else that it has led to a fascination by the patient in another sphere; either it has been projected on to another person, or it has led to his becoming fascinated by the image in his inner world. In this case nothing has been gained and much may have been lost.

The interrelation of projection and perception is therefore a useful indicator of progression and regression of the ego.

[37] The anonymity of the analyst is a fantasy more common amongst non-analytically trained psychiatrists than amongst analysts themselves.

NOTES ON THE TRANSFERENCE

Part III. *Particular Transference Manifestations*

THE DEPENDENT TRANSFERENCE

The state of dependence arises when repressed infantile contents are released and the analyst seems to fulfil the imagined role of parent. Then projection predominates over objective perception.

During this period in which the infantile patterns predominate (they never disappear) the analyst will refrain from compulsive attempts to control the direction the analysis should take, from giving advice, or from behaving too much in the many ways in which parents behave to their children. If he does this he will be dramatizing the transference projections and interfering with the aim of analysing them. However attractive this activity on the part of the analyst may be, and however therapeutically exciting and successful over a short term, it endangers the ultimate development of the patient's relation to the analyst. For this reason also social contacts between analyst and patient outside the analysis will be avoided.

The adoption of a parental role takes many subtle forms. It is even hidden in the implications of being analysed, when this means being subjected to a process understood by the analyst but not by the patient. Under this assumption all kinds of aspects of the parent imagos hide, and these have to be unearthed and analysed so as to reveal the true state of affairs.[38]

The withdrawal of projected parent imagos is an essential prerequisite for the emergence of the self and its realization in consciousness. Analyses which give continued space for the emergence of the self are almost invariably long, because of the need for gradual maturation. Indeed I am inclined to believe that length is one of the essential features of radical analyses which lead to self-realization. It is useless to object because an analysis goes on so long, and equally futile to know what is best for these patients

---

[38] Many analyses are cut short because the analyst dramatizes the parent imagos; the patient 'gets well' and breaks away from the analysis because of his improvement, but he has become a good child and so his real self is denied.

NOTES ON THE TRANSFERENCE

who cannot 'live'. They can live only in the transference, and to try to break it by any means only leads to probable disaster.

In an ideal analysis the analyst would not need any defences, nor would he display counter-transference illusions, in the sense to be defined later, but his reactions of whatever sort would be *adapted* to the patient's requirements at every point.

These requirements are manifestly complex, but they may usefully be classed under two headings: (*a*) those belonging to the transference neurosis and the repetition of infantile patterns of behaviour, termed by Freud the repetition compulsion, and (*b*) those belonging to the archetypal transference, in which the analyst can become more openly involved with the patient. The dependent transference is caused by the predominance of class (*a*), and it is often assumed that to interpret it induces an undesirable regression. The disorientation among analytical psychologists in this sphere appears to derive from the neglect of a very useful concept put forward long ago by Jung in *The Theory of Psycho-analysis*.[39] In this essay he criticizes psycho-analysts for their too great fascination with infantile sexuality, which came to be investigated in its own right, so that the importance of the present came to be neglected. He introduces the idea of the 'actual situation', which he defines as the cause of neurotic conflict and of regression to infantile patterns; he thus seems to deny the importance of fixation points. In his later writings,[40] however, it is clear that he still adheres to the relative importance of arrested development in the genesis of neurosis, though without relating it to the concept of the 'actual situation'.

The important issue which Jung raised has not yet been settled. It is still an open question how to evaluate two evident causal elements: those that lie in the present and those that lie in the past. If, however, the actual situation be defined as the totality of present causes and the conflicts associated with them, then the genetic (historical) causes are brought into the picture inasmuch as they are still active in the present as contributing to the conflicts there manifested. If we keep to this principle fruitless regression will not occur, because past and present are constantly

[39] New York, 1915.
[40] Cf. for example *Symbols of Transformation* (Collected Works, Vol. V), London and New York, 1956.

NOTES ON THE TRANSFERENCE

kept in relation with one another and only those causes that actually operate in the present are taken up by the patient. Where then does the transference come into the picture? It provides good conditions for investigating this 'actual situation', so long as the essential simplicity and sufficient 'naturalness' of the interview be maintained and the analysis be conducted with regard to the true relationship factor as well as to the illusions which appear alongside it.[41] These conditions provide the best chance of induced or artificial regressions being avoided and fixation points, to which little attention has been paid by analytical psychologists,[42] being *revealed*. The fixation theory has been overlooked, as has also the contingent problem of the relation of the self to ego development. Far from being only 'biological roots', the zones and fixation points are, in my view, also centres of developing consciousness round which archetypal motifs, as deintegrates of the self, centre in alluring profusion. The magical sense of the anal zone has recently been interestingly discussed by Dr. Whitmont,[43] who has brought the whole problem into closer relation with recent developments in psycho-analysis.[44]

The analysis of the dependent transference, which invariably leads into the infantile relation to the mother, is a lengthy and painstaking procedure. Yet it is essentially constructive since it is the only way in which many individuals can reach the growing points of their ego and so rebuild the previously inadequate structure.

THE OBJECTIVE TRANSFERENCE

In 1935 Jung wrote that[45]

[41] Cf. the projection-perception scale, *supra*, pp. 79 f.

[42] Recently, however, a few papers have appeared on this topic. Hawkey, 'Play Analysis: Case Study of a Nine-Year-Old Girl', *British Journal of Medical Psychology*, Vol. XX, Part 3, 1945; Fordham, 'On the Origins of the Ego in Childhood', cf. pp. 104 f., below; Abenheimer, 'Re-Assessment of the Theoretical and Therapeutical Meaning of Anal Symbolism', *Guild of Pastoral Psychology Lecture No. 72*, London, 1952.

[43] 'Magic and the Psychology of Compulsive States', *Journal of Analytical Psychology*, Vol. II, No. 1, 1957.

[44] Cf. Fairbairn's reformulation (op. cit) of the libido theory in which he defines the libido as object-seeking and only secondarily pleasure-seeking.

[45] *The Practice of Psychotherapy*, p. 20. Jung is not the only one to have tried manoeuvres of this type. Alexander (*Fundamentals of Psycho-analysis*,

NOTES ON THE TRANSFERENCE

All methods of influence, including the analytical, require that the patient be seen as often as possible. I content myself with a maximum of four consultations a week. With the beginning of synthetic treatment it is of advantage to spread out the consultations. I then generally reduce them to one or two hours a week, for the patient must learn to go his own way.

And again (pp. 26–7)[46]

The psycho-analyst thinks he must see his patient an hour a day for months on end; I manage in difficult cases with three or four sittings a week. As a rule I content myself with two, and once the patient has got going, he is reduced to one. In the interim he has to work at himself, but under my control. . . . In addition I break off treatment every ten weeks or so, in order to throw him back on his normal milieu. In this way he is not alienated from his world—for he really suffers from his tendency to live at another's expense.

I now wish to bring these statements into relation with another and later statement,[47] 'The bond [of the transference] is often of such intensity that we could almost speak of a "combination". When two chemical substances combine both are altered.' The question which must spring to mind is how, if the relationship is so intimate, can it be desirable for meetings to be so infrequent.

There have always been certain implications in Jung's concept of a transpersonal objective psyche which Robert Moody expresses very clearly in relation to the transference when he says of a case:[48] 'Once the animus figure had been formulated by the unconscious, it played the role of a function that led the patient step by step, and *often regardless of the analyst* [italics mine], towards the various problems that stood between her and a harmonious relationship to the unconscious.'

London, 1949), states that the Berlin Institute of Psycho-analysis investigated the value of interruption in treatment, diminishing interviews, and encouraging the patient to 'apply every analytic gain to his life outside the analysis'. The experiments were worked out in more detail at the Chicago Institute of Psycho-analysis and have apparently become part of Alexander's practice.

[46] It will be obvious to the reader that Jung, far from abandoning all methods, as he suggests is necessary in individuation, imposes a procedure with considerable vigour. The inconsistency is important because it shows that you cannot abandon method however much you try.

[47] Ibid., p. 171.

[48] Op. cit., p. 537. Cf. also, pp. 5 f. above, where an example of what Moody describes is given in another context.

NOTES ON THE TRANSFERENCE

If the unconscious is transpersonal and operates 'regardless of the analyst' and if the object be to bring the ego into relationship with it, it is clearly sensible to implement this idea by giving it technical application. It is common knowledge that Jung did this, and reference has already been made to it.[49] He enjoined his patients to write down dreams, keep records of them, and associations to them, in a book, to start painting, drawing, modelling, and extending this to active imagination.[50] All this is based on the empirical evidence that, in suitable cases, it leads to individuation. Once this process is set in motion interviews with the analyst become supervisory.

Jung frequently states that his patients are of a special kind,[51] i.e. those who have already been analysed and whose special difficulty is expressed in the symptom of a life lacking in meaning, a depressive state to which an individual solution is demanded. He claims that their problem is misunderstood if it is interpreted in terms of genetic psychology or of social adaptation. It is their individuality which needs emphasis, and therefore they may be expected to have an ego strong enough to stand the impact of the unconscious without too intense an 'alchemical' transference. For these already developed personalities the tendency to 'live at the analyst's expense' in a dependent transference must be undesirable because it derives from a misunderstanding of their problem. Breaking off treatment therefore aims at breaking up the dependent transference, which makes no sense. Jung's action therefore corresponds with his view of their problem, and not with the compulsive dramatization of the parent imagos, as is sometimes claimed.

This interpretation of Jung's statements means that there is no justification for erecting them into general rules, but they must rather be viewed as technical recommendations for the treatment of a special kind of case.[52]

[49] Cf. pp. 65 f.

[50] The aims of these techniques are defined by Jung in his essay 'The Aims of Psychotherapy' in *The Practice of Psychotherapy*, particularly pp. 46 ff. There he says: 'My aim is to bring about a psychic state in which my patient begins to experiment with his own nature.' For this is needed 'not only a personal contemporary consciousness, but also a supra-personal consciousness with a sense of historical continuity'.

[51] Cf. especially 'Principles of Practical Psychotherapy', ibid.

[52] Cf. 'Principles of Practical Psychotherapy'.

NOTES ON THE TRANSFERENCE

When I was learning to become an analyst in 1933, however, little reference to the transference was to be heard, and it seemed to be agreed by implication that if the patient's ego was brought into relation with the objective psyche a solution to his problems would appear and the transference would resolve itself without its being made more than vaguely conscious. Thus, at this period, the interpretation of Jung's statements which I have made had become erroneously generalized, and even dogmatized without adequate justification.

Jung's method must depend upon the patient's ability to introject his projections and 'raise them to the subjective plane'.[53] Out of this grows active imagination, which has become the means by which the ego is brought into a vital relation with the archetypal images. It is under these conditions that it may be assumed that the transference would become less intense; they might even signalize its termination. It is here that Jung gives only general statements such as the one already quoted: 'With the beginning of the synthetic treatment it is of advantage to spread out the consultations, I then generally reduce them to one or two hours a week, for the patient must learn to go his own way',[54] a statement which has been interpreted in various ways leading to considerable confusion. This I will illustrate by discussing two views on the place of active imagination in analysis.

Gerhard Adler in his paper 'On the Archetypal Content of Transference' says of his patient that she[55] 'soon learned to use her fantasy constructively and to practise what analytical psychology calls active imagination'. But there is no mention of the transference diminishing in intensity; indeed it would seem to have gone on as before, for he says the patient[56] 'felt her relationship to me—i.e. her secure positive transference—as a kind of temenos, of protective magic circle, inside which she was safe enough to endure this intense inner experience'.

Henderson[57] in a comprehensive review of the subject takes

[53] Cf. *Two Essays on Analytical Psychology* (Collected Works, Vol. VII), London and New York, 1953.
[54] *The Practice of Psychotherapy*, p. 20.
[55] *Report of the International Congress of Psychotherapy Zurich 1954*, p. 286
[56] Ibid., p. 288.
[57] Op. cit.

NOTES ON THE TRANSFERENCE

up quite a different position, from which he states that active imagination occurs after analysis of the transference has been completed. He defines four stages in the development of individuation, which begin only after the dependent infantile transference has been sufficiently analysed.

(1) The appearance of the self symbols while the transference is at its height.

(2) Resolution of the infantile transference and achievement of what Henderson calls 'symbolic friendship'. This term expresses the condition in which the analyst is built into the psyche of the patient as a permanent internal 'friend'. Because this has happened the patient no longer needs regular interviews with the external analyst.

(3) Post-analysis period in which a new adaptation is achieved with or without the analyst's help.

(4) Discovery of archetypal symbolism through active imagination, providing a means of self-analysis without the analyst's help.

It is therefore clear that analysts do not agree as to the place of active imagination in the transference process. The drastic difference in view could spring from a variety of roots.

(a) From differing concepts of active imagination. There is indeed a tendency to regard almost any fantasy as active imagination, a tendency which I have commented upon elsewhere,[58] and I have suggested that the term should be used only when the fantasy takes on an object quality to which the ego consciously relates.

(b) From differences in the transference phenomena due to typological differences between patients.

(c) From differences in analytic procedure arising from differences in the personality structure of the analysts.

(d) From inadequate study of the motives for differing distributions of energy.

The confusion appears to me, however, to stem mainly from differing understandings of when the synthetic process begins, and from misunderstanding of Jung's sharp distinction between methods of rational influence and those in which the dialectical relation applies, i.e. his individuation cases. In the general run

[58] 'Active Imagination and Imaginative Activity', *Journal of Analytical Psychology*, Vol. I, No. 2, 1956.

NOTES ON THE TRANSFERENCE

it is by no means easy to distinguish thus clearly. In all analyses synthetic processes are continuously in evidence, and further in my experience an objective transpersonal quality attaches itself to the vast majority of all transference phenomena, even when they are expressed most personally by the patient and whether they are more or less intense. When the former, the alchemical combination takes place. However, there are certainly patients whose capacity for imaginative activity either dissolves or masks the personal aspect of the transference,[59] so that it can only be detected with difficulty. These cases could very well develop into Henderson's fourth stage, which would seem to belong to Jung's special sphere, but they might equally well continue after the pattern of Adler's case. As far as my experience goes, the transference cannot be left out, and will sooner or later form the central feature of any thorough analysis, and though Jung seemed at one time to believe that this was not so, his later work points in the opposite direction. In 'Psychology of the Transference' he expounds his view of the 'alchemical' nature of the transference with the reservation that this need not always occur. In my view it always occurs, only with varying intensity. As we have seen above (pp. 75 f.) an apparently weak transference can be converted into a strong one by analysis. I have given this example because I believe that the indiscriminate application of Jung's thesis has led to strong transferences being too frequently overlooked because they are masked. In this connection it appears to me that there is a point in Moody's statement which is liable to a rather serious misunderstanding. It infers that transferences only occur when the analyst participates in some unstated manner and that they never arise 'quite regardless of the analyst'. This is far from the truth; indeed most transferences have the quality of autonomy sooner or later, and they all occur without anybody's willing them.

It may well be reflected that Jung's aim of getting the patient to experiment with his own nature can occur just as well through his imagination playing on the person of the analyst, who is then the equivalent of the paintings and dreams. This has to me the following advantages: it links the whole process up to a human relationship without divesting it of its transpersonal quality; it also increases the possibilities of sorting out projections and

[59] Cf. *supra*, pp. 75 f.

NOTES ON THE TRANSFERENCE

perceptions after the manner described above under the heading of 'Projection-Perception Scale'. But Jung, as is well known, prefers a mild transference,[60] and this may be one of the reasons why he takes steps to prevent a stronger transference where he conceived that the alternative method was just as much in the patient's interest. I cannot believe, however, that preferences of this kind make much difference to the development or non-development of the objective transference, which goes far deeper than conscious feelings.

Part IV. Counter-Transference

(a) Use and definition of the term.

So far we have concentrated on a number of features of the transference which are displayed by the patient either spontaneously or as the result of techniques used by the analyst. But this is only part of the analytic process, since the analyst soon becomes involved himself.

Because it was originally hoped that the analyst's personality would be eliminated from the analytic process, the counter-transference was the first class of reactions by analysts to be studied. It was soon found that the patient's transference stimulated the analyst's repressed unconscious, which becomes projected on to the patient so as to interfere with his conduct in any analysis. Efforts were therefore made to eliminate this.

The thesis which is here put forward postulates that the whole personality of the analyst is inevitably involved in any analysis, and so the counter-transference is viewed from a different basis. This must lead to reconsideration of the term. A review of it is especially desirable because it has come, as a consequence of Jung's thesis, to cover more of the analyst's reactions than emanate from the repressed unconscious. Indeed it sometimes covers all the analyst's conduct in his analytic work.

In his interesting paper 'On the Function of Counter-Transference'[61] Robert Moody describes how his unconscious led him to a reaction which seemed exactly adapted to a little girl's need, without his altogether knowing at first what he was doing.

[60] Cf. *The Practice of Psychotherapy*, p. 172.
[61] *Journal of Analytical Psychology*, Vol. 1, No. 1, 1955.

89

NOTES ON THE TRANSFERENCE

His description, in which erotic instinctive processes were mobilized within him and brought into play, would seem, according to the present view, to represent a good analytic reaction. It arose first out of Moody's unconscious archetypal response, only later to become related consciously to the patient. The idea implied in the original theory of psycho-analysis that the analyst can only safely react to his patient with his ego alone is here certainly shown to be erroneous.

It is here contended that each interpretation or other response, if it is to have validity, needs to be *created on every occasion* out of the unconscious, using material provided by the patient to give the unconscious content adequate form, and this is just what happened in Moody's case. The fact that the analyst's reactions are repeated in a similar enough form in relation to sufficiently similar behaviour on the part of patients for them to be called a technique does not invalidate their being created on each occasion, for there are always differences enough to necessitate an individual form for the same familiar themes. The fact of the analyst's reacting to a patient is maintained by Jung to be the essential therapeutic factor in analysis; the reaction differs from the patient's transference in that it has a less compelling character and is capable of integration; in other words the analyst has a living relation to the unconscious at those points where the patient lacks it. This it is which facilitates the cure. Moody's behaviour was his spontaneous archetypal response to the sexual transference manifested by his child patient. If this be counter-transference,[62] then it could be argued that all analyses are based on counter-transference, and so the term would take on a new ⸍and very wide meaning. At first I was inclined to think the extended usage was objectionable, because it blurred its original negative meaning and so opened the door to almost any unconscious behaviour by the analyst. Yet the change in our understanding of transference as a whole is better reflected by the wider usage, for *participation mystique*, projection and introjection[63] can play valuable, even essential parts in analytic procedures.

[62] Some of the features of Moody's behaviour suggest that there may have been some acting out in it; this possibility can, however, be ignored in the present context.

[63] Cf. Money-Kyrle, 'Normal Counter-Transference and Some of its Deviations', *International Journal of Psycho-analysis*, Vol. XXXVII, Parts 4 and 5, 1956.

90

NOTES ON THE TRANSFERENCE

A solution to the quandary is made possible by using a qualifying adjective and referring to counter-transference illusion and counter-transference syntony. This differentiation is especially justified because there is a need to indicate the direction in which to look in order to become conscious. In analysis there are reactions on the part of the analyst which are syntonic and can make the patient more conscious, but these are different from the counter-transference illusion, where the increase in consciousness will come about only if the analyst himself examines his own reaction.

(*b*) Counter-Transference Illusion.

The use of a recording apparatus reveals very neatly how counter-transference illusion can arise from projection. To be sure, I had found that some patients before ending their analysis would review those parts of it in which they believed I had made mistakes, and I could see that they were often right, but by then the details had escaped me; in addition, dreams about the patient give another clue, and it is possible to realize that wrong or mistimed interpretations spring from a repressed source. However an accurate verbal record shows up the phenomena far better than anything else, for it can reveal without any shadow of doubt what can happen and how the analyst's own psyche can replace the patient's by projection.

Thus one day I ended a recorded interview with mixed feelings. It seemed on the one hand remarkably successful, but there had been a part early on when I had not succeeded in making progress. The patient was a boy of eleven who had problems over his aggressive feelings. The problems were related to his school work, in which he was not being as successful as his intelligence would warrant. The relevant part of the interview ran as follows:

John: 'Why did they block that door up?' (Referring to an area in the wall of my room where the doorway had been built up.)

M.F.: 'Imagine.' (Long silence, then M.F. continued) 'I expect to keep somebody out!'

John: 'I don't!' (then, after hesitations and much fidgeting), 'Better to have the door there' (i.e. where it is at present, leading into the passage).

M.F.: 'I suppose you thought my idea wasn't sensible. I think that from the way you went so quiet.'

NOTES ON THE TRANSFERENCE

John: 'They could have easily come that way' (referring to where the door is now).

M.F.: 'I still think I am right in believing you thought your remark was more sensible—you didn't think I would agree—you didn't think I would make *stupid* remarks!'

John: 'Beg pardon' (followed by long silence).

M.F.: (Repeats statement).

John: 'It isn't really stupid, it could have been. It's unlikely.' (After a further silence he went on to talk about electric trains, inferring by asking me questions that I was ignorant on this topic.)

M.F.: 'You must think I'm an *awfully ignorant boob* if I have not heard of Meccano, because everybody has." (And later on I made a more elaborate interpretation in which the phrase occurred.) 'You didn't know you had a secret feeling that *I was a fool and ignorant* and that you were more sensible than I in some respects.'

John went on to talk about Meccano and became technical in his conversation, and gradually I was able to stop over-acting and make interpretations which did not simply increase his resistance, for example:

M.F.: 'I wondered whether your questions were not something of this sort: "Well, here's something I'm likely to know more about than him"?'

Next I began to see that it was better to be even less active and point out that in his silences he was having secret thoughts. Only when I arrived at this formulation could the analysis of the thoughts proceed.

Listening to the recording made clear to me what I had vaguely felt during the interview. My aggression against this boy had interfered with my getting to understand what was going on in his mind. I had misinterpreted the child's feelings, replacing more subtle ones by a cruder statement, owing to the repression of memories relevant to a particular period of my own childhood. Then I used to attack my mother by calling her 'stupid', a word which I had repeated in my transference interpretations to John. Evidently I had identified with the memory images and John had represented myself as a child while I, ceasing to be the analyst, represented my mother. Only when I had circumvented this reaction could I frame interpretations which brought me

NOTES ON THE TRANSFERENCE

into relation with the boy's 'secret thoughts'; only from then onwards was I able to proceed with the analysis, understanding the child well enough for him to go on to reveal himself more and more fully.

It is to this class of phenomena that the term counter-transference illusion applies. The example manifested the following characteristics: (1) there was an unconscious, or rather vaguely conscious, reactivation of a past situation which completely replaced my relation to the patient; (2) during that time no analysis of the patient was possible.

If we transpose this concept to the archetypal level, then the events would have to possess the same characteristics, i.e. the archetypal reaction would not be related to the state of the patient and the analysis would stop until the analyst was able to become conscious of the archetype in question. It is not so easy to find an illusory archetypal counter-transference, especially as a syntonic counter-transference is not necessarily positive. In his paper on 'Loathsome Women'[64] Stein has given the content of his counter-transference apparently partly syntonic and partly illusory, based on a negative anima possession, to a type of woman patient. In this paper he formulates his affective attitude, dreams, and some of his personal experiences. In doing so he has contributed towards objectivity concerning the conflicts in which an analyst can become embroiled. In my experience, when the illusion of the analyst does not become conscious for too long, the analysis ends altogether, and the patient becomes acutely aware of what is happening. But when the analyst realizes what is going on even if he cannot resolve the projection a more favourable issue may be expected.

A frequent counter-transference manifestation is the tendency of analysts to make personal confessions to patients on unsuitable occasions. When I have objected to this practice or attempted to draw analysts' attention to their motives, I have been asked: 'Why do you find it necessary to withhold information about yourself from the patient?' Assuming that this question is not aimed at what is usually covered by discretion, and has not behind it the naïve belief that personal confessions in answer to questions improve the personal relationship between analyst and patient, which usually they do not, I reply that I do not find it 'necessary',

[64] *Journal of Analytical Psychology*, Vol. I, No. 1, 1955.

NOTES ON THE TRANSFERENCE

but that I consider it essential to relate the question to another because of the special liability of confessions to cover counter-transference illusions: 'What do you want to give information to your patient for, in view of the fact that in doing so you usually give a report about yourself as you are, or conceive yourself to be, while this is not at all the person he necessarily imagines you to be?' This question often disposes of the first, but leads to another, for it is then said to be only 'human' to make confessions and also to err. The term human is contrasted with divine and animal, and if translated into psychological language refers to the ego. My answering question now changes to: 'Why do you want to introduce your ego, i.e. personal consciousness?' If the answer be that the patient wants it or needs it, then we can go on to try to define the conditions under which it is desirable, i.e. when it is adapted to the patient's requirements and when a projection. I agree that it may be correct procedure, but I must reiterate that confessions by the analyst are far more frequently obstructive than otherwise, not only because they introduce projections but also because the information is only too often liable to drastic elaboration or distortion owing to the activity of fantastic projections arising from archetypal roots. Under these circumstances the analyst as a human being (an ego) is of little consequence. During this period it is that we are submitted to the reproaches of inhumanity and the like, but this is not to be dissolved by trying to be human, i.e. by making confessions, etc. Analysts are inhuman because of the transference, and we need to know *how* to be inhuman; this is surely one of the main reasons for undergoing an analysis, so that we may understand the patient's need and, at the same time, maintain our humanity.

But as the patient's ego becomes more established[65] towards the end of the analysis it is relevant for the analyst to introduce more and more of himself—not only his ego. Then it is possible and satisfying to both parties to conduct conversations, and to interact in a more and more complete and spontaneous fashion.

Though I have never heard it stated, I have certainly thought that the introduction of the analyst's ego, as I maintain often at the wrong time, has the aim of reducing the transference, but

[65] For purposes of simplicity cases in which the aim is individuation are not included. In these cases the ego being already established the position is clearly different.

94

NOTES ON THE TRANSFERENCE

it really avoids its transpersonal aspect by pretending that to introduce 'personal and human feeling helps'. Much more effective in reducing the transference is the method of recording dreams and teaching the patients to work them up before coming to the analysis, and getting them to paint and start on active imagination. The danger of this procedure, however, needs to be kept clearly in mind: as we have seen it is liable to create an illusion[66] that the transference does not exist when it is in reality just as big but is concealed in the method which does not by any means prevent 'big transferences'. If it is not taken up by the analyst it only too often turns against him or the patient in the environment, or creates a situation for which there is no means of a decent solution.

All this does not overlook the need for the patient as well as the analyst to distinguish between the transpersonal objective transference and the conscious situation. This criticism of many personal confessions made by the analysts is based on their ineffectiveness in attaining what they aim at, not to mention exploiting the patient's belief in the truthfulness of the analyst! If, however, a statement which can be checked by direct observation of the patient can be introduced, this is much more likely to continue the analytic aim of strengthening the patient's ego and helping him to gain greater control in the transference.

A female patient was attacking and at the same time trying to seduce me because I would not stop 'being an analyst' and live with her so that she could have day-to-day 'ordinary' relations with me. She attacked me as unfeeling, heartless, and indifferent to her distress. It was as fruitless for me to deny this as it would be for me to inaugurate a more personal kind of approach, to meet her outside the analysis for instance, or to start those personal confessions for which she asked because she was the victim of a projected hermaphroditic figure. It was not until I took the bull by the horns and asserted that she overlooked that my interpretations were an expression of my concern for her condition since they were attempts to bring her relief from it, that I made any progress. This I regard as an open statement about the main root for my making the interpretations she did not like; she can confirm my motive by numerous observations of my behaviour if she wants to make them. One of these is

[66] Which we may now class as a counter-transference.

95

NOTES ON THE TRANSFERENCE

that I will go on meeting her poisonous attacks in a friendly way and seeing their positive content.

In voicing the attitude which lay behind my interpretations I am also expressing the fact of my being involved. It was only when I had said this that I broke through her defences and was able to press home my interpretations so as to relieve her of some of her anxiety, for she had been convinced that I was using concepts in order to destroy the mature love which she felt, as well as to analyse its fantastic and infantile contents.

(c) The syntonic counter-transference.

The extension of the term counter-transference seeks to undermine the idea that the transference consists in projections from a patient upon an analyst who never reacts spontaneously but remains as a kind of impervious reflector in which the patient can see his projections. This thesis holds no charms for Jungian analysts, who unanimously reject it. They hold that because of the archetypes the analyst inevitably becomes sooner or later involved with the patient in an unconscious process, which is first experienced as a projection and then further analysed.

Since the aim of analysis is realization of the self by the patient, whether it results in ego development or individuation, and since the analyst aims at performing a mediating role in this realization, all his syntonic reactions will ideally relate to the self, i.e. to the essential wholeness of his nature. Yet it is evident that the self as an integrated whole is seldom in the forefront of the analyst's behaviour, which is more often based on other archetypal forms. Yet it may be discerned obscurely by patients in their experience of their analyst as a god of one kind or another. This easily induces resistances in analysts, but it has indeed a basis of truth, since all the analyst's reactions, be they interpretations, questions, comments, or acts, are operations of their own natures.

The danger associated with the emergence of this archetypal form is inflation. But it is not necessary for analysts to feel any particular merit when this comes into the patients' consciousness, since awareness of the self is no individual achievement but a historical process, as Jung has clearly shown in *Answer to Job*.[67] The objection to being seen as a god is surely as narcissistic and dangerous as being inflated by it; indeed it reveals a negative inflation. Therefore if a patient dreams or feels I am a god, saying

[67] London, 1954.

NOTES ON THE TRANSFERENCE

that it is ridiculous, I usually ask him: 'How do you know it is?' This question has behind it the idea that the self is the prime mover behind every analytic procedure, and is a recognition that the patient's 'projection' has a basis of truth in it. My question aims at leaving the door open to a wholeness which transcends consciousness and at the same time expresses my transpersonal involvement. It is therefore appropriate or syntonic.

It is commonly believed that consciousness is one of the great aims of analysis, but this is only partly true if the analysis is based on the self. Then consciousness is the instrument we use in the analytic process, it does not embrace the whole of it any more than the self can be identified with consciousness.

As I have suggested elsewhere,[68] the self is a dynamic structure, having two definable functions; it integrates and deintegrates, and I have shown that this view of it can be used to explain how consciousness is produced and how an ego is formed in early infancy. This concept arose partly from studies in child psychology and partly from reflection upon my behaviour as an analyst. There were two ways of behaving: (1) trying to isolate oneself from the patient by being as 'integrated' as possible; and (2) relinquishing this attitude and simply listening to and watching the patient to hear and see what comes out of the self in relation to the patient's activities, and then reacting. This would appear to involve deintegrating; it is as if what is put at the disposal of patients are parts of the analyst which are spontaneously responding to the patient in a way that he needs; yet these parts are manifestations of the self. It was this that led me to see that what Jung describes as the dialectical relationship is based upon processes which neither I nor my patient can control consciously, and that analysis depends upon the relatively greater experience of the analyst in deintegrating so as to meet the patient's disintegration. Moody[69] describes the feeling accompanying this experience very well when he says: 'I decided . . . to allow myself to be drawn into whatever kind of relationship I felt her [his child patient] to be silently demanding of me.' When he did this he remarks: 'I was somewhat at sea as to what was happening, but I realized that some important development had

[68] 'On the Origins of the Ego in Childhood', pp. 104 f., below.
[69] 'On the Function of the Counter-Transference', *Journal of Analytical Psychology*, Vol. I, No. 1, 1955, p. 54.

H

NOTES ON THE TRANSFERENCE

begun to occur from the time when I allowed my ... reactions to express themselves freely.'

This experience accords with Plaut's view of incarnation. In his paper on 'The Transference in Analytical Psychology',[70] he asserts that there are two ways in which analysts handle the projected image: 'One', he says, 'will deal with it by educative procedure centred on the elucidation and differentiation of archetypal contents', while others 'will accept the projection in a whole-hearted manner making no *direct* attempt to help the patient to sort out what belongs to him, what to the analyst, and what to neither as well as to both. On the contrary they will allow themselves to become this image bodily, to "incarnate" it bodily for the patient.'

It will be observed that the way of incarnating the image leads to what is described as primitive identity, a condition which Jung has called preconscious and which I have incorporated into the theory of the deintegrating function of the self by pointing to primitive identity as the manifestation of deintegration. It follows therefore that if any new consciousness is to arise and to lead to differentiation of the ego, a lowering of the conscious threshold is inevitable and desirable. This leads to a somewhat different view of archetypal projections than that frequently held. In the case of repressed material emerging from the patient there is less difficulty in detecting projections, because they are more immediately related to memory images, but where archetypes become active, giving rise to 'fantastic images', the position is different, for owing to the concurrent primitive identity, the images can be expressed by the analyst or by the patient. This means that it can be just as valid for the analyst to know of the projection through registering its impact upon himself and perceiving it first within himself, as it is by listening to the patient and realizing it as an inference from what the patient says.[71] Thus if a patient presents infantile material to the analyst, the latter can find out the appropriate reaction from himself, i.e. whether it be a mothering or fathering attitude which he can go

[70] *The British Journal of Medical Psychology*, Vol. XXIX, Part 1, 1956, pp. 15 ff.

[71] A very similar idea is to be found, and beautifully described, in Money-Kyrle's interesting paper 'Normal Counter-Transference and Some of its Deviations', ibid.

NOTES ON THE TRANSFERENCE

some way towards meeting and out of which he can make an interpretation when the patient is ready for it. At this stage in the transference the affective stability of the analyst is crucial; he must be able to rely on the deintegrates, knowing that consciousness will inevitably arise from them. It follows that he *will inevitably find* the right form or response so long as counter-transference projections do not obstruct its development.

It is on the basis of 'incarnating' the image, which should obviously be distinguished from acting out, that explanations and interpretations can begin to find their right place, for without them the patient will sooner or later become disorientated. If, however, the analyst keeps himself apart from the patient by adopting an explanatory or superior role without incarnating the image, he does nothing but isolate the patient at just the point at which he needs a primitive form of relationship.

Interpretations are therefore to be regarded as an end product of the analyst's syntonic counter-transference. They stand, as it were, on the basis of less definable affective preconscious experiences out of which they are distilled.

Some analysts depreciate the value of interpreting the transference, but in many places Jung emphasizes the importance of making the transference conscious. For instance, in 'Psychology of the Transference' he says,[72]

> As this [breaking infantile projections] is the legitimate aim and real meaning of the transference, it inevitably leads, whatever method of rapprochement be used, to discussion and understanding and hence to heightened consciousness, which is a measure of the personality's integration. During this discussion the conventional disguises are dropped and the true man comes to light. He is in very truth reborn from his psychological relationship and his field of consciousness is rounded into a circle.

This clear statement that it is necessary and desirable to bring the transference into consciousness requires amplification. What does this 'discussion and understanding' involve? To some extent this question has already been answered, but the question of interpretation, the most powerful instrument in the hands of the analyst, needs special consideration.

[72] *The Practice of Psychotherapy*, p. 219.

NOTES ON THE TRANSFERENCE

The great majority of the statements made by the patient, including those reported, are made to a projected figure, and it is evident that the analyst needs to be constantly on the look-out to recognize who the figure may be which he incarnates. This constitutes the major problem of transference interpretation for, if it is not defined, all that he says is reinterpreted by the patient in the light of projection, and misunderstandings inevitably arise. It is for this reason that the patient is introduced to the desirability of saying all that he can about his analyst as it occurs to him either outside the analysis or during his sessions. For this reason also the analyst introduces as few complications as possible, for how he behaves is as crucial as what he says. Therefore, in order to follow what he is doing, the advantage of keeping the essential framework of the interview simple is self-evident. The simplicity also facilitates the detection of projections which can be interpreted when sufficient material has accumulated.

It follows that the interpretation of patients' material must be regarded as incomplete if its transference content is not referred to when it is sufficiently near consciousness. This applies to all reports embodying present or past occurrences, even to such simple phenomena as bits of history revealed by the patient; they all have reference to the 'actual situation', which in the case of analytic interviews is to be found in the transference.

It is sometimes held that no rules can be made as to when an interpretation should or should not be given, but this is not my experience. The following principle can certainly be formulated: when the patient has brought enough material for the analyst to make the interpretations in such terms that the patient can understand them, the interpretations can be given without hesitation. Under these conditions the patient's ego is mobilized, the reality content of the relationship is increased, and so regressive trends are brought more under control by coming into consciousness.

There is this to be said, however, against a rule—it could prevent the interpretations from being a creative act based on the analyst's past experience combined with the new experience he has of his patient; and it could short-cut the analyst's feeling of concern for the patient, the best safeguard against the use of theoretical interpretations as defences against unconscious activity within the analyst. An interpretation which violates the relationship clearly does not subscribe to the above rule which

NOTES ON THE TRANSFERENCE

aims at maintaining and improving the relationship between analyst and patient.

In 'Psychology of the Transference' Jung says:[73] 'Even the most experienced psychotherapist will discover again and again that he is caught up in a bond, a combination resting on mutual unconsciousness.' It is out of this unconscious bond that in my view interpretations best arise, for if they do not they easily become impositions of the analyst upon his patient. But this bond is not stable, because of the 'ever-changing content that possesses the patient, which Jung compares to Mercurius who, in uniting all opposites in himself, appears 'like a demon [who] now flits about from patient to doctor, and as the third part in the alliance, continues its game, sometimes impish and teasing, sometimes really diabolical'.[74] Whether the 'demon' becomes a source of consciousness or of confusion all depends on how he is handled. One useful means is to try to start every interview as though a new patient were entering the room, for this helps in getting into relation with the patient's mood of the moment.

AMPLIFICATION

In 'The Aims of Psychotherapy' Jung says,[75] '. . . it is particularly important for me to know as much as possible about primitive psychology, mythology, archeology, and comparative religion because these fields offer me invaluable analogies with which to enrich the associations of my patients'. The necessity for this knowledge is generally agreed, but it needs to be borne in mind that extraneous mythological parallels, however close, can be used to obscure rather than clarify what is going on in the transference. After the myth has been developed within the transference it will naturally give the patient a special interest in the remarkable parallels which will almost inevitably be sought out in books and will be all the more striking because he knows that their substance was first revealed to him spontaneously.

It is quite clear that what I have described is at variance with the notion of introducing intellectual knowledge when the archetypal projections are in full swing, for whether the analyst likes it or not he will inevitably embody the image, as Jung clearly sees when he says:[76]

[73] Ibid., p. 178, par. 367.   [74] Ibid., p. 188.   [75] Ibid., p. 45.
[76] 'Psychology of the Transference', ibid., p. 170.

101

NOTES ON THE TRANSFERENCE

Practical analysis has shown that unconscious contents are invariably projected at first on to concrete persons and situations. Many projections can ultimately be integrated back into the individual once he has recognized their subjective origin: others resist integration, and although they may be detached from their original objects they thereupon transfer themselves to the doctor.

There is no possibility of explaining or getting rid of them by educative procedures; if this were possible it would only be necessary to give lectures. The ultimate resolution of these projections depends first and foremost on the analyst's behaviour and experience of his own myth. Once the parent imagos are projected they stay projected till the self appears, which initiates the 'stage of transformation'.[77] Here Jung introduces the idea of the self-education of the 'doctor' as part of the analytic process. He does not, however, mean intellectual education but rather the analysis of the analyst as a means of introducing him to the inevitability of transforming himself as his patient also does.

The thesis of this essay is an extension of Jung's. It states that this mutual transformation extends to all the transference; it only becomes more significant in the 'stage of transformation' in which the mutual unconscious bond between analyst and patient becomes increasingly apparent. Amplification is used to elucidate the content of this, and is only valid when based upon the analyst's experience in the transference. That it can be used to support depersonalizing defences and mask easily verbalized transference relationships when used earlier has already been shown, and therefore I aim at using the patient's and my own experienced images first. Then if these correspond to known myths the latter can be added; then they do act, as Baynes[78] so vividly asserts, like the stains of a histologist, throwing obscure psychic contents vividly into relief, enriching the transference and leading to clearer definition of its contents.

CONCLUSION

These attempts to assess some problems presented by transference analysis will, I hope, lead to other reviews of the subject. They are especially important at the present juncture because the

[77] 'Problems of Modern Psychotherapy', ibid., pp. 69 ff.
[78] *Mythology of the Soul*, p. 424.

NOTES ON THE TRANSFERENCE

realization of the complexity of transference analysis as a two-way process in which the personality of the analyst takes an essential part can lead and has led to abandoning the attempt to define and verbalize what is contained in it, because the whole process seems too individual and subjective. I believe, however, that Jung's thesis can be used to illuminate and describe its contents. This account is more realistic and scientific than if the attempt be made to eliminate the analyst as a person and regard him as a projection screen.

I have made no reference to such practices as the patient going to two analysts at the same time,[79] or to the important question of whether the sex of the analyst is significant. These issues still appear too complex to formulate. Neither have I considered the different forms of transference due to psychopathological considerations, but have rather confined myself to more fundamental clinical problems.

The general trend of my view is that the individuality of the patient cannot be overlooked in any age group, and that the process of analysis and therefore the transference is always basically the same though patients and analysts react to it differently.

In reading Jung's essays assembled in volume sixteen of the *Collected Works* it is impossible to miss the changes that have taken place in the author's views with the passing of time. Jung is continually seeking adequate means of describing the remarkably complex and difficult field covered by psychotherapy. Fundamentally his view is the same, but the changes are often important. His tendency seems to have been to give more and more attention to the transference, and in 1951 he says, 'The intelligent psychotherapist has known for years that *any*[80] complicated treatment is an individual dialectical process.'[81] Since the dialectical process corresponds with what I have defined as transference he would here seem to be in basic agreement with the thesis of my essay.

[79] Cf. Henderson, 'Analysis of Transference in Analytical Psychology', *American Journal of Psychology*, Vol. IX, No. 4, 1955.

[80] Italics mine.

[81] 'Fundamental Questions of Psychotherapy', *The Practice of Psychotherapy*, p. 116.

103

V

THE ORIGINS OF THE EGO IN CHILDHOOD[1]

Theories in psychology are the very devil. It is true that we need certain points of view for their orienting and heuristic value: but they should always be regarded as mere auxiliary concepts that can be laid aside at any time.[2]

INTRODUCTION

THE validity of Jung's subtle and far-reaching thesis on the effect of parents upon children, both in conscious education and in the more obscure sphere of unconscious functioning, has become widely realized. It is, however, often overlooked that in his writings there can be found an outline theory of ego development as well, though it is true that careful reading is needed to reveal it and it has never been set forth completely in one volume[3] or one paper.

His general proposition runs as follows: the psychic development of children, while largely the result of natural growth, is mainly centred round ego formation. He has amplified this by showing us how to think of the unconscious as the origin of the conscious ego. These fundamental concepts have been put forward beautifully by him in a classical passage:[4]

The greatest and most extensive development takes place during the period between birth and the end of psychic puberty, a period that may normally extend, for a man of our climate and race, to the twenty-fifth year. In the case of a woman it usually ends when she is about nineteen

---

[1] Originally published in *Studien zur Analytischen Psychologie C. G. Jungs*, Zurich, 1955.

[2] C. G. Jung, 'Psychic Conflicts in a Child', Foreword to Third Edition, in *The Development of Personality* (Collected Works, Vol. XVII), London and New York, 1954, p. 7.

[3] Though much of it is assembled in *The Development of Personality*.

[4] Ibid., par. 103.

ORIGINS OF THE EGO IN CHILDHOOD

or twenty. This development establishes a firm connection between the ego and the previously unconscious psychic processes, thus separating them from their source in the unconscious. In this way the conscious rises out of the unconscious like an island newly risen from the sea.

For the purposes of this discussion it will be assumed that the unconscious, whose organs are the archetypes, is formed before birth. Since the archetypes are bound up with the functioning of the central nervous system it must presumably be there by the time the brain is formed.

ARCHETYPES IN CHILDHOOD

Through the extensive researches of Jung it is known that the archetypes first express themselves in the conscious as images. Yet in his earlier work Jung was inclined to regard the appearance of these archtypal images[5] in children's dreams and fantasies as a sort of unwelcome intrusion into the undeveloped mind of the child. This led to his interpreting them in terms of the parent's psychology. Later, however, he withdrew this idea and stated clearly that this attempt was not confirmed by the evidence at his disposal and that he had been misled by the remarkable dreams of children into believing that their apparently adult nature rendered them, so to say, unsuited to the child's consciousness.[6]

The dreams of small children often refer more to the parents than to the child itself. Long ago I observed some very curious dreams in early childhood, for instance the first dreams patients could remember. They were 'big dreams', and their content was often so very unchildlike that at first I was convinced they could be explained by the psychology of the parents. There was the case of a boy who dreamt out the whole erotic and religious problem of his father. The father could remember no dreams at all, so for some time I analysed the father through the dreams of his eight-year-old son. Eventually the father began to dream himself, and the dreams of the child stopped. Later on I realized that the peculiar dreams of small children are genuine enough, since they contain archetypes which are the cause of their apparently adult character.

It will be apparent that the view that archetypal dreams of children expressed the parents' unconscious contents, ran counter

---

[5] For the purposes of this paper the archetypal images are defined as the representatives in consciousness of the unconscious archetypes.

[6] Ibid., par. 106.

105

ORIGINS OF THE EGO IN CHILDHOOD

to the idea of the unconscious as the origin of the conscious, and so when Jung in his seminars on children's dreams changed his earlier view, he brought his ideas on children more closely into line with his earlier conception. He says[7]

The child's psyche, prior to the stage of ego-consciousness, is very far from being empty and devoid of content. . . . That such contents exist in the child who has not yet attained to ego-consciousness is a well-attested fact. The most important evidence in this respect is the dreams of three- and four-year-old children, among which there are some so strikingly mythological and so fraught with meaning that one would take them at once for the dreams of grown-ups, did one not know who the dreamer was. They are the last vestiges of a dwindling collective psyche which dreamingly reiterates the perennial contents of the human soul. From this phase there spring many childish fears and dim, unchildlike premonitions. . . . But from this sphere also spring those flashes of insight and lucidity which give rise to the proverb: Children and fools speak the truth.

Further a few lines later:

These archetypes of the collective psyche . . . are the dominants that rule the preconscious soul of the child and, when projected upon the human parents, lend them a fascination which often assumes monstrous proportions.[8]

By investigating the dreams of adult persons[9] remembered from their childhood, Jung could show the strange way they applied to the whole development of the individual. The dreams indeed gave the pattern, often pathological, of the individual's psychic maturation. They could be understood in retrospect by the dreamer, though in childhood they reached far beyond the grasp of his dawning consciousness. Though these dreams might naturally be understood as 'adult' yet they can now be understood prospectively as symbolical 'foreknowledge' of the future.

In addition to these remarkable phenomena, thrown up apparently without relation to the child's conscious, were other dreams containing images of the archetypes manifestly suited to childhood, understandable in the light of the child's situation and functioning compensatorily to the conscious attitude just as we find them doing in adult persons.

[7] Ibid., par. 94.   [8] Ibid., par. 97.

[9] Cf. Jung, *Seminars on Children's Dreams*, 1936/37, 1938/39, 1939/40 (privately circulated).

106

ORIGINS OF THE EGO IN CHILDHOOD

To me these dreams were of particular interest because I had been gradually realizing that archetypal images in childhood pictures, dreams, play and fantasy were quite relevant to children themselves. It is well known that children love fairy and folk tales, and will concentrate on them for hours, demanding repetition of particular stories over and over again. This phenomenon can only be understood in terms of the activity of archetypes within the psyche of the child. Here there is nothing pathological and nothing pecularly adult, it is a natural phenomenon of childhood, and all attempts to eradicate it, as rationalistic parents and teachers sometimes do, prove fruitless.

To clinch the matter I proceeded to interpret the children's material directly to them and found not only that, so long as the words used were understandable and the concepts simple enough, the children could understand, but also that they had ideas of their own which they had been keeping secret because no adult would listen.[10]

UNCONSCIOUS, PRECONSCIOUS AND CONSCIOUS

It will have been noticed that Jung uses the term preconscious to describe the condition of mind in which a child finds itself when under the sway of archetypal images. It will be useful to bear this in mind throughout this chapter, for the distinction clarifies an ambiguity concerning the nature of conscious states. In using the term preconscious Jung means to designate a state of consciousness in which the ego is very weak and the images representing unconscious vitality are highly charged with libido,

[10] Cf. Fordham, *The Life of Childhood*, London, 1944, and 'Analytical Psychology Applied to Children', *The Nervous Child*, Vol. V, Part 2, pp. 134 ff., 1947. It has been shown that all the most clearly defined archetypal images and themes can be found in childhood—the shadow, the anima and animus, the mana personalities, and the self. Furthermore the images of transition and initiation are of common occurrence. Cf. Fordham, *The Life of Childhood*; idem, 'Integration and Disintegration and Early Ego Development', *The Nervous Child*, Vol. VI, Part 3, pp. 266 ff.; and Chapter VI below.

Reference to Frances G. Wickes' book *The Inner World of Childhood*, London and New York, 1935, will reveal other examples, but the archetypal images are mostly interpreted in the light of the parents' psychology. That such phenomena occur cannot be doubted; they result from the identity of parent and child.

ORIGINS OF THE EGO IN CHILDHOOD

i.e. are *numinous*. In the future these will become less powerful as the ego becomes organized and a coherent conscious mind comes into being. The term preconscious is further useful to underline the emergent viewpoint and makes it possible to define a progression: unconscious leading to the state preconscious and finally to an organized conscious mind.

PRIMITIVE IDENTITY

The unconscious and preconscious conditions of the psychic life of the child are allied to the concept of primitive identity or *participation mystique*. Jung defines this as follows:[11]

Identity derives essentially from the notorious unconsciousness of the small child. . . . Unconsciousness means non-differentiation. There is as yet no clearly differentiated ego, only events which may belong to me or to another. It is sufficient that *somebody* should be affected by them. The extraordinary infectiousness of emotional reactions then makes it certain that everybody in the vicinity will involuntarily be affected. The weaker ego-consciousness is, the less it matters who is affected, and the less the individual is able to guard against it. He could only do that if he could say: you are excited or angry, but I am not, for I am not you.

The idea of primitive identity is significant for a particular reason: the concept can be used to define how the unconscious of parents seeps through into the children's psyche and forces them to live through or act out the problems of their parents; it can be used to define the psychic condition in which children dream their parents' dreams and fantasize their parents' fantasies.

The phenomena of primitive identity have been given considerable attention both by Jung[12] and by Mrs Wickes[13] without, however, the difference between primitive identity and the later identifications being made altogether clear. Primitive identity is, however, best conceived as fundamental and different from the later identifications of children with one or other of their parents as part of their emotional feeling and intellectual development. To my mind the distinction is useful because it brings out the relation with the concept of ego boundaries. In primitive identity

[11] *The Development of Personality*, par. 83.
[12] 'Child Development and Education', ibid., pp. 47 ff.
[13] Op. cit.

108

ORIGINS OF THE EGO IN CHILDHOOD

there are only hazy boundaries to the ego and apparently no boundaries to the self, or very obscure ones. By the time the later identifications occur these boundaries are far more definite and clearly marked.

INSTINCTS IN CHILDHOOD

In *Symbols of Transformation*[14] Jung states his position with regard to the physical activities of the child classed as the nutritional, presexual and sexual acts of infancy. These he accepts as established facts linked together through the rhythmical activities accompanying them. He explicitly shows that the rhythmic act of suckling is related to sexual activity, to masturbation, to arm and leg movements, and so to all sorts of cultural activities, through dancing to initiation rites, the making of fire, etc. These need no elaboration here since reference is easy to the masterly exposition which will be found in Part 2, Chapter III of that book. We may, however, get the gist of his argument from two short quotations:

We know that in infants the libido first manifests itself exclusively in the nutritional zone, where, in the act of sucking, food is taken in with rhythmic movement. At the same time there develops in the motor sphere in general a pleasurable rhythmic movement of the arms and legs (kicking etc.). With the growth of the individual and the development of his organs the libido creates for itself new avenues of activity. The primary model of rhythmic movement, producing pleasure and satisfaction, is transferred to the zone of other functions, with sexuality as its ultimate goal. This is not to say that the rhythmic activity derives from the act of nutrition. A considerable part of the energy supplied by nutrition for growth has to convert itself into sexual libido and other forms of activity. . . . As a rule, it is the other body openings that become the main object of interest; then the skin, or special parts of it; and finally rhythmic movements of all kinds. These, expressed in the form of rubbing, boring, picking, and so forth, follow a certain rhythm. It is clear that this activity, once it reaches the sexual zone, may provide occasion for the first attempts at masturbation. In the course of its migrations the libido carries traces of the nutritional phase into its new field of operations, which accounts for the many intimate connections between the nutritive and the sexual function. . . . I therefore propose to call the period from birth up to the time of the first clear

[14] Collected Works, Vol. V, London and New York, 1956.

109

ORIGINS OF THE EGO IN CHILDHOOD

manifestations of sexuality the 'presexual stage'. As a rule it falls between the first and the fourth year (par. 206).

And (par. 219):

Since the rhythmic activity can no longer find an outlet in the act of feeding after the nutritional phase of development is over, it transfers itself not only to the sphere of sexuality in the strict sense, but also to the 'decoy mechanisms', such as music and dancing, and finally to the sphere of work. The close connection which work always has with music, singing and dancing, drumming and all manner of rhythms in primitive societies, indeed its absolute dependence on these things, is very striking.

In this chapter Jung thus accepts the fact that certain zones of the body, viz. the mouth, anus, and genitalia, assume successive importance, while he refers to the skin as of essential significance in the infant's pleasure-seeking activities. To these zones we shall return; suffice it to remark here that we shall consider them from the viewpoint of centres of consciousness.

CONCEPT BUILDING

Let us now turn to an early work of Jung's on the 'Psychic Conflicts in a Child'[15] in which he describes a short but intense period of development in a little girl. This delightful paper describes the sayings, questionings and behaviour of Anna, aged three years, consequent upon the birth of a younger brother. The paper is a classic, showing on the one hand the growth in the child's awareness of the reproductive process, and on the other the relation of this process to concept building, to which the child's parents greatly contribute. Into this process come all the various elements we have so far discussed.

Jung is mainly interested in the cognitive aspect, though he takes a psycho-biological view of the development. This is no abstract process, and into it come physical facts, theories of life, death and rebirth, dreams of far-reaching significance, analogical reflection and bodily dramatizations, suggesting that the child knows the biological essentials of birth and the facts leading up to it. The child's learning seems less the result of teaching than a seeking for the right forms of expression, first in mythological images, then testing them against observations, finding

[15] *The Development of Personality*, pp. 8 ff.

ORIGINS OF THE EGO IN CHILDHOOD

them erroneous, deducing the adult reality and then again testing out whether the parents will tell the truth about her findings. Analogical reflections may be especially noted. They are derived from many sources, firstly observations on the behaviour of others, to wit, the fact of the child's mother giving birth to a new baby, the arrival of a nurse, the behaviour of a gardener; secondly from her own more intimate eating and excretory acts; thirdly from myths such as the stork and reincarnation theories. In it all we see how myth, physical observation and experience interweave, how myth and biological knowledge replace each other, and how these two processes are linked up to the relationships between the child and her parents.

It is clear that the importance of the 'truth', which to a child must in a sense remain conjectural, is none the less vital for the child's sense of emotional security in her relation to her parents. It can be said that the 'truth' corresponds to unconscious knowledge of an archetypal nature which is seen gradually finding the best form of expression.

The whole case illustrates, clarifies and makes it possible to expand our ideas of the processes already postulated: the archetypes express themselves on the one hand in bodily experience and on the other in archetypal images. The two forms of expression start like islands in the sea and, combining with ego activity, in the end coalesce to establish firm knowledge. This firm knowledge is by no means just the adult biological 'facts', as Jung clearly sees, for he says that infantile sexuality is not only the basis of adult sexuality but also the source of the higher functions: infantile sexuality lies at the root of much concept building and spiritual life.

By the age of three the little girl was evidently capable of very considerable differentiation between inner and outer reality, between thought and fantasy, between psyche and soma, between herself and others. As observations of younger and younger children accumulate it becomes evident that they only gradually develop any capacity at all to make these distinctions. Indeed at the very beginning none whatever can be made. We need to assume that from the very beginning infants experience in the act of suckling and excreting fantasies which are not differentiated from the physical experience. These fantasy systems are part of the preconscious system and must therefore express archetypes.

ORIGINS OF THE EGO IN CHILDHOOD

On this basis it can be understood that the so-called libidinal zones are preconscious centres of awareness in which the numinous images first form themselves as fragmentary units—the ego fragments.

The zones are usually thought of as discrete areas but right from the beginning analogic linkage must be found between them, since fantasy functioning is much looser than differentiated ego functioning. If as we shall consider later on these preconscious centres are aspects or, as we shall call them, deintegrates of the original self, then there will also be a tendency for them to unite one with the other, because they are derivatives of the archetype of wholeness.

The foregoing sketch will, I hope, dispel once and for all the notion that there are no concepts of psychic development, so far as the infant and child are concerned, in analytical psychology. On the contrary, the basic concepts are there, as usual set out in the main by Jung himself. These concepts and supporting observations have still been insufficiently elaborated: our aim in what follows is to see how far it is possible to do this. It is hoped that the discussion will firstly bring more order into the otherwise chaotic mass of observations at our disposal, secondly will construct a theoretical instrument which will make new observations possible. It will by now be apparent that the whole problem is exceedingly complex, and so we shall not be surprised if our discussion fails to produce an altogether coherent theory.

One perplexing fact will soon become apparent: there is little or no mention of the environment, little or no mention of the parents, who seem as it were to have been done away with. But this is incorrect, they have rather not yet appeared on the scene as persons apart from the child.

This is my justification for setting out the arguments as if there were no real parents and no real environment. It is justifiable because we are considering the states of awareness in a very small child. For him the image and concept 'parent' only gradually develop.

THE SELF IN CHILDHOOD

In 1951[16] I put forward some tentative formulations starting from the assumption that the self is the original archetype of

[16] 'Some Observations on the Self in Childhood', *British Journal of Medical Psychology*, Vol. XXIV, Part 2, 1951; reprinted as part of Chapter VI of the present book.

ORIGINS OF THE EGO IN CHILDHOOD

infancy and further that the emergence of the ego was closely related to it. I based this upon the observation that children produced pictures of mandalas, and further that when they did so a process of integration occurred in which the ego was clearly strengthened. I went on to show that very small children, even those of one year old, connected the circle with the word *I* or *me* and that here also their behaviour showed an integration comparable to that observed in older children. From this I concluded that the circle represented the self in union with the ego.

These observations ran counter to what I thought was an established concept: that the ego was not formed till much later. I therefore had to consider whether my observations were the exception rather than the rule. I knew that scribbles were regularly made by children before the second year, but I had assumed that they did not use the word *I* before the third or fourth year. If this were true the association of the scribbled circle with the word *I* in infants could not be a general phenomenon. It was therefore with some satisfaction that I discovered Gessel's work[17] which disproved the too late appearance of the word I—too late at least for my purpose. He showed that children of eighteen months used the word with some regularity, inferring that it must have appeared for the first time even earlier still.[18]

[17] A. Gessel, *The First Five Years of Life*, London (n.d.).

[18] The following phrases containing *I* are listed by Gessel p. 197: 18 months: out of 12 phrases 2 contain 'I'—'I do it' and 'I see . . .' 24 months: out of 19 phrases 6 contain 'I'—'I see Daddy', 'I want my cup', 'I want some more', 'I see Daddy go bye-bye car', 'I put it on the chair', 'I don't want to go to bed'. Gessel comments on the grammatical correctness. These phrases were reported by mothers in response to a request for 'examples of the longest combinations heard'.

Later (p. 198) Gessel says: 'The most conspicuous development in the matter of parts of speech at 2 years is the *common* (italics mine) use of pronouns, especially in the first and second persons. *I*, *me* and *you* are differentiated, though *I* and *me* are frequently confused. *My* and *mine* come before other possessives. Many children of this age still use the proper name instead of the personal pronoun in referring to themselves or others.'

It may also be remarked here that memory can be observed in the last quarter of the first year (op. cit., p. 175). These facts point to the much earlier formation of an ego centrum than Jung assumed: he puts it, possibly following Freud, at between the third and fifth year on the grounds that there is no evidence of memory till then and that the child does not use the word *I* till then. This notion seems to have been wrongly accepted

ORIGINS OF THE EGO IN CHILDHOOD

There is thus evidence from individuals which is not contradicted by statistical studies to indicate that the self is the earliest archetype of which evidence can be obtained in infancy.

A supporting but more questionable piece of evidence is the readiness of mothers, pediatricians and psychologists making special studies of infants to recognize that all the infant's important reactions are total ones involving the whole organism—they are 'self reactions' undifferentiated and complete, whilst D. W. Winnicott says:[19] 'Many infants are well on the way towards integration during certain periods of the first twenty-four hours of life.' In contrast to me he postulates a primary unintegrated state in infancy.

The difficulty however of conceiving what is meant by saying that the self is the original archetype of childhood is very great, because we are so much embedded in current biological and psychological concepts which all depend upon dichotomies: psyche, soma; mind, body; 'self',[20] environment; conscious, unconscious; ego, non-ego; we cannot conceive what it is like before these units that we have learnt to use in everyday life come into being.

In a recent paper a psycho-analytic pediatrician, D. W. Winnicott, says:[21] 'Let us assume that health in the early development of the individual entails *continuity of being*. The early psyche-soma proceeds along a certain line of development provided its *continuity of being is not disturbed*; in other words, for the healthy development of the early psyche-soma there is a need for a *perfect* environment. At first the need is absolute.'[22]

into analytical psychology, cf. Jacobi ('Ich und Selbst in Kinderzeichnung', *Schweizerische Zeitschrift für Psychologie*, Vol. XII, Part 1 (Bern, 1953).

[19] 'Primitive Emotional Development', *International Journal of Psychoanalysis*, Vol. XXVI, 1945.

[20] In this paper the word 'self' in quotation marks will be used to designate the passive awareness a child can have of himself apart from other persons and things. It is not identical with the ego though it is part of it, neither is the experience 'self' identical with the self as an archetype though we may assume that it refers to it.

[21] 'Mind and its Relation to the Psyche-Soma', *British Journal of Medical Psychology*, Vol. XXVII, Part 4, 1954, p. 202.

[22] A further recent attempt to describe something like the self has appeared in psycho-analysis under the heading of the 'body scheme'. This concept includes the cosmos and the body outline and is defined by

ORIGINS OF THE EGO IN CHILDHOOD

The notion of a 'continuity of being' in a single psyche-soma implies a condition of wholeness, but where Winnicott speaks of the psyche-soma *and* environment then the self has already been divided up even if the fit be perfect.

Jung's very method of speaking of the self paradoxically is already too far developed, and one is almost tempted to follow the method of Zen Buddhism in denying or making nonsense of any proposition, or of using poetry to help. In some sense the mystics have described the original condition, but mysticism implies great consciousness through which the self can be seen and experienced, and this is so even though some mystics try to eradicate every image. For these reasons it seems to me that we need a new descriptive phrase: original self is the one I prefer, for even Winnicott's 'continuity of being' implies time.[23]

Since writing my article on 'The Self in Childhood'[24] it has been brought to my notice that my thesis is widely assumed amongst analytical psychologists.[25] It is held that the development of the conscious in the child violates the original condition

the author as follows (Scott, 'Some Embryological, Neurological, Psychiatric and Psycho-analytic Implications of the Body Scheme', *International Journal of Psycho-Analysis*, Vol. XIX, Part 3, 1946, p. 2): 'The body scheme refers to that conscious or unconscious integrate of sensations, perceptions, conceptions, affects, memories and images of the body from its surface to its depths and from its surface to the limits of space and time. In other words the B. S. is a continually changing world scheme— the extended limits of which have to deal with what can only be called the limits of space and time.'

This concept, though welcome as introducing into psycho-analysis something akin to Jung's discoveries, is far too developed for our present purposes.

[23] I hope that in using this term the distressing tendency to imagine that it has something to do with perfection will be avoided. There is obviously nothing perfect or imperfect in this condition, but I feel bound to bring the question in because there is still too much of a tendency amongst analytical psychologists to affix it to children. It is clear *in the implication* that nothing can go wrong (psychically) with a child so long as its parents face their conflicts.

[24] Chapter XII below.

[25] Erich Neumann's valuable volume *The Origins and History of Consciousness*, London, 1954, may be cited here. On the basis of studies in myth and legend he sets out in a cultural context a thesis relevant to the present argument. But his thesis cannot be transferred to the origin and development of consciousness in children. Ontogeny does not recapitulate phylogeny (cf. Chapter I above).

ORIGINS OF THE EGO IN CHILDHOOD

of wholeness to which more mature persons attempt to return when confronted with insurmountable difficulties. Thus the retrospective tendency met with in analysis is considered as an attempt to re-establish the primal condition of wholeness termed the original self. Sometimes this condition can be approached through memories, at others a more thorough-going regression needs to occur.

THE SELF IN INDIVIDUATION AND CHILDHOOD

The activity of the self in childhood poses theoretical and practical problems for analytical psychology. The symbolism of the self has been studied and widely accepted as depicting the goal of the individuation process, but this process occurs in the second half of life, and for it to take place a strongly established ego is a necessary prerequisite. Because of this it is possible to obtain, without too great difficulty, a mass of material reflecting the behaviour of archetypal contents. This material is contained in dreams and active imagination, and as a consequence Jung and others have been able to demonstrate the order in which the archetypal images emerge into consciousness once individuation has begun.

In an earlier work[26] I pointed out (following Jung[27]) that the aims of childhood and the first half of life were directly opposite to those of the second. In consequence, whereas in childhood the goal is to develop the ego over against the self, in middle life and old age the aim is to relinquish the primacy of the ego in favour of the self. This concept has been worked out in a more general way by Jung[28] in his paper 'The Stages of Life', but he had not developed the idea so far as children were concerned. He has, however, conceived of the self as the origin of the ego as the following quotation from 'Transformation Symbolism in the Mass'[29] shows:

The term 'self' seemed to me a suitable one for the unconscious substrate, whose actual exponent in consciousness is the ego. The ego stands to the self as the moved to the mover, or as object to subject,

[26] Cf. Chapter XII below.
[27] *Modern Man in Search of a Soul*, London, 1933.
[28] Op. cit., pp. 109 ff.
[29] *The Mysteries*, Papers from the Eranos Yearbooks, New York, 1956.

116

ORIGINS OF THE EGO IN CHILDHOOD

because the determining factors which radiate out from the self surround the ego on all sides and are therefore superordinate to it. The self, like the unconscious, is an *a priori* existent *out of which the ego evolves. It is an unconscious prefiguration of the ego.* It is not I who create myself, rather I happen to myself.

There is an obvious conclusion to be drawn from the regular progression of archetypal images in individuation: in childhood one would expect them to appear in the reverse order to that found in individuation, i.e. instead of the progression, shadow, animus, or anima, mana personalities, self, we should find the self first followed by the mana personalities, animus or anima and lastly the shadow. Search for such a progression in children is beginning to bear fruit, but the problem is difficult in infancy because the lack of ego makes the recording of images impossible and we have to rely on behaviour alone to confirm or disprove our hypothesis.

THE CONCEPT OF DEINTEGRATION

In comparing the self in childhood with the self in individuation we are also comparing the process of integration with another one for which I propose the term deintegration. This term is used for the *spontaneous* division of the self into parts—a manifest necessity if consciousness is ever to arise.

In choosing this word I have in mind a distinction from disintegration, a condition which is associated in experience with destruction or splitting of the ego into a number of fragments. It presupposes an ego which is already formed, and consequently the experience is a danger to its whole integrity. Deintegration on the contrary is conceived as a spontaneous property of the self behind ego formation. Expressing the idea anthropomorphically one might say that it springs from a desire of the self to become conscious, to form an ego by dividing itself up, leading to a state which would be described from the ego standpoint as unintegrated. Therefore, when Winnicott refers to a primary unintegrated state he looks at the progression from the position of ego psychology; from the level of the self it is a deintegrated state.

Since the term disintegration will be used in a later essay this is an appropriate place to discuss it. This term, like the

ORIGINS OF THE EGO IN CHILDHOOD

phrase unintegrated states, refers to ego psychology. The self cannot disintegrate, for only the ego can be destroyed or split in pieces. Therefore the term disintegration can be defined as a condition in which the ego integrate regresses, often but not necessarily catastrophically. If the process is catastrophic the ego does not return to an earlier integrate, either because there is none, as seems to be the case in schizophrenia, or because the disintegration causes too much anxiety for the regression to proceed to the earlier and less developed level. Where the disintegration is complete a simpler integrate appears naturally and an earlier state of stability is re-established.

Jung has shown us that when we think we have discovered a new concept, myths will certainly have reflected it before, and further that through the study of myths we can not only gain support for the concept but also amplification of it. The concept of deintegration is no exception.

The most probable source of parallels to the deintegration concept lies in cosmic creation myths, and indeed they are to be found amongst our Western cosmogonic myths, the Greek ones showing the essential features most clearly. In the Orphic cult we find the cosmic egg as '. . . the symbol of what gives birth to all things and in itself contains all things'[30] and the *Clementine Homilies* say: 'Orpheus likened Chaos to an egg in which was the commingling of the primaeval elements.'[31] From the cosmic egg springs Eros, he '. . . revealed and brought to light everything that had previously lain hidden in the golden egg'.[32] I would here emphasize the spontaneous character of the process.

According to Jung[33] the *scintillae* are said by the alchemists to be 'seeds of light broadcast in the chaos, which Khunrath calls "mundi futuri seminarium"'.[34] In his interesting discussion of the phenomenon Jung compares the *scintillae* to the archetypes and says that at the same time they '. . . correspond to tiny conscious phenomena'. In so saying he implies that the origin of consciousness lies in the archetypes, and so we can conclude that

[30] Plutarch, cit. J. E. Harrison, *Prolegomena to the Study of Greek Religion* (2nd ed., Cambridge, 1908), p. 628.
[31] Cit. Harrison, ibid., p. 627.
[32] C. Kerenyi, *Gods of the Greeks*, London and New York, 1951, p. 17.
[33] 'The Spirit of Psychology', in *Spirit and Nature*, Papers from the Eranos Yearbooks, New York, 1954, p. 401.
[34] The seed bed of the future world.

ORIGINS OF THE EGO IN CHILDHOOD

deintegrates, if not identical with, are at least closely related to them. Jung goes on: 'If the luminosity appears in monadic form as a single star, sun, or eye, it readily assumes the shape of a mandala and must then be interpreted as the self.'[35] This brings the deintegrates into a close relation to the self.

Other instructive parallels are to be found in the Upanishads. In the Brihad-Aranyaka Upanishad, we find:[36]

> In the beginning nothing whatsoever was here. This world was covered over with death, with hunger—for hunger is death.
> Then he made up his mind: 'Would that I had a self!'
> So he went on praising. From him, while he was praising, water was produced. . . .
> The water, verily, was brightness.
> That which was the froth of the water became solidified. That became the earth.
> On it he [i.e. Death] tortured himself. When he had tortured himself and practised austerity, his heat and essence turned into fire.
> He divided himself threefold: fire one third, the sun one third, wind one third. He also is Life divided threefold.

Of special interest here is the idea of hunger being at 'the beginning', but the spontaneity is also very clear. Again:[37]

> In the beginning this world was Soul (Atman) alone in the form of a Person. Looking around, he saw nothing else than himself. He said first: 'I am.' Thence arose the name 'I'. Therefore even today, when one is addressed, he says first just 'It is I' and then speaks whatever name he has.

Here is the notion of the word 'I' as a creation of the self, a topic we shall take up later.

The hypothesis of deintegration is simple in so far as it posits a spontaneous division of the self. For this indirect evidence can be gained from various sources, from myths such as those quoted above, from dreams of adults and children, from fantasy and play. It becomes difficult when the earliest deintegration is considered, for we are bound to try to think out just how the first element of consciousness arises, how, in short, an image is formed.

We can best consider the matter figuratively by taking the

[35] Op. cit., p. 410.
[36] R. E. Hume, *The Thirteen Principal Upanishads*, London, 1921, p. 74.   [37] Ibid., p. 81.

119

ORIGINS OF THE EGO IN CHILDHOOD

image found in small children, the circle, to represent the original self. This, however, is wrong, for there is really no image with which to represent it. We can next imagine the circle dividing itself up into fragments like the *scintillae* of Paracelsus but without form.

We can describe a deintegrate by saying it is a readiness for experience, a readiness to perceive and act, but there is as yet no perception or action. Both come into consciousness together without distinction between subject or object. It will, however, appear from outside as if the infant were object seeking and were trying to express itself in specific ways and selecting its object with the utmost care. Indeed we assume that only when the object exactly fits the deintegrate can a correct perception occur,[38] for only then can we conceive a state of affairs when there is no distinction between subject and object so far as the infant is concerned.

By way of amplification we may consider what happens if the correspondence between object and deintegrate is not exact. In the first place it will not be perceived at all and nothing will happen, but later on there develops a tolerance of the object failing to fit exactly on to the deintegrate. From this springs a dawning awareness of a distinction between subject and object.

IMAGE, SCHEMA AND ARCHETYPE

If, as appears inevitable, the original wholeness is an imageless condition, the study of how images arise must give us further understanding of how preconsciousness develops from the original wholeness by deintegration, for we assume that images are the first evidence of consciousness.

Amongst analytical psychologists there seems to be some confusion upon this point. Archetypes are, for example, frequently identified with their images. Yet it is not easy to understand the fact that specific images refer to specific archetypes. If the archetypes are innate, why not the images also?

There is one great objection to the hypothesis of innate[39]

---

[38] Cf. Winnicott's perfect environment, *supra*, p. 114.

[39] The term innate is preferable to hereditary because the only real hereditary units are the genes within the sexual cells. All characteristics are the consequence of the interplay between these genetic units and the environment. Cf. Julian Huxley, *Evolution: The Modern Synthesis*, London, 1942.

ORIGINS OF THE EGO IN CHILDHOOD

images, namely that it can never be shown that they themselves are not derived from perceptual sources. But the opposite hypothesis of complete derivation gets into difficulties when the images do not mirror exactly the object they are supposed to represent and it has, of necessity, to be assumed that they are changed or recombined in various ways in the process of perception. There is without doubt such an enormous perceptual field that all images can be derived from it approximately in one way or another. This is a consequence of cultural development and the special characteristic of man who, in contrast to the animals, provides for his offspring and transmits to it all the advantages and disadvantages civilization has built up. Culture and ego-consciousness must indeed be regarded as largely the consequence of nurture. But even here the distinction between nature and nurture is not altogether satisfactory since it is man's nature to nurture his children and himself. We may perhaps get some light on the quandary from the study of infants and animals.

According to our hypothesis a perception cannot be conceived as a passive act, it is rather part of an affective process and part of object-seeking activity.

Recent studies in instinctive behaviour in animals are interesting in this connection, for it has been shown that a highly specific perception releases an instinctual response. The perception acting through a postulated 'innate release mechanism' results in highly specific behaviour, for example, the baby gull already cited above (p. 12). It is just *as if* the baby gull were ready to perceive the spot and when it saw it knew exactly what it was and accordingly behaved in a specific way. It is almost an example of the environment exactly fitting a deintegrate.

The idea that the instinctive behaviour is *released* is highly suggestive, for an instinct does not comprise all possible patterns of behaviour but only one of many. We know that many other forms of behaviour can be released by other perceptions, and so it is clear that all forms of instinctive behaviour are contained *in potentia* within the organism at and before birth. The comparison between the deintegrate and instinctive behaviour is indeed impressive, and if we further consider that Jung has regarded the archetypal image as the representative in consciousness of the instinct our hypothesis begins to build itself into current analytical theory.

ORIGINS OF THE EGO IN CHILDHOOD

From a totally different quarter comes an almost identical concept. In recent years Piaget has published a series of monographs embodying the study of his own children from immediately after birth. From numerous observations he concludes that a schema lies at the root of imitation, play and intelligence. These schemata are unconscious elements upon which the whole psychic life of the infant is organized. They are total 'global' reactions to which all objects are assimilated and they thus have a 'centre'. Piaget says:[40]

In view of all we have seen regarding assimilation we may hypothesize that every assimilatory schema tends to conquer the whole universe including the realms assimilable by means of other schemata. Only the resistances of the environment or the incompatibilities due to the conditions of the subject's activity curb this generalization. So it is that the child sucks everything that touches his mouth or face and learns to co-ordinate the movements of his hands with those of sucking as a function of his pleasure in sucking his thumb. When he will know how to grasp he will suck everything he will have in his hands. Concerning what he sees or hears, if the nursling does not try to suck this from the outset it is perhaps less because these realms have no connection with sucking (it often happens that he makes sucking-like movements as soon as he hears a sound) than because it is difficult for the child to do two things at once (looking attentively and making sucking-like movements, etc.). But instead of immediate co-ordination between sucking and sight it is possible that there exists nevertheless excitation of the sucking cycle in the presence of especially interesting visual images. The remarkable protrusion of the lips observed in the youngest children . . . in states of great attention could not be other than sucking-like movements if it cannot be explained by a purely automatic or tonic postural mechanism. In the same way, with regard to the visual, hearing and grasping schemata, etc., the child will try little by little to see everything, hear everything, take everything, etc. This is well put by C. Buhler when she says with regard to the first sensorial reactions that the response to an excitant during the first months depends more on the subject's functional needs than on the nature of this excitant.

And further (p. 35):

Now this schema, due to the fact that it lends itself to repetitions and to cumulative use, is not limited to functioning under compulsion by a fixed excitant, external or internal, but *functions in a way for itself*. In other words, the child does not only suck in order to eat but also to

[40] *The Origin of Intelligence in the Child*, London, 1953, pp. 84–5.

122

ORIGINS OF THE EGO IN CHILDHOOD

elude hunger, to prolong the excitation of the meal, etc., and lastly, he sucks for the sake of sucking. It is in this sense that the object incorporated into the sucking schema is actually assimilated to the activity of these schemata. The object sucked is to be conceived, not as nourishment for the organism in general, but, so to speak, as aliment for the very activity of sucking, according to its various forms. From the point of view of awareness, if there is awareness, such assimilation is at first *lack of differentiation* and not at first true generalization, but from the point of view of action, it is *a generalizing extension* of the schema which *foretells* (as has just been seen) *later and much more important generalizations.*[41]

But how does it happen that the mere perception becomes a symbolic image? Piaget again has interesting observations to make in this connection. He shows that imitation is based upon schemata which can be perceived in the child by adults and it is only upon these schemata that imitative behaviour can be built. The child cannot imitate anything, indeed the behaviour to be imitated must correspond closely to the schema already expressed by the child. Here again we find a less rigid but still clear need for the outer object to comply with what seem to be inner requirements so that it can become organized into the infant's psyche. Piaget traces with much supporting evidence the manner in which imitation leads on into play and symbolic activity. His observations indicate that if we assume his schema to be a deintegrate the deintegrate is capable of developing through imitation to play and symbolic activity as a whole.

We here come up against the whole problem of early object relations in infancy. It is now widely recognized that small children *need* objects, whether they be parts of themselves or parts of others. Through these objects it seems that the child's consciousness of himself as a whole person grows, as also does his image of other persons as whole beings.

We have inevitably changed from the notion of perception to that of image. How the transition occurs we do not know. Piaget thinks it occurs in his sixth stage, that is at about one year. The image is at first of an object that is not present and is clearly linked up with the development of memory.

[41] The italics are mine. Piaget bases his investigations on quite a different set of concepts. He believes that the first reactions of the infant are based upon reflexes and that the schemata are the representatives of reflex action.

123

ORIGINS OF THE EGO IN CHILDHOOD

We are thus in a position to suggest a progression from perception as part of a release mechanism to perception as part of imitation leading to image formation. We may suppose that once images are formed apart from the object they may be used not only to represent absent objects but can also, as it were, be taken hold of by the archetype, used and altered so as to make up archetypal images.

We can now turn to another study more specifically directed to the problem of how images not only form but evolve. This excellent study of some 100,000 children's scribblings and early pictures has been made by Mrs. Rhoda Kellogg in her nursery schools in San Francisco.[42] The studies are on much older children, but the work is so much concerned with images and so suggestive that we shall describe it in some detail.

Starting from rhythmic body movements the child produces a set of twenty 'Basic Scribbles'. These comprise various obviously rhythmic records, dots, lines (curved and straight), loops, circles, spirals and irregular jumbled up scribbles.

It appears that the jumbled up scribbles are the most creatively important because a great number of figures and irregular shapes are to be found in them. These make possible the picking out of shapes ('Diagrams') which seem most significant to the child. Out of the jumble of lines it appears that the child 'abstracts' five Diagrams: two forms of cross ($+$ and $\times$), the square, the triangle, and irregular-shaped enclosures. One 'Diagram', the circle, is carried directly over from the 'Basic Scribbles'.

Following this 'Combines' of the diagrams are made, far the most important of these being the mandala, from which is derived a sunlike figure and then a human being by modification of the mandala and combination of the modification with circles.

Thus the child has created an image of a human being by a process combining rhythm, random activity, 'abstraction', and combination. The human figure which results is thus recognizable but is not copied directly from his perception of human beings; indeed it seems as if the pictorial representation is only recognized

[42] In what follows I am giving my own interpretation of what Mrs. Kellogg has recorded and classified in a preliminary pamphlet. In consequence Mrs. Kellogg cannot be held responsible for what is set out here, though I hope I have not distorted her views and observations, which are not yet published in detail.

ORIGINS OF THE EGO IN CHILDHOOD

as a human being after it has been made, and only when this has happened can it be given a name.

How far the child's perception of objects in the external world comes into this apparently regular progression we do not know, but its regularity suggests an inner libidinal development which cannot be explained by imitation. It is a process of expressing his needs and perceiving what he does. Perhaps the best illustration of the selecting quasi-purposive process is the 'abstraction' of diagrams from the most confused scribbles.

There thus appear to be two processes by which image formation occurs. Firstly the instantaneous 'recognition' of an external object releasing either an instinctual or an imitative response, and secondly the building up and separating out of images from the infant's own activity. In the latter process 'recognition' takes a part, but it is only the end result of the process.

Mrs. Kellogg's researches were undertaken on pre-school children, Piaget's on babies, but both point to the importance of models. From Mrs. Kellogg's material it seems justifiable to assume that the process called abstraction corresponds to what we have termed deintegration, and if this be so we cannot fail to notice three processes at work: (*a*) random activity, (*b*) abstraction or deintegration, and (*c*) combination or integration. All these processes seem to be depicted in the scribblings and pictures— they all take part in the development of the conscious in children of this age.

In spite of the fact that Mrs. Kellogg's work is all done from an educational standpoint, her material is highly suggestive. It is most striking that from the mandala all sorts of separate images are derived but especially the human figure. Is it going too far to see in this a record of the birth of the ego out of the self, in a manner comparable to my own observations upon mandalas and the words *I* or *me*?

EGO INTEGRATION

As a consequence of deintegration and the images formed as a result of it, we arrive at the position which Jung described when he spoke of fragments of ego consciousness, or alternatively the preconscious state. He went on to say that these unite to form a centre, the ego.

ORIGINS OF THE EGO IN CHILDHOOD

The conception I want to put forward is that it is the self which integrates the ego fragments and so produces the ego centre.

The conception of the self as the prime mover in the integration of ego fragments[43] sprang from the observations already described in which the child's drawing of circles was related to the words *I* or *me*. These circles correspond to the later more elaborate mandala figures coming at periods of integration in which the ego showed an evident development. This form of integration is most easily seen when the child is alone—it needs a temporary isolation of the child from its environment.[44] It is under these conditions that my observations were first made; in them the child indicated directly or indirectly its separating from myself or others.

But this is not a necessary feature of the integrative action of the self whose functioning can be seen within analytic transference situations as well.[45]

No doubt the reader be aware that many other psychic activities besides those of the self enter into the growth of the ego. We may therefore list some of them, but it must be pointed out that all these presuppose a relatively firm ego before they can seriously contribute to its further development.

[43] Gerhard Adler, 'The Dynamics of the Self', *British Journal of Medical Psychology*, Vol. XXIV, Part 2, 1951, puts this significance of the self interestingly. He says (p. 98):
'Where, as in the later stages of life, the personality needs to limit the ego-sphere in favour of the non-ego sphere (that is to say, where the individual is faced with the task of adapting to the "interior world" of the archetypes), the non-ego becomes so charged with energy that the ego has to retire in order to make room for the higher energy of the non-ego. The situation is reversed in childhood: here the non-ego has the upper hand at first, and the self charges the ego-function with sufficient energy for it to establish itself against the non-ego, so that it can fulfil the demands of adaptation to the outer world. In both cases the self operates as an image of potential wholeness behind the psychic processes and bends them towards the realisation of this wholeness, which appears as the synthesis of ego and non-ego, of conscious and unconscious, of the inner and outer worlds.'

[44] Cf. Chapter XII below.

[45] See my 'Integration and Disintegration' (cf. p. 131, note 1). In a state of integration it is next to impossible to distinguish the ego from the self, so that the self united with the ego gets called *I* or *me*. In more mature personalities this union of the ego lends to inflation, a pathological state. But in infancy it must be regarded as normal.

126

ORIGINS OF THE EGO IN CHILDHOOD

(*a*) There is the recognition of similarities. Using the example of Anna[46] this would be that the mouth is like the anus in being a hole that can open and shut to let things out.

(*b*) There is association in time. We may here instance the infant's tendency to pass motions at the same time as feeding and as a consequence he can feel the two acts as part of one whole.[47]

(*c*) Infantile logic. Again we may turn to little Anna. She concluded that babies came out of the anus because faeces came out there. There are many other examples in Jung's case. Logic comes much later than (*a*) and (*b*).

(*d*) Allied to logic is concept building to which (*a*) and (*b*) contribute.

(*e*) In all these processes instinctual aspects of the archetypes, expressed as drives, play their part. Anna's infantile sex instincts were the motive force behind her sexual interest. Associated with this is the pleasure in discovery and the pleasure in fantasy.

(*f*) Next comes the activity of archetypes inasmuch as they become expressed in consciousness by images and contribute to the preconscious state. The numinous effect of the images can, though it need not necessarily, have an integrative effect, because behind them lies the self, as we have already seen.

(*g*) Education. This subject can only be listed here; it clearly calls for a volume to itself.

DEINTEGRATION AND INTEGRATION OF THE SELF

We are now in a position to consider the relation of deintegration in the formation of an ego nucleus. I regard it as periodic; the two processes being necessary to the growth of the ego.

The sequence can be conceived as follows: the original self deintegrates spontaneously, it is a release phenomenon comparable to that discovered from the study of instinct. The deintegrates represent a readiness for experience, a readiness to perceive, a readiness to act instinctively, but not an actual perception or action. The next step is to perceive and act according to the patterns of the deintegrates; for this a perfect fit with the

---

[46] Cf. pp. 110 f., above.

[47] It is clear that we are here abutting on the whole problem of synchronicity into which there is no space to go here.

ORIGINS OF THE EGO IN CHILDHOOD

environment is necessary. If this fit occurs there then develop reaction patterns based on archetypes which differ from instincts in their innate predisposition to represent themselves in a preconscious image.

It is, however, only through the integrative action of the self that these deintegrates which have grown into ego nuclei get brought together so as to contribute to a single ego nucleus or centrum as Jung[48] calls it.

But if the ego be formed in this way it cannot grow if the self remains integrated any more than consciousness could begin without deintegration. Therefore further deintegrations must take place, since manifestly the ego does not fail to develop and various specialized units of consciousness and various differentiated behaviours occur.

RECESSION OF THE SELF AND THE STRUCTURING OF THE PERSONALITY

Structuring of the personality comes about as the result of the rhythm of integration-deintegration of the self, for it creates an ego nucleus. When this has happened we can speak of a conscious-unconscious dichotomy. There arise areas of the personality easily accessible to the ego and areas, i.e. archetypes, which are never completely, but only indirectly, accessible. It is also supposed that consciousness develops of itself and differentiates. This development in the conscious runs parallel to a corresponding deintegration into unconscious archetypes which become relatively discrete entities as we have stated before in reverse order to the individuation process. As this occurs the self sinks more and more into the background and it appears as if the ego takes its place.

'SELF' AND ENVIRONMENT

We may briefly make up for a grave deficiency: the slight reference to the significance of the environment in the early development of consciousness. This deficiency is especially great as we

[48] It will be evident that once a central ego nucleus has formed the deintegration process will be a threat to it. The ego will be in danger of being torn apart by the deintegrating self. Since this is not the case it may be assumed that the ego separates from the self before it deintegrates.

128

ORIGINS OF THE EGO IN CHILDHOOD

have learnt so much of its essential importance in child development. It will, however, be clear that it is not really underestimated but rather that we have been considering early ego development in periods when the dichotomy 'self'-environment is absent or not at all clear. The whole subject merits another paper and we must therefore be content here with a brief note upon a matter of much practical importance.

In the first place it is not possible to separate out self and environment, but once deintegration has occurred we can begin to distinguish an environment exactly fitting a deintegrate. After this a progressive differentiation must occur between what is at first a bit of ego and a bit of environment. While there is a perfect fit between these two there can clearly be no differentiation between them. The separation must therefore occur as a consequence of failure by the environment to fit the deintegrate. These bits of differentiation can be assumed to occur if the frustration involved is tolerable. As time goes on it must be assumed that the infant is able to stand more and more frustration till a working duality is established between the 'self' composed of the ego nucleus and with it a whole body image, and the environment. It is then that the process of taking in, rejecting and ejecting can begin to occur. This will happen first in terms of feeding and excreting, later in terms of conscious psychic equivalents. This organization is the prerequisite for conscious learning.

It is in the preconscious state that the environment, particularly the emotional environment, exerts its greatest influence owing to the lack of clear boundaries to the ego.[49] This preconscious condition is always there and is expressed in play fantasies and dreams, but its importance sinks into the background as the ego progressively increases in strength.

CONCLUSION

Although in this discussion we have confined ourselves to a theoretical outline sketch and have avoided the use of illustrative case material, this will be supplied in a later chapter.

The ideas certainly need development and will in all probability be changed out of recognition as new viewpoints and new facts

[49] Cf. Jung, *The Development of Personality*, Sections III and IV; Wickes, op. cit.

ORIGINS OF THE EGO IN CHILDHOOD

are brought to light. They are manifestly a starting-point rather than a finished product.

It is a hazardous undertaking to launch into the realm of early ego development in the infant because of the almost inexpressible nature of the processes. But if we are ever to penetrate this difficult realm theories are essential. Even if they are incomplete they are needed for their 'orientating and heuristic value'; they are the vital tools of those who like discovery.

VI

SOME OBSERVATIONS ON THE SELF AND THE EGO IN CHILDHOOD[1]

INTRODUCTION

IT is often assumed that, in their psychic growth, children progress from a totally unintegrated state towards one of increasing integration, starting when the ego forms and increasing as it grows. This simple formula is however inadequate; firstly because during development some psychic experiences regularly become disintegrated and repressed, secondly because the essentially unconscious archetypes never can be integrated within the ego. Only parts of the psyche can, then, be integrated into the conscious mind, but Jung has shown that the ego is not the only centre of integration in the personality. Amongst the archetypal images are those of wholeness and order which represent a controlling influence over the unconscious functions; it is also known that they represent a potential integrate of the ego and its 'inner objects', the archetypes.

It is evident, therefore, that research has established two kinds of integration: in the first place integration through the growth of the conscious mind, i.e. through ego development, and in the second through the general tendency towards wholeness, in which the conscious mind and the unconscious become united. Jung has demonstrated the symbolism of this comprehensive synthetic process in adult subjects, so that the self, the term he has given to the integrating factor, has moved from the region of

[1] This paper is derived from two publications: 'Some Observations on the Self in Childhood', *British Journal of Medical Psychology*, Vol. XXIV, Part 2, 1951, and 'Integration and Disintegration and Early Ego Development', *The Nervous Child*, Vol. VI, Part 3, 1947.

131

OBSERVATIONS ON SELF AND EGO IN CHILDHOOD

abstract concept and has become, to borrow a phrase from Toynbee,[2] an 'intelligible field of study'.

MANDALA SYMBOLISM

In four important works, Jung[3] has demonstrated and discussed mandala symbolism, but he has nowhere shown that this symbolism occurs in children.

According to Jung a mandala is a magical enclosure which need not necessarily be round, though this is the most usual shape. He says[4]: 'The round or square enclosures . . . have the value of magic means to produce protective walls . . . they prevent an outburst and a disintegration.' That is conceived as a 'peril of the soul'. Though he refers here to disintegration it is clear that they are also needed when a new element is to be integrated or, as will appear, when the process I have termed deintegration begins to occur. This means that integration, deintegration and disintegration are closely related.

The contents of a fully developed mandala are variable but in every case they are arranged about a centre. The space between the centre and the circumference is divided up in various ways. The most frequent and stable number of the divisions is four, or a multiple of four, and Jung has put forward the view, elaborated in many of his works but above all in *Psychological Types*,[5] that these represent the fourfold structure of the psyche.

Apart from these contents Jung lays considerable emphasis upon the centre and remarks that its meaning '. . . is simply unknowable and can only be expressed symbolically through its own phenomenology, as is the case, incidentally, with every object of experience'.[6] The centre, its surrounding contents and the circumference represent the self which in adult persons is to be differentiated from the ego. This differentiation is, however,

---

[2] A. J. Toynbee, *A Study of History*, London, 1946.

[3] Cf. *The Secret of the Golden Flower*, London, 1935; *Psychology and Religion*, New Haven, 1938; *Psychology and Alchemy*, London and New York, 1953; 'Über Mandalasymbolik', *Gestaltungen des Unbewussten*, Zurich, 1950.

[4] Cf. *Psychology and Religion*, London, 1938, p. 105.

[5] London, 1938.

[6] *Psychology and Alchemy* (Collected Works, Vol. XII), London and New York, 1953, par. 327.

132

OBSERVATIONS ON SELF AND EGO IN CHILDHOOD

by no means clear in children. Indeed if the ego grows out of the self it would be inevitable that the two should be in close relationship. This consideration needs to be kept clearly in mind when interpreting the material of infants in the early stages of ego development. With a view to examining these early stages and their repetitions in the course of development I have studied the scribblings of infants and the more developed mandala forms of older children. This investigation has been made more significant by Mrs. Kellogg's study, to which reference has already been made (cf. pp. 124f.), and also by some observations reported in Herbert Read's volume *Education Through Art*.[7] Read found a class of adolescent children between the ages of fourteen and sixteen years who were taught to make 'mind pictures'. The teacher described his procedure as follows:

When I take a class in 'Mind Pictures' I tell them (the children) to close their eyes and relax and try to feel at peace, not thinking of anything—to try to get away from physical things as one does just before going off to sleep. Some girls get a mind picture quite soon, in a few minutes (sometimes instantly), others take ten minutes or even longer, and some do not see them at all. I try to make them understand that if they do not see one they must be quite honest and say so, and that they are not in any way 'odd' if they do not see them.

Amongst the pictures produced in this way were many mandalas.

The type of study made by Mrs. Kellogg and Read cannot, however, give an adequate idea of the dynamism represented by the image in relation to the personality. These investigations are subject to an educational interpretation or to various other explanations ranging from the aesthetic to that of an exercise in muscular co-ordination. There are many factors which can be separated out of the activities of scribbling and painting, but only by studying the context of the activity in individuals can the meaning be elicited. The following studies are based upon this consideration.

CIRCLE, SELF, AND EGO INTEGRATE

A one-year-old boy whose vigorous and healthy personality marked him out from other children will serve as a point of

[7] Read, *Education Through Art*, London, 1943.

OBSERVATIONS ON SELF AND EGO IN CHILDHOOD

departure for discussing the imagery of circles. His parents had allowed him to scribble on the walls of his nursery, and he made good use of the opportunity. After a period of squiggles he started on circular movements in which he became preoccupied to the exclusion of all else and gradually innumerable more or less perfect circles emerged. For some weeks this continued, his whole self became absorbed into the activity and then one day, as if by revelation, he discovered the word 'I'. Then the circles stopped. The relation in time between the discovery of the circle and the discovery of 'I' suggests that the circle represented the matrix of the self out of which the ego arose. The self seemed to prepare the ground for its emergence, to create a *temenos* in which the event could occur.

This accords almost exactly with the theory of ego development set out in more detail elsewhere,[8] and if this be accepted and the child's behaviour be born in mind it seems almost inconceivable that the 'I' does not refer to the ego.

In this connection Stein's researches into the origin of the word 'I' are significant. He says:[9] 'The linguistic development . . . reflects a process by which the ego is separated from the self. . . . It is born as the child is born from its parents.'

Far from contradicting our interpretation, Jung's observations that the circle represents an archetypal non-ego confirm it, even though his researches are on individuation in which the separation is essential and this research is based upon the concept that the separation has not yet occurred. This inversion is a logical consequence, as we have seen, from Jung's theories (cf. pp. 116 f.).

It seems then that the small child identifies the word 'I' with the circle, but we need not assume that he means it is 'I' in the sense of an organized ego, it is rather an awareness of himself as a whole, as a circle, as somebody inviolable, complete, if only for a moment. It is a state of wholeness, of integration, which according to my view indicates that the ego and self exist together as a self-ego axis.[10] The circle thus represents the boundary of the ego but refers at the same time to the self.

[8] Cf. 'The Origins of the Ego in Childhood' in the present volume.

[9] L. Stein, 'On talking or the communication of ideas and feelings by means of mainly audible symbols', *British Journal of Medical Psychology*, Vol. XXIV, Part 2, 1951, pp. 113–14.

[10] The concept of a self-ego axis has been introduced by Neumann.

134

OBSERVATIONS ON SELF AND EGO IN CHILDHOOD

The possibility that this circle refers to the state of uroboric incest can also be considered here since its symbol, according to Neumann, is the circle. Neumann says:[11] 'The initial stage symbolized by the uroboros corresponds to a pre-ego stage, . . . in the history of individual development it belongs to the stage of earliest childhood when an ego germ is just beginning to be.' This 'initial stage' is conceived by him as *participation mystique* in which the psyche is identical with the environment and no boundary exists between the two. Observation of this child and the others to be considered points in just the other direction. The phenomena indicate that the identity is broken at this time by the appearance of a clearly defined boundary.

An important part of Jung's analysis of mandala symbolism is its integrative and protective function against a 'peril of the soul'. Can this be applied to the child? If so, it must be assumed that some danger threatens him, but this is not apparent and would indeed be difficult to perceive since the ego is so little differentiated from the self. Let us therefore consider other cases of elder children in whom greater differentiation makes the dangers manifest. Such examples may well throw light on our problem.

In the *Life of Childhood*[12] I described the case of a little girl aged two and a half years who had attracted my attention because of her lively and attractive appearance. As I was interested in children's scribblings I took her on my knee and gave her some chalks and paper. The series of scribbles which she then made ended with a circle, after which she got off my knee and went to join her brother. The earlier scribbles had been aggressive, and I had concluded that her apparent acquiescence had been under secret protest; it was only when the circle appeared, however, that her ego could express itself in action. It seemed to represent the statement that my power had become neutralized and that there was now a magical boundary between herself and me which made her position safe; no aggression from me was now possible.

Jung states that the circle is a protection against the 'perils of the soul' thereby relating it to psychical functions rather than to real persons. This contradiction is, however, more apparent

[11] Erich Neumann, *The Origins and History of Consciousness*, London and New York, 1954, p. 266.
[12] London, 1944.

OBSERVATIONS ON SELF AND EGO IN CHILDHOOD

than real, for the child must have seen me as a danger—I would not have pressed her to scribble had she not acquiesced. The danger was due to a projection of the 'soul', in this case the father imago. If I had been more active the projection would not have been withdrawn, therefore in cases where the environment is dangerous or hostile the projection becomes indissoluble because it is 'true' and strong indissoluble defences are set up against it.

This state of affairs had clearly come about in a boy aged eight years, incontinent both of faeces and urine, who was totally inaccessible to my friendly approaches owing to the projection of terrifying parent imagos. When he started drawing numerous pictures of children, their faces appeared as empty circles, there were no eyes, nose, ears or mouth, and so no way of getting in or out of them. This child had been through many difficult times. His desperate parents had lectured him, beaten him, cajoled him, bribed him, and threatened him because of his incontinence, till he was unable to grasp any coherent sense in their treatment of him. There can be little doubt that the circle was an image expressing his defensive inaccessibility. As he tested out whether I was going to behave like his parents, and as he became more and more sure I would not do so, he revealed his feelings more and more, and then his pictures began to show faces peering out under a large hat.

But the peril can come not only from parents, but also from within the child's psyche itself. The girl of two years old, to be discussed in detail later (pp. 148 f.), who suffered from fits, had regressed to an early stage of integration based on a more dependent relation to her mother. This girl drew a circle at a point where she began to become more independent. Since, therefore, her regression came about as a result of an inner threat (the fits) the circle would here seem to protect against this danger.

Elder children recognize the relation of a circle to protection from inner dangers and may put various objects inside their pictures of the circle so as to control psychic contents which are causing anxiety. For instance, a very aggressive and sadistic delinquent boy put the Nazi swastika inside a circle, thus revealing his desire to control the processes in which he had previously gloried. Again a girl, aged seven years, with night terrors, painted a picture of 'the bad world' enclosed entirely in a circle.

OBSERVATIONS ON SELF AND EGO IN CHILDHOOD

Previously she had projected her fear into the German aeroplanes that dropped bombs, and her mother had supported this, since the family had actually been bombed, but without personal damage to them. At this period the child was increasingly able to release fantasies of the inside of her mother's body which contained 'babies, blood, and bones'. These fantasies had previously been too bad and dangerous for her to reveal.

Having now shown that children draw circles in relation to danger situations and that if there is a good environment they more readily appear as part of the psychic activity of the child, we can now return to the question asked earlier: What is the peril of the soul in the case of the one-year-old boy?

The danger is clearly from the child's psyche itself, and if it be accepted that he had made an image of the self from which the ego is budding off, then the danger to the ego can come only from the self. The theory of the self as a deintegrating-integrating system is particularly relevant here, for the deintegration of the self can be conceived as the danger to the ego which can thereby be torn to pieces if the two are insufficiently separated. But, it will be objected, the self is in its integrating phrase. True, but this is at its maximum, and according to the principle of enantiodromia[13] it will now tend to swing over into its opposite phase at just this point, and thus there is no theoretical difficulty in postulating the self as the source of danger to the ego.

These observations and reflections point to the circle as representing a delimiting or protective magic used to ward off real or imagined dangers from without or from within, or a danger inherent in the condition itself, a condition which provides the circumstances out of which the ego can come into being.

THE DEVELOPMENT OF A MANDALA

Before considering the example of a child aged seven years[14] who was simply allowed to paint pictures, some of which I published previously,[15] we may consider briefly the amplification which will be employed.

[13] The tendency of all psychic phenomena, if allowed freedom, to swing over into their opposite activity. Cf. Jung, *Psychological Types*, London and New York, 1923.

[14] I am indebted to my wife for the use of this material.

[15] *The Life of Childhood.*

OBSERVATIONS ON SELF AND EGO IN CHILDHOOD

In order to elucidate the material I shall bring forward a number of parallels from Jung's essay 'Psychology of the Transference',[16] where he uses for the purpose of demonstration a series of alchemical pictures from the *Rosarium Philosophorum*, first published in 1550. Jung considers the process shown in the pictures to be the equivalent of the individuation process in which the self is formed as the result of the conjunction of opposites.

In drawing parallels the similarities in the process of the alchemical opus will be brought out, and the difference in the specific images ignored. It is evident that the child's experiences are expressed in images which are familiar to her, just as the alchemist puts his experience into the form of chemistry. The alchemical work contains the detailed elaboration resulting from centuries of conscious scholarship and unconscious revelation of which the alchemical pictures are the result, and which contrasts greatly with the child's spontaneous expression. Thus amplification aims at defining an unconscious essence of which the various images are the manifestation. As far as I was concerned, the whole meaning of the series was thoroughly obscure until I started to look at the alchemical pictures and read Jung's text with its full quotations.[17] In what follows I shall proceed somewhat differently from my own procedure so as to make the demonstration more orderly. If this method lacks something of the force of the discovery I hope that what is lacking will be compensated in greater clarity and coherence.

The first picture painted by the little girl (Pl. 1) consists of a mass of red blobs ('rain') which comes from the sky. In the sky besides the sun is a cloud, projecting downwards, from the centre of which emerges a bifurcated phallic object connecting with a

[16] In *The Practice of Psychotherapy* (Collected Works, Vol. XVI), London and New York, 1954, pp. 163 ff.

[17] In using amplification intuition is inevitable and a friend of mine once humorously remarked that the method was comparable to that of an amateur fortune teller who read meaning from the tea-leaves in a tea-cup! But he overlooked the importance of perceiving the similarity in the images. If the analogy 'clicks' there is an experience of excitement and conviction. This is due to the activation of an archetype within myself. After it has occurred a long sorting-out process is needed and at the end the material begins to make sense. In my experience the feeling of value comes relatively late. To work out an analogy therefore appears to engage all the four functions of the psyche.

138

OBSERVATIONS ON SELF AND EGO IN CHILDHOOD

ship. The phallus is continuous with a yellow figure, probably a man, on the vessel which catches a large quantity of the rain. The main body of the picture is surrounded by a kind of frame which, however, is broken on the right-hand side. Since the blobs were described by the little girl as rain the picture must be taken to depict a dynamic process. The phallus in the sky is at the same time a cloud from which the rain descends into the sea but mainly into the boat. I surmise that the yellow figure in the boat is a man so that there is a conjunction of opposites, the male in the body of the feminine vessel; the female contains a male as the female genital contains the phallus. Two analogies to this can be found in Jung.[18] The first picture in Jung's book (here reproduced as Fig. 1) shows a 'vas hermeticum', alternately termed the uterus, containing water which flows into it from an upright fountain with three spouts. A later picture (Fig. 3) is also analogous, for the rain comes down from heaven upon a bisexual figure contained in a vessel.

The child's second picture (Pl. 2) consists of a rectangular outline in two colours—within it are the red blobs, attached to white strokes so as to make numerous phalli. These are joined to a central mass with a blue core.

Here the combination begun in the first picture has proceeded further. The phallus has come inside the containing outline or vessel, joined with the central mass and, in addition, has greatly multiplied. In this picture the conjunction of opposites is clearer than before.

The alchemical parallel is also to be found in Jung's book (Fig. 3), elaborated in the chapter on the 'Conjunctio', and shows a couple, the king and queen, copulating in a circumscribed sea which at the same time contains the sun and moon. The 'king' is clearly analogous to the phallus, later multiplied, and the 'queen' we may assume is the analogue of the surrounding vessel or womb and also of the brown in the centre.

A point which attracted my attention was the blue inside the brown, which seemed to have no sense in it till I hit upon the following quotation: 'But the water I have spoken of is something that comes down from heaven, and the earth's humidity absorbs it, and the water of heaven is retained with the water of the earth, and the water of the earth honours that water with its lowliness

[18] Op. cit.

ROSARIVM

Wyr sindt der metall anfang vnd erste natur/
Die kunst macht durch vns die höchste tinctur.
Keyn brunn noch wasser ist meyn gleych/
Ich mach gesund arm vnd reych.
Vnd bin doch jzund gyftig vnd ödtlich.

Succus

Fig. 1.

and its sand, and water consorts with water and water will hold fast to water and Albira is whitened with Astuna.'[19]

This quotation seems almost made for our purpose, connecting the child's first picture with her second. By means of this amplification it can be concluded that the blue in the centre is

[19] Cf. Jung, op. cit., p. 271.

PHILOSOPHORVM

ABLVTIO VEL
Mundificatio

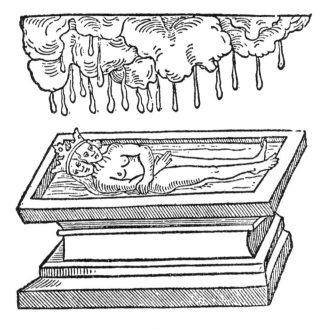

Hie felt der Tauw von Himmel herab/
Vnnd wascht den schwartzen leyb im grab ab.

Fig. 2.

the water in the earth and surmised that the water from 'heaven', the red raindrops in the first picture, joined with the waters of the earth.

A further parallel is to be found in connection with the appearance of white; the text runs: 'and Albira is whitened with Astuna'. Though no hint can be found as to what or to whom Albira and

OBSERVATIONS ON SELF AND EGO IN CHILDHOOD

Astuna refer, the whitening process is a regular feature of alchemy which often follows the black stage of putrefaction; it is the light which follows the darkness, the emergence of consciousness out of the unconscious. In the child's picture white follows and joins with the red, an apparent contradiction, but other alchemical parallels show that the red and white are regularly represented together. In a book by Herbert Silberer[20] it is stated: 'The red and white reveal themselves as man and woman, and the last aim is . . . the sexual union of both.'

The next, the child's third picture (Pl. 3), is one in which the circular mandala is seen forming, though at the same time the former images are seen in dissolution. There is a circle and a number of irregularly radiating lines which could be imagined as forming a nucleus.

Taking the child's second picture (Pl. 2) in conjunction with the third (Pl. 3) the following quotation from the *Rosarium* is helpful. 'Then Beya [the maternal sea] rises up over Gabricus and encloses him in her womb, so that nothing more of him is to be seen. And she embraced Gabricus with so much love that she utterly consumed him in her own nature and dissolved him into atoms.'[21] 'Atomization' may be interpreted as the negative aspect of multiplication followed by the dissolution of the phalli (Gabricus) which are completely contained within the framework (the body of Beya) and, as it were, invisible from outside.

On this subject of the conjunction Jung says:[22] 'the real meaning of the *coniunctio* is that it brings to birth something that is one and united. It restores the vanished "man of light" who is identical with the Logos in Gnostic and Christian symbolism and who was there before the creation.' The 'man of light' is 'the perfect all-round man, the *filius philosophorum*, the divine child'. These various forms express an unconscious content which can also be represented by the mandala, the 'perfect all-round man' as Jung has shown at length in *Psychology and Alchemy*.[23] The mandala, an orderly arrangement consisting of a wheel with eight main spokes, follows in the child's fourth picture (Pl. 4), so that we find the result which the alchemical parallel predicts.

[20] *Problems of Mysticism and its Symbolism*, New York, 1917, p. 54.
[21] Jung, op. cit., p. 246.
[22] Ibid., p. 248.
[23] Collected Works, Vol. 12, London and New York, 1953.

CONIVNCTIO SIVE
Coitus.

☽ Luna durch meyn vmbgeben/vnd suffe mynne/
Wirstu schön/ starck/vnd gewaltig als ich byn.
☉ Sol/ du bist vber alle liecht zu erkennen/
So bedarffstu doch mein als der han der hennen.

ARISLEVS IN VISIONE.

Coniunge ergo filium tuum Gabricum dile=
ctiorem tibi in omnibus filijs tuis cum sua sorore
Beya

Fig. 3.

The conclusions to be drawn from this material are in part negative and in part positive. The imagery does not indicate that the individuation process has necessarily been constellated any more than the child is an alchemist because her material is analogous. All that these analogies suggest is that in each case the same unconscious process is at work in alchemy, in the individuation process, and in the child. The common feature in all

OBSERVATIONS ON SELF AND EGO IN CHILDHOOD

this is the emergence of an image of wholeness as the result of a conjunction.

The change in the child we have been discussing was quite unusually marked. By simply allowing her to introvert and to express the processes going on within her, she changed from a miserable woebegone person almost completely absorbed in crying into an independent personality quite able to fend for herself. In other words her ego had developed.

FURTHER OBSERVATIONS ON IMAGES OF THE SELF

Naturally the imagery of the self does not necessarily appear in pictures, and in order to suggest something more of it the following case will illustrate its appearance in relation to the inflationary pressure leading to 'omnipotence of thought'. The case is one of an introverted child aged eight with a schizoid disintegration.

As a consequence of an interpretation of a dream the child became aggressive and threatened me (indirectly) with a monster. The monster had 'enormous eyes that could see everything, enormous nose that could smell everything, and enormous ears that could hear everything'—the image of totality comes out in the repetition of 'everything'. This monster was also a dot. The necessary parallel to this theme occurs in the Katha Upanishad: 'The Self, smaller than small, greater than great, is hidden in the heart of that creature.'[24]

Then one day the child became very insistent on the subject of whether I knew God before I was inside my mother's stomach when I was a dot inside God (repetition of the monster theme, on the basis God=monster, circle and centre). When at length I interpreted this insistence as being his wish to be sure that I could not contradict him if he asserted that he knew God in reality, a change occurred in his whole demeanour and he poured out a long and elaborate series of *ex cathedra* thoughts which expressed mental concepts of the following kind—'Because there is *something* there must be *nothing*', or 'Spirits are *nothing* because they can go through you and you can stick things through them—but that is *something*.'[25] He was thinking in opposites

[24] Katha-Up., I, ii, 20. Cf. *Hindu Scriptures* (ed. Nicol Macnicol), London, 1938, p. 199.

[25] Cf. D. T. Suzuki: *Introduction to Zen Buddhism*, London and New York, 1948.

144

1. The Golden Rain

2. The Conjunction of Opposites

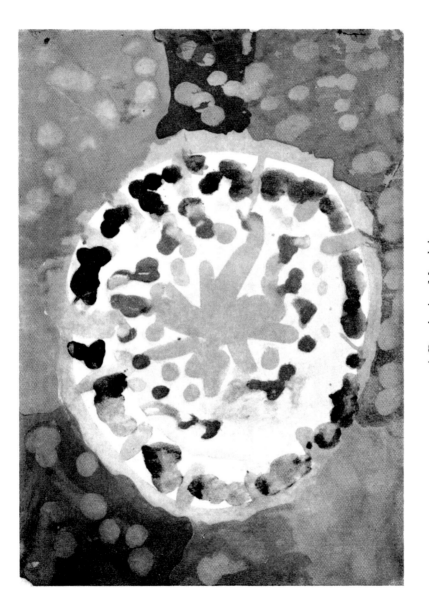

3. A Developing Mandala

4. The Final Mandala

OBSERVATIONS ON SELF AND EGO IN CHILDHOOD

and behind these thoughts lay a psychical dynamic which expressed itself in a cosmology of fairies, witches, devils and a god. Interspersed with this there gradually developed evidence of positive ego functioning, for the child was able to explain how he felt and to relate his feelings to the present and other situations. For instance, going away from my room presented a difficulty, since at this point his feeling of omnipotence was threatened. I should explain that as he left I always mentioned the day when I would see him next in order to try to preserve continuity. On one occasion he replied to my interpretations about his difficulty in leaving the room that he was sad at going away from mother and he thought going away from me reminded him of that. Here his God-almightiness had sunk into the background and the ego was clearly in evidence.

Mandala images could be inferred from the monster and the dot, and they came out later in many other ways, e.g. in a statement that the house in which a bad witch lived was surrounded by trees, and again in a series of what were apparently resistance phenomena in the form of mazes, tricks, and riddles which were related to the circle imagery.

The dark aspect of mother comes out clearly as the central content of the house surrounded by trees, but a postman also enters the enclosure and we get a hint of a *coniunctio* in a negative form. The witch and the postman are very fond of each other, and in consequence because they are bad they like to be away from each other. Gradually, as his anxiety lessened the *coniunctio* became positive, the separation of the parents changed into their sexual union. This the child revealed in his play and fantasy of the primal scene.

Later there developed a series of notions about the relation between good and bad which became less and less clearly defined and mixed up. Taking good and bad as conscious qualities or values in contrast to those of the self which unites the opposites and is consequently beyond good and bad, the changes must be related to the appearance of the self which would necessitate modifications in the standard of conscious values of which good and bad are examples.

There were reasons in the child's development why he should have at first expressed himself abstractly, but his defences were greatly enhanced because his thought fascinated both himself and

OBSERVATIONS ON SELF AND EGO IN CHILDHOOD

others. He could use it to obtain a measure of control over the external environment as well as his own affects when nothing else would do and it therefore had a useful function in his relationships with others as well as in his relation to his internal world. For this reason it led to his maintaining the omnipotence of his thought through which the self first became manifest. This success of his mind, however, had divorced him from the instinctual basis of his life with which he needed to re-establish contact.

Previously it has been noted that the archetype expresses itself in the form suitable to the collective matrix in which the individual is enmeshed. This child is no exception. In the midst of the one-sided omnipotence of thought appeared images which reflected the process leading to a new orientation through a necessary disintegration. This necessary event was followed by reorganization of his personality on a firmer and more complete basis.

This material clearly shows that images of the self can be found in children. Subject to confirmation by others this can be regarded as established. Further it seems clear that it can be seen to function in the child in such a way as to integrate the child's personality. As the result of this integration the ego develops.

DEINTEGRATION

A puzzling feature was the lively nature of the first picture painted by the child described above (pp. 138 f.), since she was apparently in a resistant and disintegrated state before starting to paint. She had looked woebegone, having been accused of a 'crime', sex play with her brother, which she did not understand and had then been brought to me presumably for further punishment. This did not occur, hence the change; it was as if good had happened to her instead of the bad she had anticipated and the good was represented in the picture.

The unity of the phallus and the numerous raindrops suggests in itself a release or deintegration. This meaning can be amplified from the myth of Danaë[26] in which a deintegration manifestly occurs. Danaë, the daughter of Acrisius, was fated to bear a son who would kill her father. Acrisius therefore shut his daughter

[26] For this amplification I am indebted to Mrs. Jung.

OBSERVATIONS ON SELF AND EGO IN CHILDHOOD

in a bronze chamber. However, Zeus visited her there in a shower of golden rain and she conceived and bore a son, Perseus. This myth contains the erotic conjunction following a spontaneous deintegration of the unitary god, numerous golden particles of rain.

A further suggestion of deintegration is the multiplication of the phalli within the forming mandala in Pl. 2.

In the case of the eight-year-old boy (pp. 144 f.), when I interpreted his wish to be sure I would not contradict him if he asserted that he knew God in reality, there followed a release of numerous mental concepts based upon opposites. This also is subject to the interpretation of a deintegration of the self, my interpretation converting a fear of disintegration into a deintegration. It was followed by positive ego functioning in as much as he was able to explain his feelings better than heretofore.

This example raises interesting possibilities, for it would seem that there is a relation between deintegration and conscious discrimination. Conscious discrimination separates out one set of ideas from others and clarifies them. But whence comes the motive power for this? The apparent answer is that it derives from the self. Furthermore, it would seem that the conscious process of correlating separate concepts, of relating them to each other as the child started to do as well, is based upon the integrative processes based upon the self.

This formulation accords with Jung's statement about the relation of the ego to the self: 'The self is an unconscious prefiguration of the ego.'

Another example is of a small boy of four years who had been referred for bedwetting and fears at night. Singularly little material was expressed on this topic and I was compelled to conclude that though bedwetting disturbed his parents it did not disturb him. His material was nearly all anal and he drew many pictures of faeces of many sizes and shapes in the process of appearing from the anus. It gradually became clear that he was concerned about the behaviour of the faeces, what they would do, whether they were pleasant or dangerous. Gradually as his anxieties changed the faeces in his drawings took on the faces of people and gradually acquired bodies.

In the theoretical chapter it was stated that the so-called libidinal zones became centres of consciousness. This case confirms

OBSERVATIONS ON SELF AND EGO IN CHILDHOOD

the thesis. The common phenomena of anal interests depend upon this event.

But further the faeces can be interpreted as deintegrates of the self because they have the characteristic of being beyond control of the ego. From this stems the fantasy of dangerous faeces; it is because they threaten the ego. But there was no serious threat in this child's fantasy which played round the process of defaecation, they were dangers which could easily be circumvented. For this reason it appears clear that the process depicted was deintegration.

In this case and the earlier one of the rain where urination was implied, the interpretation of deintegration seems equally applicable. Images of the deintegration process may clearly be looked for in the excretory processes in each of which substances, at one time a part of the body, become separated from it. This physical fact gives sufficient basis for the projection of the psychic process under discussion.

THE CIRCLE, INTEGRATION AND DISINTEGRATION

A little girl of just over two years was brought to see me because of fits from which she had been suffering for a year previously. In these fits she became completely unconscious. She was lethargic after them and had to be kept in bed for several hours. Apart from this the child hung on to her mother almost all the time and could do none of the usual things for herself which might be expected of a child of two; she could neither feed nor dress without help. Her elder sister was far more robust and bullied her incessantly.

Administration of luminal resulted in diminishing the fits to about one every week, but did not alter the regression.

At the first interview it was soon clear that the little girl was much too anxious to leave the waiting-room on her own, so I asked her mother to bring her along to the play-room where little could be done with the child, whom I let stand by her mother while we discussed the problem. The next time mother and daughter came together as before, but I gave the mother a chair to sit on just outside the door of the play-room. Very timidly the child came into the room; the door was left open. I gave her some chalks and a piece of paper. At first she did not do

OBSERVATIONS ON SELF AND EGO IN CHILDHOOD

anything, then she did a slight scribble and to my surprise made a circle, looked up in my direction and said quite distinctly 'me' (meaning herself). Almost at once her whole manner changed and she got down off her chair and played with some toys for several minutes. Then she trotted out of the door back to her mother who confirmed my earlier good impression of her by taking the situation in a natural way so that the child soon came back on her own.

One day, after she had established a more positive transference and so was feeling 'at home', an object fell on the floor and broke. This provoked severe anxiety and she ran back to her mother as before. But she soon returned, and when she did so and had started playing I gave the broken object a name and said, 'mother broken'. This produced an increase in rapport, since I had been able to make her realize that I understood her fear.

I then started making mothers in plasticine and these she broke up. After a time she wanted a baby made by me. This she tore to pieces in the same way as she had done with the mother. I tried making a father but he was left alone; at no time did she make any destructive attack on the father figure.

At this point I introduced a further remark, and that was to stigmatize the mother and baby as 'naughty'. It increased the activity. I did this in order to reinforce the 'good' part of her and because this was, as it were, her counterattack against the 'bad' (dark) aspect of the images in question, and also because I felt sure an enantiodromia would occur, i.e. the child's constructive impulses would emerge if the activity were supported.

Her mother made an interesting observation at this point: she told me that whenever her daughter saw a baby in a perambulator she would have to go and look at it and was not content till she had done so.

Gradually the child wanted the bits and pieces of the figures representing mother and baby put together again and she tried to do this. It annoyed her when the bits of plasticine would not adhere, and she enlisted my help. By now she could stand her mother staying in the waiting-room, and I judged that the essential process for which the child came had been sufficiently worked through, so I suggested dropping the luminal; no fits occurred. In addition, her mother reported a progressive maturation, so that the child, from appearing backward and listless,

OBSERVATIONS ON SELF AND EGO IN CHILDHOOD

had become independent, lively, and extremely competent at handling her own affairs, seeming even precocious. A feature particularly pleasing to the mother was that the child was no longer bullied by her sister, and could co-operate in enjoyable games with her. Five years later I heard from the little girl's mother. Her daughter's development had been most satisfactory and she had started school with pleasure and success.

The discussion of this little girl's play is facilitated if it be divided up as follows:

(a) The difficulty in separating from her mother.

In my estimation the failure to come with me was not caused by the mother who was not unduly anxious, or embarrassed by the child's anxiety, and further she readily brought her daughter with me to the play-room. The anxiety of the child must therefore have been due to the projection of a terrifying image on to me.

(b) The events before the destruction of the object.

Of these the most striking was the drawing of a circle and the naming of it. This can be interpreted as a picture of the self and ego in union bringing about increase in security and establishing the ego for a brief period. The relief of anxiety can be compared with the tendency to unite with her mother, whose physical presence was needed by the child at this period. The circle united with the word 'me' can therefore be equated with the periodic union of mother and daughter which proved necessary at this early stage.[27]

Apparently the necessity for the child is to maintain an image of a whole integrated self which it would seem disintegrates easily.

(c) The breaking of the objects.

The breaking of the object confirmed her worst fears that things and so people go to pieces easily. The tendency to disintegration can lead to the following conclusion on the basis of *participation mystique*. Equation: object = herself = mother. Running back to her mother brings with it necessary reassurance or real stability which can come about in the following ways.

(1) It could revive the memory of the whole self image. In support of this it can be said that without memory of a whole mother the little girl could not have gone back to her mother in the crisis of anxiety.

---

[27] Neumann (op. cit.) holds that the mother is the first carrier of the self. This observation would confirm his hypothesis.

OBSERVATIONS ON SELF AND EGO IN CHILDHOOD

(2) It could be that the stability arose because of the reassurance derived from matching the fantasy with reality. If in fantasy her mother was broken up, to find her body whole would bring reassurance that her fantasy was not true about her mother.

(3) If the fantasy was very powerful another alternative arises; that the mother had disintegrated but had (magically) been made whole again.

My naming the broken object as her mother was based upon the identity of object and mother. The naming was possible because of the knowledge that she could be an integrate, a whole child, and that she had distinguished between fantasy and reality.

My activity in making mothers in plasticine—I made them with breasts and named them—was a test to see what she would do. In breaking them up she was acting out intentionally that which, according to her feeling, had previously happened magically. Between dismemberment and disintegration there is an essential difference; it is the difference between being torn to pieces and tearing to pieces—the difference between archetypal and ego activity. Neumann[28] says in this context: 'Consciousness = deliverance: that is the watchword inscribed above all man's efforts to deliver himself from the embrace of the primordial uroboric dragon [the mother].' He is speaking of the history of consciousness in man, but the same principle applies.

Dismemberment in myths is a regular feature of the cults of the Great Mother who is herself the destroyer, she is the terrible mother who castrates and destroys her son.[29] Through all the differences the same archetypal form reveals itself—the terrible mother who is the self, who is everything and upon whom life depends.

The little girl was in the grip of an archetypal experience of dismemberment, and if we are to judge by the good results of working through the event, this must have been one cause of the symptoms, the fits, and the regression, the other being its occurrence before enough ego was formed to convert the event into words or fantasy.

The concept of deintegration assists in understanding the child's disorder, for the source of the fits is the dismemberment

---

[28] Cf. Neumann, op. cit., p. 105.

[29] Cf. *Symbols of Transformation* (Collected Works, Vol. V), London and New York, 1956.

OBSERVATIONS ON SELF AND EGO IN CHILDHOOD

of the ego by the deintegrating self, a process described as disintegration. This leads to a regression to a level where the mother and child again represent the whole integrated self from which the child can be separated at her peril. But that mother herself is in danger when any progression is attempted, particularly when any artificial or imposed attempt to separate mother and child is made. That must have been the original fear of coming to see me. And yet that separation of the ego from the self is essential if progress is to be made. It all depends on how it happens.

In order to study this problem I have taken separation anxiety as a paradigm of the general problem and studied the effect of not separating mother and child till the child did so herself.[30] This can be carried on until the child exerts her ego and sends her mother away. If the situation be handled thus the essential basis of consciousness is developed, the child's ego separates from the self and with it comes increased spontaneity in the form of play. This fits in with the deintegration theory, for the spontaneity of play may be conceived to stem from the deintegration process. It seems to me clear that the most important consideration is that the intention to separate must come from within the child.

The next step taken by the little girl was to ask for a baby to be made, and this she tore to pieces; it is the same dismembering process as that which occurred before but on a different plane. Is it meaningless to the child's play that the rites of dismemberment are associated with fertility? or can we assume that this child has in herself an archetypal unconscious knowledge of the relation between birth and death? But she as the mother destroys the baby—it is the next step in consciousness, nearer to the developed myths of Attis and Osiris—myths contain much more consciousness than is contained in the play and fantasy of little children. There was no younger child in the family, she is the baby—this she knows—and she is now expressing what happened to herself. In doing so some detachment occurs, the baby is no longer herself but another child or baby in the perambulator. Again it is necessary to realize the magical nature of the whole process represented in her play. The various processes postulated when the fantasy of a disintegrating mother were at their height

[30] Cf. Chapters VIII and IX.

OBSERVATIONS ON SELF AND EGO IN CHILDHOOD

apply when it happens to the baby. It would seem that she has to go and look either to be sure that the whole baby has not really been destroyed, or to revive the memory of a whole baby, or else to discover that it has been magically reconstructed.

(*d*) The remaking of the objects.

What are the sources of the constructive play initiated by the little girl? Has her mother shown her the desirability of mending broken objects? If so she has applied it to new spheres, since she has played the game of demolishing models of mothers and babies only with me. Is it guilt that impels her to a constructive effort? If so I was not able to detect any sign of it. It is not, however, necessary to enter into these speculations, for the constructive play follows from the hypothesis already formulated: that seeing her mother intact and seeing the baby whole gave rise to a fantasy of their both having been reconstituted magically. Somebody had done it, so she would try. At first she could not do it alone, and I had to be that other person, then she could do it without my assistance.

In the little girl's play the process of deintegration can be inferred behind the disintegration. On this hypothesis the pathological process derives from the ego being torn to pieces by the self as it deintegrates and so instead of a progression in which consciousness grows, a regression results. This regression leads to a level at which an earlier integrate is found based upon the unity of mother and child together. The fits can now be understood as the discharge of the energy which might have gone into a progressive deintegration.

In the play the child worked through the disaster in a modified form and re-established the position of her ego, *vis-à-vis* the self whose deintegrates expressed themselves in growth of the ego, a more independent and positive relation to her mother and co-operative play with her sister.

CONCLUSION

The collection of case material marshalled here needs to be read in connection with an earlier one 'The Origins of the Ego in Childhood'.[31] The earlier chapter owes much to the case material, and vice versa. The mandala pictures and the one-year-old boy

[31] Cf. Chapter V above.

OBSERVATIONS ON SELF AND EGO IN CHILDHOOD

and the little girl with fits were indeed the crystallizing points round which the whole theory developed.

The temptation to refrain from publishing material and theories in an incomplete state of development is strong. To do so is to risk misunderstanding or rejection, but they have already received some measure of acceptance and this has encouraged me to think the formulation is not altogether inadequate.

I have made some references to Neumann's pioneering work on the origins of the ego with which my concepts bear a close relation, particularly that of the self-ego axis. If I have reservations about some of his ideas it is because I have not as yet sufficiently assimilated them.

VII

CHILD ANALYSIS[1]

THE literature on child psychology, enormous as it is, contains few contributions by analytical psychologists. Jung's essays have recently been collected together in a volume: *The Development of Personality*.[2] In all his investigations he underlines the effect which the unsolved problems of parents have upon children, and focuses attention on the unconscious mind of parents as the source of children's difficulties. He sees that children are forced to experience and act out essentially adult problems; it is the parents who are the most frequent and main cause of behaviour disorders and neurotic symptoms.

In her book, *The Inner World of Childhood*,[3] Mrs. F. G. Wickes goes into this aspect of children's problems or, as we should rather say, this aspect of the parents which is revealed in the children. Though she touches on the actual analysis of children themselves, she does not go far along this line.

Oddly enough the concept underlying this caution seems to be that of causality. Because in the majority of cases the parents are, or were, the cause of the child's disorder, therefore they have to be the object of the main analytic endeavour. This, it may be pointed out, is quite at variance with the prospective or finalistic view of analytical psychology as a whole, which has come to recognize that causes represent only part of the total picture.

Since much of what I shall have to say may appear to run counter to current teaching in analytical psychology, I want to

[1] Originally published as 'Analytical Psychology Applied to Children', in *The Nervous Child*, Vol. V, Part 2, 1946, pp. 134 ff. The present version is greatly revised and expanded.

[2] Collected Works, Vol. XVII, London, 1954.

[3] New York and London, 1935. A brilliant recent descriptive essay from her pen has recently appeared: 'Three Illustrations of the Power of the Projected Image.' *Studien zur Analytischen Psychologie C. G. Jungs*, Zurich, 1955.

CHILD ANALYSIS

state here and now that I still regard the investigation of the unconscious of parents as of the first importance when a child becomes the presenting symptom of a family conflict, but I seek to supplement Jung's thesis and counteract the one-sided developments, based on too restricted experience, which have resulted from it. The cautiousness and open-mindedness of Jung's view, of which Mrs. Wickes became the main exponent, undoubtedly lays emphasis upon the treatment of parents, but it does not exclude the analysis of pathological children. The general thesis has, however, resulted in a neglect of child psychology amongst analytical psychologists as a whole which I have spent much time and energy in trying to change.

Apart from my own publications in recent years a small literature has begun to accumulate. M. Hawkey[4] and E. Lewis[5] have published some studies, and J. Jacobi[6] and W. Zueblin[7] in Switzerland have also contributed, whilst E. Neumann[8] has recently published an interesting theoretical article on early ego development in relation to his concepts of automorphism, uroboric incest, centroversion and the self-ego axis.

In spite of this growing interest in still appears necessary to discuss a view amongst analytical psychologists which though widely assumed, has never, so far as I am aware, received public expression till it was set out concisely by Dr. Cahen;[9] to him I am much indebted for this statement though I shall disagree with almost the whole of it. It is always of the greatest value to have clear statements which can be refuted! Dr. Cahen attributes his view to Jung, but its somewhat extreme position goes further than I can find that Jung does anywhere in his writings.

[4] 'The Witch and the Bogey', *British Journal of Medical Psychology*, Vol. XXI, Part 1, 1947; 'The Use of Puppets in Child Psychotherapy', ibid., Vol. XXIV, Part 3, 1951; 'The Function of the Self in Adolescence', ibid., Vol. XXVIII, Part 1, 1955.

[5] 'The Function of Group Play during Middle Childhood in Developing the Ego Complex', ibid., Vol. XXVII, Parts 1 and 2, 1954.

[6] 'Ich und Selbst in der Kinderzeichnung', *Schweizerische Zeitschrift für Psychologie und ihre Anwendungen*, Vol. XII, Part 1, 1953.

[7] 'Die aktive Imagination in Kinder Psychotherapie', *Studien zur analytischen Psychologie C. G. Jungs*, Vol. I, Zurich, Rascher, 1955.

[8] 'Narzissmus, Automorphismus und Urbeziehung', ibid.

[9] 'Psychotherapie de C. G. Jung', under 'Methodes Psychothérapeutiques', in *Encyclopédie Medico-Chirurgicale*, Paris, 1955.

156

CHILD ANALYSIS

Dr. Cahen's argument is divided into four sections, and is directed to showing why individual analysis is undesirable in childhood:

(a) l'organisme psychique de l'enfant est trop délicat et trop dépendant du milieu parental; il est le lieu réactionnel par excellence sur lequel agissent et se concentrent les tensions du groupe familial et les forces sociales collectives.

Quite apart from the widely recognized usefulness of individual psychotherapy in all age groups of children, or at least from two years to adolescence, this statement is open to criticism for its theoretical looseness.

There is one characteristic of childhood which stands out above all others; it is that it comprises more different, changing states of psychic organization than any other age group. The changes in an infant between birth and one year are, for instance, vastly greater than the changes that occur in an adult in any corresponding one-year period. The rate of change during infancy and childhood thereafter diminishes, but still remains far greater than in any corresponding adult period; between the ages of five and six years, children become relatively stable till adolescence. New and rapid changes reveal themselves at this time.

Therefore it is clear that the term 'child's psyche' means too many things to be of more than very indefinite meaning. When talking about childhood it is just as well to designate the age group to which reference is being made. A useful set of divisions is the following: infancy, between birth and two years; childhood, between two years and five and six years; the middle age group, between five and six years and adolescence; finally adolescence itself.

If Dr. Cahen be referring to infancy[10] he would gain much greater support for his thesis, less for childhood, less still for the middle age group, and least of all for adolescence.

A further consideration to be borne in mind is that it may be questioned whether the different states comprised under the heading 'child's psyche' have the common characteristics of being too delicate and too dependent, for analysis rests as much on the sensitivity and capacity to tolerate dependence on the part of the analyst as it does upon the nature of the child's psyche. On various grounds the analysis of children is more difficult than

[10] Cf. Mrs. Sandford's interesting study, 'Some Psychotherapeutic work in maternity and child welfare clinics', *British Journal of Medical Psychology*, Vol. XXV, Part 1, 1952.

CHILD ANALYSIS

adult analysis, and in this sense Dr. Cahen's view is wholy justified. If this be what he has in mind it is not the usual idea which combines with his view. On the contrary, it is commonly held that child analysis is easier, and I have even heard it said that those who are insufficiently mature to become adult analysts can successfully handle children! With this I find myself in complete disagreement. The analysis of children requires a special gift, but it also requires very great maturity on the part of the analyst. Children are nearer to the archetypes and have less ego than adults and in consequence require more restraint and more sensitivity in their handling. They can tolerate fewer 'mistakes' and make larger emotional demands. Jung's thesis on the subject of parents and children furthermore makes it seem desirable for a child analyst to be an adult analyst first, because he is then able to see both sides of the problem and to avoid the tendency to identify himself too closely with the child or his parents.

We may now turn to the statement that the child is the indicator of family and social tensions. Though no exception need be taken to this concept as such—it is indeed valuable and highly illuminating—yet the whole question is by no means simple. We still need to know much more about the relationship between parents and children than we do at present, and it is consciousness of our ignorance in this remarkably complex region that has made me try to develop a theory of ego development in childhood.[11] As a consequence of these researches it has become clear to me that the problem is one of strength or weakness of ego boundaries in relation to primitive identity. It may, however, be remarked in passing that the differences between adult and child are not quite so great as Dr. Cahen implies, for though the pressure of family conflicts is important for the child, social or collective conflicts are greater for the adult because the child is largely protected from them.

Dr. Cahen continues:

(b) le pouvoir d'intégration du Moi de l'enfant est trop faible.

This statement depends upon the kind of analysis that Dr. Cahen envisages and upon the theory of ego psychology on which he bases his assertion. In the rest of his paper, which is a lucid exposition of the 'Psychologie de Jung', he does not

[11] Cf. Chapter V in the present volume.

CHILD ANALYSIS

necessarily imply radical analysis, but it is difficult not to believe that he has this in mind, for he states under his final heading

(d) une tentative thérapeutique directe peut détourner l'enfant vers les mondes intérieurs, loin des nécessités adaptatives de son âge.

The classical radical analysis in analytical psychology involves just this turning towards the inner world of the objective psyche in order to bring the patient into relation with the images of the inner world. As the result an inner progression comes about in which the archetypes of the unconscious, so to say, direct the ego towards realization of a transpersonal control point—the self.

If this be what is meant by analysis, then Dr. Cahen is correct in deprecating its implementation in children of whatever age group. But if it is, he misunderstands the whole orientation, the whole nature of the psychic organization of the child, which is directed towards ego development in which the self sinks more and more into the background. The self functions not as a super-ordinate 'personality' to which the ego has to give way, but as a seeding ground for the ego out of which it is generated. This thesis can be confirmed by clinical observation, for in the last chapter of the present volume it is shown that by allowing a little girl to 'retreat' into her inner world the ego developed. A case in which the inner world features will also be demonstrated later in the present chapter. Both the cases come at the border between what I have termed childhood and the middle age group, but another case of a child aged two is worth study in this connection (cf. pp. 148 f.).

A fascinating study of the same phenomenon has been observed in the middle age group by Dr. Lewis.[12] In her researches she shows how groups of children of this age form gangs held together by a central archetypal experience of the self. She shows how the various children orientate themselves to this experience according to their type and particular problems and how when this experience is worked through the group disintegrates and each child has developed his or her ego.[13]

[12] Op. cit.

[13] Dr. Zueblin, in *Studien zur analytischen Psychologie C. G. Jungs*, Vol. I, Zurich, 1955, has made similar observations, though I find myself in disagreement with some of his theoretical formulations; in particular the idea that active imagination is a phenomena of childhood. The ego is not engaged sufficiently and I consider the term imaginative activity better.

159

CHILD ANALYSIS

The pattern as it presents itself in adolescence has been taken up by Miss Hawkey,[14] who has shown how in an adolescent case the self leads the way to integration into the ego of certain aspects of the shadow.

There has thus grown up a body of independent observation indicating that the fear expressed by Dr. Cahen is based upon a wrong assumption. It must, however, be recognized that the danger Dr. Cahen envisages is not without substance, but only if the child's problem be mishandled; if, for instance, it were not understood that a child only becomes fixed in the inner world when persons in the outer world become, in his fantasy, too terrifying for him to face. This phenomenon is an everyday problem of child analysis, and it is necessary to discover whether the outer world has become terrifying owing to maltreatment of the child, or to projections from the unconscious of the child, or to a combination of both conditions. Techniques for handling these states of affairs are definable.

Turning to Dr. Cahen's third proposition he says:

(c) si on parvient, en particulier en bas âge de l'enfant, à traiter la mère, qui est pour lui le trait d'union avec le monde et qui préside aux intercommunications avec celui-ci, si on normalise la mere en tant que volant d'entrainement de la vie et vers la vie, on place l'enfant dans une situation psychologique et humaine telle que le plus gros de l'œuvre psychothérapique individuelle sera obtenu sans traitement individuel de l'enfant.

This most attractive proposition is the one which in early years of investigating child psychology caused me most heart searching. The prophylactic implications of this view in relation to other children in the family who would benefit from 'normalization of the mother' are evident.

Unfortunately the practical application of this ideal is most disappointing and I have gradually come to realize that it is in numerous cases a false assumption, for there are pathological children quite apart from abnormal parents.

Dominated as I was at the outset by the propositions set out so clearly by Dr. Cahen, my experience in Child Guidance Clinics gradually forced me to realize that children are far more capable of fending for themselves than I had previously supposed.

[14] 'The Function of the Self in Adolescence', *British Journal of Medical Psychology*, Vol. XXVIII, Part 1, 1955.

CHILD ANALYSIS

Some of them even seem able to take a considerable part in changing the attitude to the parents themselves, so that I could not help being reminded of another trend in Jung's writings in which he talks of the parents as mere instruments in the service of the evolving psyche of the child.[15] On the other hand there are also children who are extremely susceptible to home influences which, if really abnormal, damage them beyond repair; this damage becomes incorporated into their psychic organisms so that they require treatment quite apart from whether the parents' problems are solved or not. This fact was finally driven home to me during the 1939 war when I was in charge of a group of hostels for children evacuated from the large towns.

Many of these children were seriously damaged beyond repair. A good environment made it possible for them to improve, but it did not heal them. Thus I obtained first-hand confirmation of what now seems so obvious.

Before going on to illustrate the complexities of the problems involved in child analysis, it will clarify my position if I set out briefly the possible origins of the disorders of children in relation to family life.

(1) Children can show permanent or transitory symptoms as the result of unconscious conflicts of their own. An example of a severe disorder will be found on pp. 148 f. of the present volume. The child aged two years suffered from fits and was cured without any analysis of the mother; there was no evidence of conflict in the mother other than natural anxiety over the condition of her child.

(2) Children can, owing to the fact of primitive identity when the child has relatively few ego defences, express the conflicts of

[15] *The Development of Personality, The Collected Works of C. G. Jung,* Vol. XVII, London, 1954, par. 97: '. . . behind every individual father there stands the primordial image of the Father, and behind the fleeting personal mother the magical figure of the Magna Mater. These archetypes of the collective psyche, whose power is magnified in immortal works of art and in the fiery tenets of religion, are the dominants that rule the preconscious soul of the child and, when projected upon the human parents, lend them a fascination which often assumes monstrous proportions.'

And par. 93: '. . . it is not so much the parents as their ancestors—the grandparents and great-grandparents—who are the true progenitors, and . . . these explain the individuality of the children far more than the immediate and, so to speak, accidental parents.'

CHILD ANALYSIS

their parents. In this case analysis of the parents results in a true resolution of the child's problem.

(3) As a result of later identifications, i.e. after the ego has developed to a considerable degree, the same result can follow, but it is not so serious or far-reaching as in the case of the second heading. This is because the child has sufficient ego to keep significant areas of his psyche intact.

(4) Owing to special problems of the parents there can be a period in which the child is damaged. The parents' conflicts can, however, be sufficiently resolved. The damage has however been suffered by the child and incorporated into his psychic organization. It is not changed by the resolution of the parents' conflicts.

(5) As in (4) only the parents' conflicts are still unresolved. In spite of this the damage to the child has become part of his psychic organization.

The following case will illustrate some of the complex factors here listed.

Case 1. This boy, A.B., aged six years, suffered from partial hysterical paralysis of the left leg—he was wheeled about most of the time in a perambulator and presented a wizened, under-nourished and undersized appearance.

His mother had the greatest difficulties over the physical expressions of physical sexual love. She did not have sexual intercourse for several months after her marriage because her sexual organs were said to be malformed and it was only after an operation to her vagina that it became possible. She always had severe menstrual pain, whilst she found sexuality repulsive and painful. She had the feeling that her womb was a bad one and when her first child, A.B., was born, much underweight, she became thoroughly convinced that she was malformed and was fated to produce physically weak children. Her sense of guilt over all this made her unable to express her love in a natural way and forced her to repress her maternal feelings because she felt they would harm her baby—instead of loving him she worried over him; as we shall see this was not so as he got older. A.B. could never walk as well as other children because he had 'weak legs', and when he was five years old his left leg started to 'fly out' and he began to fall down. He was thought to have various physical diseases but investigations proved negative; it was only very much later that the

162

CHILD ANALYSIS

correct diagnosis of hysteria was made. There were other causative factors in the history, but these are not relevant to the present discussion.

No analysis was possible with the mother throughout the time that I treated the child, because if I started to investigate her problems she simply ceased to attend though she would bring her child. I state this as a fact without justifying it; the failure was due to her overwhelming sense of guilt. Possibly had I been more skilful I might have got further, but, as will be seen, this does not matter so far as the present discussion is concerned.

In the circumstances I took the child on for analysis and the leg improved, but only partially. It tended to relapse when the child's mother had one of her periodic fits of depression. It seemed a fair assumption that the mother's depression was at least the precipitating cause of this, and she was persuaded to let A.B. go away from home to a hostel.

At first the analysis was discontinued, but, though the child improved in various ways, becoming more alive and eating better, the partial paralysis remained. The analysis was therefore continued after two months' break; the leg at once improved, but still was not cured. The child's relation to his mother was maintained throughout all this period and he went home from time to time, but each time he left the hostel the leg got worse. The striking fact was, however, that it got worse directly he saw his mother in the distance, and this confirms the view which I had been developing, namely that the child's fantasies about his mother were more important than the actual psychological state of the mother herself, even though she was abnormal.

The analysis did not as yet show this quite clearly—it was, however, evident that the child had a strongly negative transference to me, the content of which did not reveal itself, though it might have been deduced that it was based upon the fear of his fantasies about his mother's body.

An interesting and, as I learned later, most important fact was the hostel matron's observation that he was not capable of accepting any physical affection. If she went to tuck him up in bed at night he made no response to her, and if she so much as attempted to kiss him good night, he disappeared under the bedclothes to the bottom of the bed.

One day, in analysis, the whole system of resistances collapsed.

CHILD ANALYSIS

The child suddenly stopped the aggressive games he had been playing; he sat quite still in his chair, leant his head on his arms, complained of being sick and wanted water to drink. After a time I suggested that he should come nearer to me; he not only did so but climbed into my lap, curled up there, and lay in my arms sucking gently with his lips. At the end of the interview he got down and walked quite naturally to the door for the first time.[16]

This case demonstrates:

(1) that the child's neurosis does not clear up if he is removed from home; it is merely relieved in some respects;

(2) that the child shows the same reaction to physical love from the matron as from his mother, for the type of physical affection the matron expressed was quite possible for her. It does not depend upon his mother's psychic state;

(3) that the appearance of his mother brings up fantasies related to what has become the child's nature of which his mother has become the instrument;

(4) that when his resistances collapse, the most resistant symptom disappears apparently as the result of his being able to live through a regression.

We may, therefore, conclude that disturbances in the parent-child relationship can produce disorders in the child's psyche which cannot be handled simply through the parents even if, in the first place, their attitude is the main causative factor.

This case poses a problem of considerable interest arising from the observation that this particular mother could be a good mother to her child when he ceased to make excessive demands on her. His demand that she should not express her capacity for physical love in any form whatever, because it appeared extremely dangerous to him, put too severe a strain upon a woman able and needing to show physical affection in ordinary ways to her son.

The danger which the child imagined stemmed from the nutritional or oral phase in his development; witness the rhythmical sucking he was able to allow when he sat on my lap. This belongs to the period at which his mother was known to be inadequate. Reference to the child's history showed there had been a

---

[16] This did not constitute a permanent cure—he only walked normally for a few minutes, then the old attitudes returned. It did, however, dispose of the possibility of his symptom being due to an organic birth trauma.

CHILD ANALYSIS

conflict at this time. The mother's erotic and sexual feeling had as we know been masochistic, and her whole attitude was too undeveloped for her to be an adequate mother to her baby. From this stemmed the child's main difficulties, though other factors also were of great importance.

The special theoretical point that I want to underline is this: that many mothers can be good mothers to their children at a particular age or in particular ways, but not at or in others. They can be good mothers to babies but bad mothers afterwards, or like this mother, they can be inadequate mothers to babies but adequate mothers later on.

It was only after some years' work that I could conduct analyses of children with enough confidence to feel any conviction of their value. I attribute this partly to my theoretical preconceptions but also to the fact that the analysis of children is more difficult than in the case of adults; one is confronted, as Dr. Cahen has also seen, with a complex and delicately balanced organism whose nature is relatively unknown to the child, and about which one has to find one's way with less direct verbal help from him than is the case in adult analyses; a situation which is due to his being unable to aid the inquiring analyst in the same way as an adult can. Another difficulty arises because it is not always easy to distinguish clearly between those phenomena which belong essentially to the child's own psychology and those which belong to the environment.

Because the child is relatively unaware of himself he involuntarily hides himself from others, only giving, by means of allusions, hints about the real feelings which dominate his life at a particular time. One may try to penetrate behind this into the child's psyche by means of question and answer, but this only gets a certain way, and in some cases, particularly where there is a persecution fantasy at work, it produces an almost insuperable resistance.[17] One may, on the other hand, try to let the child reveal himself by remaining passive and watching what goes on: so-called passive therapy.

At first I approached the problem haphazardly, largely intuitively, and for many years I studied the products of children's

[17] This method can produce interesting information (cf. the work of Piaget) but in analysis it can be positively dangerous because it plays on powerful phobic mechanisms.

CHILD ANALYSIS

play without succeeding in getting into much closer contact with the actual child. I studied children's pictures, trying to analyse them for my own profit, but though I was led to interesting conclusions, I was unable to apply them to the actual analysis of particular children. The same thing happened with other forms of activity, with play, with the things they did with toys and materials of various kinds.

This preliminary theoretical work was of interest because it confirmed the wide application of Jung's theory, since over and over again in play, in fantasy as well as dream, patterns could be found closely analogous to those revealed by the parents. Only later did I suddenly realize that, quite apart from what parents put into the child's psyche, open as it is to external influence, the child projects into the parents an enormous quantity of its own nature; thus I had arrived at the other side of Jung's view of the parent-child relation, a view not dependent upon causality but upon his final, developmental concepts.

His thesis is that the psyche contains within it a series of inherited archetypes whose images give us forms of expression for psychic energy. The energy can flow now in one direction, now in another, and in so doing brings to life one or other of the images.

The theory can explain the remarkable plasticity of children and their variable response to different situations; it can explain why they appear neurotic or difficult under one set of circumstance, for instance, at home, but normal and adapted away from their parents. This phenomenon is frequently reported by parents and school teachers and leads to conflicts between them, each accusing the other of misunderstanding or mishandling the child. There is usually something to be said for each view since the child is usually showing one aspect of his nature to each set of adults. Another comparable response was that shown by children evacuated from London and other English towns. I was very much struck by the fact that they tended to behave 'well' in hostels where there was a strong assumption on the part of the staff that they would do so. Where this expectation was not in evidence the children behaved 'badly' but were more alive and natural.

The nature of these problems can be grasped more easily by analytic means. Consider the following observation: a child of the middle age group came to see me for the first time and remained

166

CHILD ANALYSIS

almost mute; he stood stiffly to attention during the interview; when going away he skipped with a lively, carefree air along the street. Without considering the deeper implications of this, it is self-evident that the child has quite different feelings in the two situations, and I needed to determine what was the nature of the child's feelings in the interview, i.e., how he was reacting to me within the transference. In other words, what did he think or feel about me, and why was he so carefree when he went away from the interview? That child was a delinquent and thought that he would receive punishment from me. The most usual notion such children have in their minds is that they are to be sent away from home to an institution, and they think I am the person who will decide about this. They cannot grasp that I am simply concerned to understand them, and so project on to me their previous experience of adults with authority and power over them. It is therefore important to decide: What sort of person does the child think the analyst is? The boy who cannot express himself is incapable of doing so because he imagines the analyst is a person of one of the following kinds: teacher, policeman, or father, and these derive their power over him, not so much from the real character of teacher, policeman, or father as from the power of the archetype; in this case the father archetype which produces a spell-binding influence. To put the matter in another way, the child is all the time reacting not so much to a reality situation as to a system of fantasies based on the archetypes.[18] The threats of parents made in the heat of the moment, the conversations with other children about remand homes or about approved schools contribute, but the child actually believes that retribution is to be meted out to him even when nobody intends it in the way he conceives it. He conceives it as an all or none proposition; either he will be sent away or else he will not, and this all or nothing quality is one characteristic of the archetypes. When he finds that nothing of this kind happens he is reassured and released from the spell.

Experiences like this encouraged me in my attempt to apply Jung's theory of archetypes to the psychology of children, which

---

[18] We thus arrive at a position which is, in important respects, the same as that taken up by Melanie Klein. Cf. *Psycho-Analysis of Children*, London, 1932, and *Contributions to Psycho-analysis 1921–1945*, London, 1948.

167

CHILD ANALYSIS

was beginning to bear fruit, and I was able through this kind of experience to approach nearer to a real child.

I was then struck by Jung's idea that the unconscious mind 'personates', it expresses itself in the terms of 'persons' who are not complete but fragmentary personalities. This supported me in the idea that if one is going to analyse a child one must always be concerned with the question: 'What sort of person does the child think the analyst is?' i.e. what is the content of the transference?

It is easy to see that a question will not produce a reliable answer with such a boy as is described above, because he fears, as it were, that the thunders of Jove will be visited upon him unless he preserves the most correct and respectful attitude. Therefore I refrain from asking questions which may suggest to him that I consider him naughty or bad but concentrate straight away upon helping the child by explaining why he behaves as he does, and letting him know that I understand it even if he does not, i.e. I start to interpret the transference. Insofar as I succeed in showing the situation to him using material which he provides for this purpose I shall succeed in finding a secure basis upon which he and I can build a relationship. Only when the relationship is secure will a question produce an aswer of value.

Let us consider other ways of trying to exploit the situation. In the first place, one might use the projection to make the child play or paint; in this way one gets more or less valuable information about him. If this is to be done with a view to developing the relationship, words are important: an order will produce a different kind of response, even a different kind of picture, from a request. In the second place, one might deliberately take a delinquent attitude—for instance, offer the child a cigarette or something to make him think you side with him or at least do not oppose his evil doings, in this way rejecting the projection. Though this can produce a startling change, great difficulties are attached to it, for it gives the child real grounds for thinking or feeling that you are on his bad or shadow side. To collaborate with the child on this basis can produce awkward situations and can involve one in physical assaults or in damage to one's room and furniture; the violence with which a child will attack any object which he thinks bad can reach the most extravagant degree. More important than the destruction involved, however,

168

CHILD ANALYSIS

is the fact that this kind of behaviour tends to obstruct the child's efforts to alter his dark side and may plunge him into a state of anxiety from which he cannot find relief. It is wrong to give the child grounds for identifying the analyst with his own bad 'self'.

One can, however, approach the child as I have suggested above by more strictly analytical means, and we may now proceed to inquire what this involves by considering the following questions, all of which depend upon restricting the inquiry to the phenomena revealed in a single interview. In child analysis the handling of the transference is the essential problem.

(1) What is the particular fantasy system at work in the transference?

(2) How can the analyst help the child to understand what is going on?

(3) How can he help him to handle and transform, where necessary, those parts of himself which he feels to be bad?

These principles appear to me the fundamental ones which have to be observed; the rest of the analysis grows out of them. As we know more, accumulate more knowledge, we shall be able to analyse better and more quickly, but I do not think these basic ideas will be easily altered. As the result of our knowledge, for instance, we find that children's main difficulties lie in personal relationships, in adaptation and in the development of the ego. In this respect they are quite different from those who are past the climax of life, who have mastered, to a very large extent, the problems of their personal life and are concerned to review the past in the light of wider or religious experience. It follows from this that archetypes need to be treated differently. The theoretical consideration behind this idea is that the archetypes are the functions, which, if allowed to work, will, through their own activity, heal the child, i.e. they act as compensatory functions just as in adult life.

Before continuing with the subject of child analysis a few points about interviews with parents of children who are being treated need to be mentioned. On the whole, if a child is being analysed it is not desirable to see the parents often, especially when the child is trying to express his negative feelings about them. It is usually necessary to arrange interviews about which the child knows nothing, or else to see the parents in the presence

169

CHILD ANALYSIS

of the child. This is particularly so if the fantasy is one of persecution by his parents. A frequent and difficult symptom supported too often by husbands and neighbours is the tendency of mothers to blame themselves for their child's difficulty. This seemingly sensible idea is one of the easiest pitfalls for the inexperienced to fall into. The subject can only be mentioned here; it needs a chapter in itself. Where a mother shows this symptom I have found it best to start off with the child alone even though the mother is neurotic; because when he improves the genuine problem of the mother is more liable to come into her consciousness. It is valuable to show such mothers that they are not as responsible as they imagine, and when the child improves they have more security in themselves and are consequently more able to look after their child in an adequate way. Then they can view their neurosis in relation to their own needs. This is the time for them to begin analysis, not before.

This appears to run in direct opposition to Dr. Cahen's proposition criticized above. The difference is not, however, so much one of principle as of method of approach to the family problem. There are very serious objections to assuming on theoretical grounds that a mother is responsible, and acting directly upon what appears obviously true. The direct application of this theory plays on the one hand upon the mother's sense of omnipotence and increases it, for too many mothers like to imagine they have their child completely in their power; on the other hand it can lead to a disastrous deception which cannot be undone without great difficulty if analysis of the mother be advised. This arises from the mother's half-conscious knowledge that the child is really abnormal. If the analyst simply assumes that the mother is at fault she may well accept the idea because she believes the analyst must know the truth. In these circumstances the analysis starts on the basis of an illusion and the mother will be tempted to conceal her knowledge at almost any cost. The analysis then becomes relatively meaningless and no change occurs in the child. In the case that helped me to realize this the mother's analysis could proceed when the child himself started treatment.

It is not possible to clinch the matter on this evidence, for the mother had certainly developed a resistance, but a case did come to my notice in which a mother had been in a good analysis.

CHILD ANALYSIS

Fundamental changes occurred certainly transcending 'normalization'. She had gone into analysis on my recommendation because her child showed serious symptoms and was failing at school; he was a gifted boy whose prospects of gaining a scholarship were reduced to nothing because of emotional disturbances. In spite of the mother's radical development no change was to be noticed in her son. Recognition of this led to the boy being given the deep analytic treatment he needed, with the most favourable results.

On these grounds it is desirable to keep in mind the question: What is it in a child which constellates the unconscious of his parents? This means recognizing the child as abnormal. The seriousness of a particular disorder in a child can be judged by many means, but they all depend upon combining the presenting symptoms with their duration.

These considerations lead to most interesting phenomena, of which the following is an example. A child of eleven years was referred for compulsive symptoms. His mother was completely absorbed in her family and her creative work, and apart from a manifest sense of guilt there was no indication for treatment as far as she was concerned. The boy was treated, and has now remained stable for four years. The next child, aged three years, was referred because of phobias and enuresis. The phobias derived from a traumatic incident, and it was evident that they persisted in spite of the mother's excellent handling of the phenomena they presented; it took some 200 interviews extending over three years to resolve his difficulties, which gradually led more and more into the mother's psyche. While the child was being treated an elder girl developed transitory symptoms which, however, soon went; she did not require further analysis. Finally the fourth member of the family, an elder brother, came for an interview out of curiosity as to what was going on.

Throughout all this period of several years the mother was seeing an analytically trained psychiatric social worker, and though her problem was apparent there was no indication that she felt the need of analysis. Only when the small boy's symptoms had practically gone did the mother's unconscious react and begin to produce the infantile sexual material which had been preventing the cure of the child's enuresis. She is now in an analysis which is thoroughly meaningful to her.

171

CHILD ANALYSIS

This result is the consequence of following the movements of the unconscious within the family group. In this way and in this way only is it possible to get a sound result. If the mother had simply gone into analysis she would not have had access to the unconscious because it was not only projected on to the children, but the projection was also true. They for their part would not have been able to resolve those conflicts which had become part of their natures as the consequence òf their development. It was these that fixed the projections of the mother in such a way that she did not have access to them. If a long time was spent on the children, this time, I venture to predict, will shorten the mother's analysis by a comparable period.

We will now proceed to consider some aspects of a second case through which it will be possible to grasp the analytical procedure better than by further theoretical discussion, which in any case can never succeed in describing the living process at work.

Case 2. C.D., aged six years. My first impression was of a boy in whom the pressure of activity was such that he could not continue with one activity for more than a few minutes. This pressure was so great that I made a note to the effect that the child was like a hypomanic adult, his play corresponding to the flights of ideas in such an adult. In the midst of his activity he would look apprehensively in my direction. I left him alone for a whole hour, merely acting in a friendly and helpful way when it seemed indicated. In this first interview it seemed clear that he was afraid I was going to do something of which he was terrified. I accordingly told him, when the same symptoms manifested themselves at the second interview, that he was frightened of me, and that I knew doctors often did things to children which they, the children, did not ask to have done to them and which they could do nothing to prevent. The result was enthusiastic agreement. He told me how he hated doctors because they were always wanting to operate on him or stick things into him. When talking about operating he pointed to his eye which had a slight squint, meaning that the doctor wanted to operate on it. Though on this occasion he said no more, yet later he told me that he suffered from hay fever and had been treated by injections. He had become terrified of doctors, partly because of the pain, but also because directly after one injection he got a severe attack of hay fever so that he

CHILD ANALYSIS

was confirmed in his underlying belief that the doctors did him harm. Unless I had first cleared away this difficulty I should have had to wait perhaps for weeks before he would have been able to establish sufficient positive feeling to proceed. As it was, his whole relation to me changed in a few minutes and he gave me a large quantity of information covering the following subjects. He had the same kind of anxiety about the behaviour of school teachers as he had about doctors but for different reasons. In the case of teachers he feared that he would be punished by being hit with a stick. He had difficulties in controlling his use of swear words, and was afraid of other boys at school. In this connection he said that he had almost given up any hope of being good, since he could not stop himself talking about 'bad things'. He was also able to tell me that he had dreams about giants who were associated with the war between the white and the black peoples. He knew the story of Jack and the Beanstalk, and this brought out the fear of being devoured by a giant.

The analysis proceeded by my observing the activities of the child and framing remarks and interpretations to keep the process going. The child's play soon began to show his fear of his own violent impulses which he had to control lest they should produce devastating results, hence the shift from one type of activity to another. He was afraid of the gigantic nature of his power which appeared as something almost objective and in relation to which he felt helpless.

The war between black and white I assumed to mean the conflict between good and bad impulses. The giant, like the one in 'Jack and the Beanstalk,' was associated with the bad, i.e. the black people. A further statement about his wickedness is contained in the child's remark on another occasion: Nazis were terribly bad people, 'the worst people in the world'—worse even than giants, blacks, redskins, yellow 'people'.

The giant, as the dream points out, symbolizes the forces within himself which he fears. He rationalizes the conflict with them into the conventional good and bad system of morality in order to keep them at bay. The giant is, however, an archetype which belongs to the level of instinct and has a different kind of morality associated with it; it is nearer 'jungle law' than the notions of right and wrong which one might call policeman's

CHILD ANALYSIS

law. In order to bring the child out of his level of good and bad it is necessary to diminish his sense of guilt so that he can react in a more natural and instinctive way.[19]

I can best illustrate how I attempted to help the child by the following example: On one occasion he played at bombing a Nazi train with lumps of plasticine. I remarked: 'You know, I think you *like* to feel that there are people, I mean the Nazis, who are worse than yourself.' To this he replied: 'That's right, the Nazis line up people and shoot them.' This conversation establishes that he feels bad and it helps him to say so. I next took the further step of trying to raise the conflict on to the subjective plane with the following remark: 'I think that the Nazis do the things that you would like to do but dare not', to which he replied: 'Yes, I am afraid because of the Police.' It was then that he produced his remark about the Nazis who were worse than the giants, they were 'blacks, redskins, yellow'. Following this I tried to get further understanding on his part by saying: 'You were blowing up the train. There is another meaning for "blowing up"; it means exploding, getting in a temper, and that is perhaps what happens to you.' To which he replied: 'Mummy gets bothered inside; she gets sick; all the bad things come out. She gets hot and then she gets cold.'

I infer that, in reality, it is he that gets 'bothered inside', for this would actually explain a great deal of his behaviour during my interviews with him. In other words, when he talks of 'mother' he refers to the 'mother' inside himself—the archetypal mother with which he has become identified.[20]

This example illustrates that the essential process of analysis, namely, the interpretation of the unconscious process, can be applied to children.

In adult analysis we use the methods of dream analysis for which associations are required. In child analysis associations are not usually obtained without previous interpretation, as the case of C.D. illustrates; the constant activity of play and imaginative activity as a whole replaces the associations. Much of the

[19] If the giant is merely understood as the father or, because of the devouring theme, the mother, we avoid all the extra insight which has been gained by Jung's work.

[20] At a later date he produced fantasies of his stomach being enormously fat. Inside were mother and father squabbling. This fantasy was a spontaneous one—it was quite unexpected by me.

174

CHILD ANALYSIS

child's play can simulate active imagination inasmuch as he reacts in play to active images, but I believe there is an essential difference of a quantitative kind. This difference arises from the strength of the ego and in consequence I prefer to call the corresponding phenomena in childhood imaginative activity, of which C.D. gave a good illustration. He had an imaginary companion named 'Pilot', a figure who, at one time, became associated with a small girl, the mother of many children. His mother had observed that the 'Pilot' would do all the things, in fantasy, which the child himself was forbidden to do in reality. In some respects, therefore, the figure corresponded in many ways to the shadow figure of adult analysis, and was the means the child used to detach himself from those impulses which he could not altogether stop. By means of the 'Pilot' he kept the material conscious without provoking the disapproval of his parents, who instead of being angry were tolerant and even amused.

According to the child's statements 'Pilot' did magic, he could appear and disappear at will, he could do tricks of various kinds and cared 'for nobody but his own stomach'. He made plots against his parents; 'the only thing he got afraid of was the two flying bombs which fell on his house"'! 'Pilot' was rude, used swear words and kept the child in fits of laughter with them.

This case answers a problem posed by Dr. Cahen, who fears that the analysis of the unconscious of children will result in turning the child's libido towards the inner world at the expense of the necessary adaptations of his age. Exactly the reverse occurred. The child lived in his fantasy because of his fear of the violent and fear-ridden instinctual impulses. His imaginary 'Pilot' was not created by the analysis but was there before; as the result of analysis the guilt about the content of 'Pilot' was diminished and the magical content of 'bad behaviours' removed.

But what of my interpretation of the explosions? This must surely direct too much attention to the inner world. That it did not do so must be attributed to the emergence of images representing how he felt. With the aid of these he could bring his feelings into closer relation with me and realize that I was not the terrible policeman he had felt me to be.

I am convinced that the fear of pushing the child into the inner world is not based on experience with children, but rather upon a failure to realize the difference between adults and

CHILD ANALYSIS

children. The difference between child and adult analysis rests not on any essential difference in principle but in realizing the needs and nature of children at the different phases in their development. Directly it be grasped that the psychic organism of the child is directed towards ego development, whatever persons, parents, teachers, or analysts do, then many of the anxieties concerning the undesirable features of child analysis vanish.

Let us now turn to a theoretical question, arising out of the case material, of how consciousness develops in a child of this age. Upon our knowledge of this subject turns the whole method of child analysis. We have noted how the 'Pilot' was the instrument through which C.D. was able to retain in consciousness a part of his personality which would otherwise have been repressed or else would have brought him into serious conflict with the environment. The contents of the 'Pilot' complex are felt by the child to be bad, and this enables him to keep himself good whilst at the same time getting used to the bad 'Pilot'. This suggests that the problem of becoming conscious is concerned with that of the opposites, felt by the child as goodness and badness.

I am convinced that the deeper understanding of this problem will lead to our greater appreciation of children's anxieties arising in ego development. Psycho-analysis understands the opposites solely in terms of pleasure and pain, and in doing so makes clear the roots of the matter for extraverted psychology. Bad objects are aggressive ones (aggressive either in fantasy or in reality), they are objects which inflict pain, which are sadistic, and which stand in the way of the emotional satisfaction experienced as pleasure. This mechanistic concept, with its corollary of the need for release from tension and necessary frustrations, takes no account of why or how consciousness grows. In order to obtain any insight into the process Jung's constructive conception is indispensable, for it is necessary to postulate a forward striving tendency to account for the occurrence of any development at all.

From the position of analytical psychology it appears that the development of consciousness necessarily involves a division in the psyche—it involves the formation of a dark side out of which any new consciousness emerges. Once the initial event has occurred[21] there results a more or less permanent struggle

[21] Cf. the concept of deintegration, elaborated in Chapter V, pp. 117 f.

CHILD ANALYSIS

between the light side and the dark side, between consciousness and the unconscious. The attainment of consciousness immediately expresses itself in the feeling of guilt, a feeling which is illustrated in mythology. Here we find that the attainment of consciousness is a crime against God, a crime which brings in its train retribution of one sort or another. The myths of the Garden of Eden or the theft of fire by Prometheus are typical examples.

My work with children goes to confirm this view; namely that consciousness comes about through the conflict between what the child and what the parents conceive to be bad; with the struggle between the child and its real external parents, or his inner struggle with the inner parents or archetypes. This is the problem with which our patient is confronted, the conflict between himself and the giant.

If we look at the various forms in which the opposites appear in childhood we soon see that they are always in conflict: the good fairies and the bad witch, the good magicians and the bad ones, and white people and the blacks, the cowboys and the Indians, the detective and the crooks, the English and the Nazis, and so on.

The most important element in the conflict gets a special afflux of libido and becomes the hero whose conquest over the enemy brings him power and glory. This theme appears not only in 'comics', children's story books, on the films, but is frequently incorporated in children's games. The hero appears in schools and is often given formal recognition by the award of various insignia. He is the 'Pilot' in our case of C.D.

According to Jung, the hero has his roots in the mother archetype and his struggle aims at overcoming her monstrous form, the monstrous fact of incest. Freud, on the other hand, viewed the hero's conflict in terms of the father, who represents the incest taboo. The apparent difference is not as difficult to overcome as it may seem at first sight, and we can offer a theoretical solution. In early years the conflict occurs between mother and child; the child's fantasies centre round his mother's body.[22] The conflict reaches a climax and is resolved in favourable circumstances. As a result the child attains greater independence from his mother and his affects, but the same motive remains, only this time the battle is transferred to the father. Inasmuch as the situation is

[22] Cf. Melanie Klein, *The Psycho-Analysis of Children*, London, 1932.

CHILD ANALYSIS

not worked through in relation to the mother owing to unfavourable circumstances, the father appears in a persistently negative light. As a consequence the oedipus complex is especially difficult to solve; indeed, it cannot be solved until we go behind the negative fixation of the father into the realm of the mother.

A particularly interesting form of the hero motif occurs in the case of delinquent children, in which they become the object of admiration and win for themselves a special role in the society of children. This occurs most markedly when the delinquencies are directed against parents or their surrogates.[23]

I was once able to watch the transformation of a neurotic child of ten years, an outcast from the society of children, into a robust and healthy individual while in a hostel for difficult evacuees.[24] This change occurred while he was still involved in many delinquent acts. We may well pause to consider this case somewhat further, because it shows how analytical knowledge can be applied to handling a difficult child. The boy's relation to the matron was not good; she was unable to get adequate rapport with him. He was nervous and pinched-looking, his hands were continually twitching and it was impossible to get them even reasonably clean. As time went on he started to retail the most exciting adventures in which he was the hero and in which he would pretend to discover amazing things—on one occasion, for instance, he told of an enormous store of money hidden down a hole in the road nearby.

The negative relation to the hostel matron fitted into the same picture as the stories, since we know that the hero grows out of the resistance to the mother.

When at the height of his stealing he had two dreams: in one he was liberating animals from captivity in a field, making a breach in the hedge through which they could escape by pulling up a tree; in the other he was freeing his friends who had been wrongly captured by the police, i.e., negative view of the father which is the result of the bad feeling he has about the mother.

At this time he won a negative position among the children

[23] The 'Pilot' in the case of C. D. illustrates the bad quality associated with the hero.

[24] 'Evacuees' were children removed into the country from the bombed areas in England during the war. The more difficult ones, who could not settle in billets, were collected together into hostels.

CHILD ANALYSIS

as the 'hostel thief', he even gained some collaborators, but it was not until he took a 'bashing' from the other boys that he was finally established among them.

Because the delinquencies were known to be a sign of inner development which grew out of the unsolved mother fixation, the matron refused to be provoked into being what the child must see as a bad mother. If she could avoid this role she stood in a good position to improve her relationship with him. Accordingly the situation was handled in the following way: the matron refrained from using punishment, she allowed the delinquencies to go on, even though they involved considerable inconvenience to her, strain on her patience and financial loss. In addition she attempted to live through the fantasies with the child without siding for or against them. In this way she succeeded in gradually improving her relationship with him and it became firmly established. As this occurred he established himself in the society of children, his physical health improved, he lost his nervous habits and became altogether more alive and happy. In addition, he had far greater control over his fantasies which had previously been the source of his neurosis.[25]

If we consider the actual qualities of the hero, not only in myths but also in the life of children, there is one which stands out; namely, that he is individual. It is on this account that a child who is playing out this role tends to collect round him a group of boys, a gang, because though he participates in the collective emotion, the collective desires, he always stands out as the leader. In other words, he stands for, or symbolizes, the principle of individuality.

The growth of a child's consciousness is most clearly dependent upon parents, nurses and teachers, but this kind of consciousness is simply taken over from the adult and leads the child to form patterns of thought and behaviour which are generally acceptable

---

[25] I do not intend to generalize about delinquency from this single case; nevertheless, it is common for a delinquent child to regard his delinquency as a heroic act. The question whether the hero motif takes on a delinquent trend, or whether it comes to receive social sanction, depends, in the case of a relatively normal child, upon the way the child's problems are handled by the environment. In the case of abnormal children, it usually depends upon the past environment, though some cases defy our efforts to grasp why they behave as they do. These children form the hard core of the cases which come before the Juvenile Courts.

CHILD ANALYSIS

to society. The hero, being the expression of individual powers, leads, on the contrary, not so much to collective as to individual forms of knowledge which are inclined to become involved with the dark side of the parents. In our case (C.D.), the individual enterprise (Pilot) had led to the use of power words of an obscene nature which gave him a position which he would not otherwise have gained in regard to other children and adults. It was in this sphere that he was individual, not so much in the use of particular words as in his notions about them and of the ways in which he combined them.

In this article I have tried to cover what I conceive to be the subject of child analysis, and if I have paid more attention to method than to conclusions it is because this branch of analytical psychology is only beginning to find its feet. If, however, we look into the future we can hope to find it one day not only bringing relief to children in their difficulties, neuroses and psychoses, but also contributing in a considerable degree to our knowledge of how to bring them up and educate them.

VIII

NOTE ON A SIGNIFICANCE OF ARCHETYPES FOR THE TRANSFERENCE IN CHILDHOOD[1]

THE archetypes are defined by Jung as the organs of the unconscious; because of their unconsciousness they can only be perceived indirectly through typical behaviour in human beings. This definition covers actual patterns of behaviviour—sometimes called instinctive behaviour—at one pole, and imaginative activity at the other. In the case of children the two, i.e. imagination and behaviour pattern, are more closely united than is the case in adults; the manifestation of the union is to be seen in play, but the union pervades the child's whole life, giving to it that spontaneity which is less in evidence, or even lacking, amongst adult persons.

On the basis of the above definition, I have begun to study behaviour in standard situations of the first interview between parents, child, and myself, with a view to separating out behaviour patterns and relating them to primordial images when they emerge in the subsequent analysis of the child. I have found it an increasingly interesting method of research, and wish to call attention to some of its possibilities.

In order to simplify and standardize the initial contact between the child, his parents, and myself I have adopted the following procedure in order to set the first interview in motion:

The mother and child (father too if he comes) are conducted to the waiting-room by the receptionist, but they are not brought to my consulting-room. Instead I go to meet them in the waiting-room, announcing myself as 'Dr. Fordham'. I next say that I

---

[1] Read to the International Congress of Psychotherapy, Zurich, 20–24 July, 1954, and published in the *Acta Psychotherapeutica*, Supplementary Vol. III, Basel and New York, 1955.

181

NOTE ON A SIGNIFICANCE OF ARCHETYPES

would like to see the child first (using his or her christian name) and the mother afterwards, and wait to see what happens. This initiates simple or complex behaviour patterns varying from acquiescence in my proposal to screams and confusion. According to the behaviour I decide to proceed with my stated plan to take the child in alone, or to abandon it and to take the mother in as well.

Much can be learnt from this situation alone which gives access to many fields of the child's and mother's experience, both in relation to each other and to stress situations in the past. Here I shall not take these much into account, but shall study the phenomena mainly in terms of typical archetypal psychology.

I think it is possible to see that an archetypal transference forms at once. Coming to see a doctor is a typical event, a doctor is a 'mana personality' in the community, as Jung recognizes in *Two Essays on Analytical Psychology*,[2] because through projection he acquires mysterious prestige. This mysterious prestige is originally projected on to the parents and expresses itself in the parent imagos. It later becomes associated with doctors and becomes specifically expressed in fantasies about the body. As the result of the projection of 'mana' I enter into the fantasy world of the child at once (the fantasy world is one form in which archetypes express themselves).

I have found it useful to keep in mind a list of the possible contents of this situation:

(1) First it is necessary to consider the child's consciousness. The child may only know that his mother has brought him to see a doctor; alternatively he may have been told beforehand why. Whether he has been told or not may be very significant or unimportant—it depends upon his real and fantasy relation to his parents. But clearly if has *not* realized the reason and purpose of his visit it will increase the unconscious fantasy as to what it is all about.

(2) Secondly the child's unconscious. In this lie past experiences of doctors as 'mana personalities'. In this part of the list I shall give first the fantasy and secondly the actual situation to which it corresponds. Doctors may have been experienced as:

(*a*) persons with special powers of searching out bad internal

[2] *Collected Works*, Vol. VII, London and New York, 1953.

NOTE ON A SIGNIFICANCE OF ARCHETYPES

objects. This corresponds to history taking and physical examination;[3]

(*b*) persons capable of finding that bad internal objects are *not* there and that the insides are good and so of reassuring the child. This corresponds to the negative outcome of an examination, followed by verbal reassurance;

(*c*) persons capable of being tricked about bad internal objects which have been safely hidden away. This occurs when the child has a persistent secret fantasy of his insides as bad. If the doctor finds nothing wrong he has, in fantasy, been tricked;

(*d*) persons with dangerous powers of injuring the child's 'good' objects outside or inside the body surface in various ways: for example the mouth (tonsillectomy), anus (rectal examination, suppositories and enemas etc.), genitalia (circumcision); or as persons who attack invisble objects (abdominal operation); or as persons capable of injuring the child's good insides indirectly, i.e. by giving medicines which the child conceives as poisonous;

(*e*) as persons capable of removing or otherwise eliminating bad objects. The same objective situations apply as in (*d*).

With suitable alterations the scheme can be adapted to children who fantasy about their interview in terms of bad behaviour (i.e. delinquents) or bad thoughts (i.e. psychotic cases). In these cases the children may not associate their visit with the bodily fantasies so much as with anxieties about their bad behaviour or bad thoughts; in consequence being brought to a doctor is less dangerous than to a policeman, clergyman, or psychologist.

The other person in this meeting is the mother, and we need to assess how far the typical anxieties enumerated above have been appreciated, consciously or unconsciously, by her and how far she is capable of handling them herself and so of being a good secure mother to her child.

Some indication of this can be obtained by the way the mother behaves when the child shows anxiety directly he hears I want to see him alone.

The manifestations are:

(1) Animus opinionating covering shame and anxiety.

(2) Open irritation and aggression.

[3] The term internal object is derived from Jung's distinction between the internal and external object; cf. *Psychological Types*, London, 1923, pp. 210, 591.

183

NOTE ON A SIGNIFICANCE OF ARCHETYPES

(3) Good behaviour and concealed hostility.
(4) Agitated reassurance.
(5) Calm reassurance.

ILLUSTRATIVE CASE

I will now illustrate and elaborate my thesis by describing and interpreting the case of a child, John, aged three years.

When I went into the waiting-room and explained that I would like to see John first and then his mother afterwards, the child showed manifest signs of apprehension—he clung to his mother's legs and viewed my proffered hand with fear and distaste. I took no further action but waited. His mother looked anxious and made some attempt to get her son to detach himself from her, i.e. showed in this and other ways signs of concealed hostility. She behaved as in the third heading of my list. After a short time, when no further developments were likely, I suggested that they both came along together to my room. When in the room the mother told her story in the presence of the child. The following is a compressed version:

He was restless at night from birth, but breast feeding proceeded well. He was starting to get dry at night when, at the age of two years, he became frightened by children dressed in grotesque head-dresses at a party. The fear lasted three months, but then he became ill with an undiagnosed illness, the symptoms being catarrh, red patches on his face, and persistent diarrhoea. At two years and nine months he had a mild attack of mumps, his enuresis became a more serious problem from now on, and he got restless at night as well, developing a fear of ghosts. One further fact was mentioned by John's mother: he had been found masturbating with another boy and since then was reported by his aunt to masturbate openly; his mother had not observed this.

The behaviour on my appearance can correctly be called separation anxiety, but we do not believe, in these days, that this gets us far. We need to know the contents of this anxiety, which can only be grasped fully from subsequent developments within the transference, though much can be inferred at once.

There are two methods of proceeding: if the source of the anxiety is easily accessible it can be directly linked with the ego by interpretation. Where it is not accessible it is gradually

NOTE ON A SIGNIFICANCE OF ARCHETYPES

presented in the form of images of a more or less mythological character, which amplify the problem and reflect the sources which only gradually come more and more into the open as they emerge from the collective unconscious in which they have become immersed. John's reaction could not be analysed with any certainty at the time, indeed the full import of it only gradually emerged in subsequent interviews. In these the primordial images appeared in the child's play and statements, and through them it was possible gradually to reach and work through the sources of anxiety. All the images I shall mention are well known, so that no mythological parallels will be required.

(*a*) The image of a terrifying ghost which John said did 'horrible things', came down the chimney. This I could show was reflected in his original transference anxiety by pointing out that his fear of me was like his fear of the ghost. This comparison produced his anxiety and a renewed retreat to his mother.

(*b*) An imaginary sky world where things are not as they are in the real world. For instance, there was 'no wind because there were no trees'. There was 'only a sun up there'. He lived up there for much of the time and 'came down by rocket'. Since ghosts are associated with the world of spirits, and so are liable to ascend, I conjecture that this fantasy system developed as the result of the loss of anxiety about the ghost, which, so to say, ascended into the sky and deintegrated into many and different forms.

(*c*) Through his secrecy over his bed wetting it was possible to reach his castration fears in which I as the doctor played a dangerous part.

(*d*) Fantasies of an enormous giant. The giant expresses the feeling of gigantic, magical physical power; John's giant had enormous legs which stretched out of the window of my room, across the street into a hospital opposite—the giant was not hostile and did not appear at any time as a dangerous figure. This fantasy came when his relation to me was more positive and when his earliest fears of my body were going. It will, however, be remembered that in his anxiety he clung to his mother's legs, which were good and helpful objects. Thus there are two associative connections here: (*a*) to the development of a positive transference feeling to my body, and (*b*) to his mother's body which was reassuring because real in contrast to the unreal ghost.

(*e*) Anxieties about unnamed animals which terrified him in

185

NOTE ON A SIGNIFICANCE OF ARCHETYPES

bed. These were of interest because of their connection with faeces. He had earlier on attacked me with sand and made me 'dirty' in this and various other ways. Further he had been developing fantasies about excrement of all kinds. At first the faeces were lumps, but later they developed eyes and faces, to turn finally into people. When I related the fears of animals with the fantasies, the fears were resolved and the fantasies changed. I conclude that he was working through his feelings of dangerous inside objects which he was afraid would get loose and against which he was not strong enough to defend himself and so needed my aid.

(*f*) A dangerous wind which killed him, in contrast to the good sky world where there was no wind.

(*g*) Dangerous men who shot him without making a hole in his body. This could be related to his fears of strange and dangerous forms of intercourse derived from his actual sex play mentioned in the first interview by his mother.

As a result of the analysis of this material it is possible to conclude that the early anxiety contained the concentrate of all the material which emerged later. In this is found fear of a fantastic ghostly figure that would not only castrate and kill him but also find out about the dangerous internal objects (the animal faeces) which he harboured inside his body.

Together with this emerged helpful figures, first as his mother's body, then far away in the sky world, then as the giant, and finally in myself who could remove and change the dangerous objects inside and around him.

Such a demonstration must be incomplete and so unconvincing, but I hope that I have at least shown how the concept of the archetype with its dual form of expression in behaviour and image can relate the phenomena of the initial interview to much of the subsequent behaviour.

In conclusion I cannot refrain from a final comment upon the significance of the archetypes in the counter transference.

It is usual to consider the counter transference as the evoking by the patient of individual and personal contents of an unconscious 'belonging' to the analyst. On this basis the counter transference is supposed to be a phenomenon which should really be under the control of the analyst's ego. At the level of archetypes, however, the counter transference must be regarded as a

NOTE ON A SIGNIFICANCE OF ARCHETYPES

usual and, so to say, normal phenomenon since archetypes are the organs of a general unconscious. These manifest themselves in the spontaneous unconscious interchange between analyst and patient as human beings.[4]

This concept can be referred to childhood: where the archetypes are expressed in play they give a theoretical basis for the child analyst's entering into the child's imaginative activity and relating to the child within the images; this is sometimes called 'playing rôles', but such a statement supposes the analyst to be deliberately controlling the situation, of which spontaneity is an essential part. The capacity to enter into the child's imaginative (sometimes inaccurately called 'inner') life can be vital, especially where the sense of outer reality is markedly impaired and where verbalization is limited or imaginative expression inadequate.

During my treatment of John this spontaneous activity could be increasingly allowed to display itself in games and fantasy, particularly as his anxiety diminished and he could allow himself to be 'killed' and 'brought to life'.

[4] Cf. 'Notes on Transference Analysis' (*supra*, Chapter IV), where a distinction is drawn between counter transference illusion and the analyst's syntonic reaction to the patient.

IX

A CHILD GUIDANCE APPROACH TO MARRIAGE[1]

OBJECTIVES IN THE FIRST INTERVIEW

CHILD guidance is commonly associated with the team approach to family problems which have as their presenting symptom some distress of which the child is the manifest cause. Over the course of years I have come to make use of the team personnel in a special manner which seems worth recording in outline because, whilst recognizing the value of each member of the team, I have come to think that the usual method of handling the first interview by deploying all members of the team is unsatisfactory.

Critical examination of this first interview reveals a somewhat complex situation: the child sees two persons, the psychologist and the psychiatrist; the mother also sees two, the psychiatric social worker and the psychiatrist. Neither child nor parent knows what is going on during the time he or she is occupied; they can only imagine what is happening and their imaginings are not brought to light. This consideration made me realize that fantasies must be more or less active during the whole procedure. This perhaps is not important in the long run, but it must make a difference to the assessment of the dynamics of the interpersonal relationships which are the subject-matter of this study. To be sure these considerations are advisedly ignored in the team approach because another consideration is put in the forefront. The classical operation aimed not so much at studying the interview processes as at getting a complete and objective account of

[1] Based on a paper read at a meeting of the Medical Section of the British Psychological Society on 26 November, 1952, and published in *The British Journal of Medical Psychology*, Vol. XXVI, Parts 3 and 4, 1953.

A CHILD GUIDANCE APPROACH TO MARRIAGE

the problem presented by the child right at the beginning. The psychiatrist aimed at getting as good a grasp as possible of what the child was like and how far he was aware of the problem for which he came to the clinic. He was, in short, expected to make a 'diagnosis' of the child's condition. Before this the psychologist had taken an intelligence quotient, made observations on how the child behaved, and used such other tests as seemed relevant and as time allowed. In the meantime the psychiatric social worker had interviewed the parent, and amongst the information she was expected to get was a history of the child's development, and secondarily, an impression of the mother and some inkling of family relationships, to which we may add the collection of reports from school and other agencies.

Throughout this procedure the aim may be considered in terms of collecting information and arriving at a diagnosis or a conclusion which was often recorded by filling up an index card on which the various symptoms and conclusions were entered. Admirable as this may (or may not) be, it presupposes a static scheme, a structure or a frame of reference of a fixed kind. We need not here enter into the merits or demerits of this procedure; all that need be brought out is that apart from the complexity of the interpersonal relations involved in the team method, the aim is different from the one here put forward. Here it is to initiate a process in which information as such is subservient to the actual dynamics of the interview. From this position it is useful to distinguish between all that occurs during and in relation to the interview, and what may be termed reporting or hearsay.

To illustrate from the team procedure: the I.Q. is the consequence of an actual situation created by the test, as also is that part of the psychiatrist's interview with the child in which he makes direct observations on the child. But he also receives the child's report about home, school, and his symptoms; and the history given by the parent is a report, involving complicated memory processes, giving a number of more or less accurate facts which are stated to have occurred. On the other hand, the way in which the history is told, whether or no it is told spontaneously at all, is significant both with regard to the kind of mother who is talking and what her attitude is to the interview and interviewer. Directly we take this set of phenomena into account the static reported facts start to become dynamic

189

A CHILD GUIDANCE APPROACH TO MARRIAGE

because they are related to the present immediate situation of the interview.

In order to allow the dynamics of the interview to display themselves more easily I have adopted the following guiding principle: the mother (or parents if the father has come too) and the child are allowed to form or construct the interview within the framework to be described. This leads to a very unstable interview content, varying from the whole being filled with a full report by the mother of the child's symptoms and their history, to a very limited and in many respects incomplete statement. For instance, there may be a negative reaction from the child followed by vituperation on the part of his mother against him because his ingratitude makes it seem unlikely that he will bring her the consolation she hoped for since she lost her husband.

The kind of procedure here adopted makes no claim to originality, but the problems it creates are far from being solved. Thus, when listening to a conference in a psychiatric clinic a case was presented by a psychiatric social worker (who was handling a series of therapeutic interviews with a student) which showed many of the features of the present procedure. She described the first or 'intake' interview from which the material was very scanty on account of the inhibited condition of the patient. When she invited comment, many of those present were unable to comply. Some of them complained and attempted to prevent another conference of this kind being held. They thought the material should be presented as a whole.

But this kind of tidying up is an end-product. If the interview is based on the idea of finding out what kind of relationship any particular person, child or adult, can make under the circumstances of a first interview one does not necessarily get a tidy or complete picture. The integration of the bits and pieces comes about gradually, mainly through the use of interpretations. The psychiatric social worker in the case mentioned above had not given verbal interpretations, but had maintained a passive attitude of acceptance to the material. It appears, however, that interpretations are usually asked for by implication not only before the parent and child leave the clinic, but also when sufficient material of emotional significance emerges. Because of this need for interpretation of the material presented I prefer to get only enough information to initiate the interpretative process, even if this is

A CHILD GUIDANCE APPROACH TO MARRIAGE

based upon bits and pieces and before a whole image of the supposed total situation can be grasped.

ANALYSIS OF THE FIRST INTERVIEW CONTENTS

In what follows I shall describe, in conjunction with a further outline analysis of the first interview, the procedure I have come to adopt as the result of a critical estimation of the team procedure. The idea is to outline three nuclear points and to leave the rest flexible. The nuclear points can be studied comparatively because they are static; the others are not so easy, and, indeed, at the present stage I do not feel able to give a general descriptive account of them.

The nuclear points are the following:

(1) The beginning of the interview—the particular point of importance being the separation of mother and child which is required.

(2) The change-over from seeing the child to seeing the mother.

(3) The end, when mother and child are reunited.

This pattern is varied from case to case and may be almost completely disrupted: the child may not separate from the mother, and if he does so, he may want to be present during the interview with his mother, and in consequence the reunion may not occur at the end. Yet to keep in mind the general pattern is useful, since deviation from it at any point indicates abnormality.

(1) *Beginning of the interview*

It seems to me an advantage to fetch the child myself, so I go into the waiting-room and explain to mother and child that I want to see the child first and the mother afterwards.

At this point three things may happen:

(*a*) The child hastens off at once as if leading the way.

(*b*) He comes along, letting me lead him.

(*c*) He shrinks away from me with varying degrees of fear, he may even scream or howl. In this extremity he may run to his mother, cling to her skirts, bury his face in her lap; alternatively, he may not go to his mother but shrink backwards in fear or look mutinous.

Just as there are standardized responses of children to the arrival

191

A CHILD GUIDANCE APPROACH TO MARRIAGE

of the psychiatrist, so there are standardized ways in which mothers react to anxiety on the part of their children. The most usual is to try various ways of persuasion, amongst which is the one of constructing a fantasy of a good doctor with whom the child should go; on the other hand, she may get anxious about the impression her child is making on others and which reflects upon their estimation of her as a mother. In other words she shows varying degrees of anxiety and guilt if the child does not do as he is requested.

I remain inactive, and if the child does not overcome his hostility or anxiety easily I then ask mother and child to come along together. The subsequent interview in which the child is left to his own devices is conducted as if I were seeing the parent alone, that is, I ask the parent to give me an account of the difficulties. Naturally this excludes more or less material which might have come out had the child been absent. It is usually less rather than more!

It is clear that the first formula does two things which are a guiding line in the whole procedure. In the first place, it is phrased on the assumption that I have authority and so in some measure will show the relation of the child to his parent and to authority in general. Secondly, it puts the child first, or as I prefer to put it, in the centre of the picture.

He is kept in the centre when his anxiety or hostility, or both, are taken seriously—which I show by my rapidly giving in to his desires to be near his mother, and so mobilizing his feeling of omnipotence. These I have learned to make use of in later interviews by separating child and parent only when there are clear intimations that the child wants the parent to go away.

(2) *Change-over from seeing the child to seeing the mother*

When a child has been interviewed, he is given the opportunity to be present while his parent is seen if he wants to, but it is explained that it does not matter so far as I am concerned. Three choices are open to him: either he does not mind, or he opts to go out or to stay. All these responses are useful, but as an example of how significant they can be, the following pattern may be cited. When the child will tell nothing of significance, and when he opts to be absent when the parent is seen, one can then predict a hostile parent. Again, should the child want to stay, this points

A CHILD GUIDANCE APPROACH TO MARRIAGE

to anxiety, often of a paranoid kind, with regard to what is going to be said.

(3) *Reunion of parent and child*

The reunion occurs without the psychiatrist being present. I have therefore not been able to make this a subject of study, but subsequent interviews often reveal what has happened.

ILLUSTRATIVE EXAMPLES

I shall now describe and comment upon the content of two interviews, one of which went according to plan, while in the other the child refused to be removed from his parents, both of whom had come for the first interview. The interviews are described as I think they were conducted. It will be noted that in the first case there was no detailed account of the symptoms for which the child was referred because the mother assumed that I knew them, though in fact I did not.

Case 1. *June, aged eleven years*

June was seen on her own, i.e. she complied easily with the first formula, but soon it became clear that she regarded the difficulties, whatever they might be, as now in abeyance, and this view I interpreted. She then revealed that she had been worried by the French teacher who was too strict, but she agreed that she, June, got more upset by her than the other children. There had also been trouble about her little sister who always clung round June. Recently, however, the sister had broken her leg, and because June had known what this was like, having done it herself in the past, they had become more friendly. In addition, during what was a friendly conversation, she remarked that she had felt home was a strange place when she came back from hospital where she had been when she was ill. She preferred to wait outside while I saw her mother.

At first the mother took the same view, viz. that the troubles were in abeyance. She gave a number of explanations of difficulty over discipline which she assumed I knew about. These explanations were, first, that it was due to the jealousy of her sister, and, secondly, that it was due to the illness; she thought that the hospital ought not to have sent the child back so soon.

o 193

A CHILD GUIDANCE APPROACH TO MARRIAGE

The interview was threatened with a breakdown at this point, so I showed her that I was not in disagreement with her view of the case. Then she gradually began to talk more easily under the influence of interpretations of her feelings of hostility towards the interview and what she had supposed a child psychiatrist to be like. June had got to know an older girl and the mother was astonished at how dishonest the child became. She started taking letters from her brother's drawer. The letters were from his girl friend, aged fourteen years. The girl June had known was more free, owing to her 'parents' comparative neglect'. They gave her money to go to cafés and cinemas, and this June was not allowed. The mother was much upset by the way children carry on today. She was a country girl who did not have a mother, and her father would not allow her to go out with boys until she was seventeen, although she did so without his knowing. Interpretation of the girl's sexual interest made the mother more easy and produced more information. June started menstruating when she was eleven. There were difficulties over menstruation, which was irregular, and the periods have only recently 'settled down'. I reassured the mother by telling her that some girls started menstruating at eleven. She then at once went on to talk about the child's illnesses: a fractured bone when aged six followed by an abscess in the place of the fracture a year later. June went to a convalescent home at this time for fourteen weeks. I remarked that it seemed these events must of necessity have made for difficulties in growing up, and the mother remarked that June was nervous when she came back from the convalescent home, and had been nervous of the night and the dark ever since. The difficulties of growing up led to the fact that the child was shy on the one hand and on the other liable to get hysterical. Further, June was born during the war when they had a very 'bad time' with the bombs. This led to my interpreting the mother's feelings of guilt about June, and to incipient tears and a hint of the mother's own anxieties.

The features of the child's interview which interested me were the statements about the problems being solved, combined with an explanation of a kind which seemed to exclude me from the picture. One might say that she framed the interview in such a way that I was redundant, while at the same time giving unconscious hints of guilt and relief from it because of the sister's

A CHILD GUIDANCE APPROACH TO MARRIAGE

broken leg—suggesting a possible solution of her conflict on the basis of castration.

But whatever credence might be given to the view she presented, the fact that she firmly preferred to be absent when her mother was there pointed to the contrary, for opting to go out points to present conflicts between herself and her mother. This supported me in not accepting the almost complete identity of the child's and mother's views of the problem, and made me certain that active interpretative measures were required and being asked for in indirect ways.

The appearance of ready-made explanations (animus opinionating) points to uncertainty in the mother's feminine position, and there seems to be further evidence of castration anxiety linked with masturbation and fantasies of internal damage resulting therefrom. This conclusion is reached through the association of menstruation and disease, leading on to remarks about the fracture and an abscess at its site. This anxiety about her own failure and guilt struck me as being combined with feelings of powerful destructive components directed towards June, violent enough to be projected into the bombing. The interpretation of her guilt resulted in incipient tears and so brought us to the heart of the mother's conflicts and to the reason for the defensive position first seen in the daughter, and then more elaborately expressed by her mother.

I regard this example as a good one for illustrating the conversion of an apparently static situation into a dynamic one. For this purpose interpretations were essential. The interview led on to the production of a good deal of dynamic material at the next interview, at which much more historical material came pouring out, so that the significant facts could be seen in relation to the mother's guilt and anxiety.

Case 2. John, aged four years

On requesting John to come with me, I was met with an emphatic 'no', so I attempted to remove him physically, i.e. took him by the hand, but when it became apparent that he was prepared to fight I desisted and asked the mother and father to come in also. The parents were embarrassed at talking in front of the child and tended to lower their voices, but the child played on his own without embarrassment for the whole interview, taking

A CHILD GUIDANCE APPROACH TO MARRIAGE

no apparent notice of us. There was good co-operation between the parents over the child, but it appeared that neither of them could handle him, though at one time his father had been more successful than the mother. Description of the symptoms started spontaneously and went forward smoothly. These symptoms consisted of banging his head on the wall, screaming during the day and at night, inability to play with his parents or other children on formal occasions, getting violent in public—for instance, when the mother took him out shopping—and hitting other children. These symptoms would disappear if he became ill, when he would be good. Recently, however, when he was taken to hospital for the treatment of an ulcer on his eye, he got nervous and developed facial contortions. He had good characteristics: a very good memory and a very good side which he showed in public, especially when not expected to co-operate with other children.

He was said to have been 'a perfect baby', breast-fed and 'no trouble at all'. Certain peculiar features were, however, early in evidence. For instance, he did not seem to 'learn to walk' but 'suddenly started walking' at eighteen months. It was at this time that the screaming began for no apparent reason, but conflicts arose from this difficulty between the mother and the paternal grandmother in whose house the parents were living. These conflicts persisted until recently. The mother showed some hesitation in mentioning this in front of her husband and did so apologetically, hoping that he did not mind, but he was able to say that it was all right. At one time the screaming aroused the ire of the neighbours, who banged on the wall, and this terrified the child so that he got a phobia about the room in which the noise occurred. Until recently the child had slept in his parents' room, and it was only recently that the family moved to a house of their own. Reasoning and smacking have both been used in attempts to control John, without much success, and here the father volunteered the opinion that the child did not feel the smacks.

In the first place this case shows how the child demonstrates the very aggressive symptoms about which the parents had come. They are patently within the child and come out in relation to authority; it looks like a resistance against imposed control.

Not only does this confirm the parents' contention for my own benefit, but it improves the rapport between the parents and myself for them to see I take the behaviour seriously and cannot control it.

A CHILD GUIDANCE APPROACH TO MARRIAGE

My offering the child a hand is a test of the rigidity of his response. Many more healthy children, having asserted themselves, will swing over to the opposite and come along quite easily if they are given the chance.

The second phenomenon is the parents' embarrassment at talking in front of the child, though all their statements covered topics about which the child must either be aware or have known about in the not too distant past. This we may fairly conclude is being based on the fantasy of the innocent or perfect child (he was a 'perfect baby'), the so-called divine child who is not only divinely good but also uncontrollable. This theme has been dilated upon at length by Jung and Kerenyi,[2] where Jung says it points to the original condition of unity in childhood, and would indicate a significant degree of infantilism on the part of the parents, confirmed by the fact that they lived till recently in the paternal grandparents' house, a fact which might easily have been erroneously taken as a purely social (economic) arrangement.

A crucial point in the parents' relation was the mother's concern about exposing the father's family to criticism. The interchange between father and mother at this point, as well as exposing their common concern about the situation, indicated a significant component of brother-sister pairing as an element in the marriage. An account of the facts expressed by either parent would not have done this so well, and the value of having the father there is well illustrated in this interview.

There are many familiar reasons why fathers tend to delegate to the mothers the task of taking the child to clinics, so it is worth while reflecting on why this father came. With a child of this kind it is, I think, more usual for the mother to find all the difficulty and for the father to find either relatively little, or else none at all, in which case he vents his critical feeling upon his wife with varying degrees of vehemence. This had been the case with the parents of John, but latterly the father had found matters as difficult as his wife.

This must have been the overt reason, but I think the brother-sister content of the marriage is the more striking, for it tends to lead to a closer identity in feeling between the parents.

[2] C. G. Jung and K. Kerenyi, *Introduction to a Science of Mythology*, London, 1951.

A CHILD GUIDANCE APPROACH TO MARRIAGE

SOME CONCLUSIONS

We have arrived at last at the relationship between mother and father who constitute the particular interpersonal relationship which we call marriage. At first sight the children are the offshoots of this, but in reality they are part of it because of the complex of identifications which come about during the child's development so that disorders in marriage become reflected in the children of that marriage.

The first case clearly shows the child revealing the same pattern in the interview as her mother, and though nothing of a direct kind emerged about the relation between the parents, it can be inferred through the attitudes of mother and child to the whole clinic procedure. This was one of anxiety and, as gradually emerged, it was based on a fear of condemnation. It would not be going too far to conclude that conflicts arise when the husband takes up his position as father.

Apart from this conclusion, based upon observable phenomena, the first case brought up the following problems of marriage:

(1) The place of control (discipline) in family life.

(2) The responsibility of parents in relation to adolescent children, leading to

(3) The contemporary tendency of mothers to go out to work.

(4) Geographical problems, i.e. the differences between bringing up children in large towns and in country districts.

(5) The tendencies of mothers to take over control of the children in crises.

Thus as an offshoot of the interview, significant problems are posed and useful information becomes available outside the essential dynamics of the situation.

INDEX

Abaissement du niveau mental, 48
Abenheimer, K. M., 83n.
Abstraction, 124, 125
Acquired characteristics, 10
  inheritance of, 19
Acrisius, 146–7
Acting out, 70n., 77–9, 90n., 99
  case illustrating, 77
  in children, 155
  as defence, 78
  in interview, 78
Active imagination, 73, 74, 76, 85, 87, 95,
    116, 175
  case of use of, 75–6
  and childhood, 159n.
  and imaginative activity, 33
  reveals archetypal activity, 4, 5
  and transference, 80, 87
Adaptation, 67, 71, 85, 169
Adler, G., 62, 64, 74–5, 78, 88, 126n.
Adolescence, 157, 160
Affects, 65, 78, 146
Aggression, 92, 135, 183
Aggressive:
  feelings, 91
  games, 164
  objects, 176
Aim(s):
  of analysis, 70, 96, 97
  of childhood, 116
  of first half of life, 116
  spiritual, 72
  vocational, 68, 72
Albira, and Astuna, 140–2
Alchemy, 59–60, 66, 138ff.
  and individuation, 143
Alexander, F., 83n.
All or none proposition, 167
Alpha rhythm, 17n.
Amplification, 101–2, 137, 138, 140
Amygdaloid nucleus, 14
Anal zone, magical sense of, 83
Analogy, 138n.
Analysis, 82, 158, 165, 170–1 176
  aim of, 70, 96, 97
  ascetic nature of, 70n., 170
  of children, *see* Child Analysis

of children's unconscious, 175
deep, of child, 171
and life, 71–3
of mother, 172
outside the interview, 174
of parents, 162
personal, 64
therapeutic factor in, 90
training, 63–4, 69
transference, 102
  central in, 66
  complexity of, 103
Analyst:
  analysis of, 102
  anonymity of, 80
  archetypal reactions, 64
  and child, relationship, 67
  conflicts of, 93
  dependence of, 157
  as 'differentiated object', 79
  ego of, 94, 186
  explanatory or superior role of, 99
  imaginary, 74
  as parent, 81
  and patient, *see* Analytic relationship
  personal confessions of, 93–4, 95
  personality of, 63, 87, 89, 103
    therapeutic element in, 64
  as projection screen, 70, 103
  relation to unconscious, 90
  repressed unconscious of, 89
  sex of, 103
  therapeutic reactions in, 64
  training experience of, 69; *see also*
    Analysis, training
  unconscious bond with patient,
    102
Analytic:
  process, 102
  relationship, 63, 64, 68, 76, 93, 168
    archetypes in, 187
    difference in parties to, 69
    social contacts during, 81
    transference not peculiar to, 70
Analytical method, 44
  place of transference in, 66
  see also Technique

199

INDEX

Analytical psychology, ix, 180
  analysis in, 159
  finalistic view of, 155
  and new physiology, 18
  and synchronicity, 47
Anima, 107n., 117
  of prima materia, 60
Anima possession, negative, 93
Animus, 43, 107n., 117, 183
Animus figure, 5, 7, 8, 75, 84
Animus opinionating, 195
Animus possession, 43
Anna, 110, 127
Anxiety, 118, 136, 149, 150, 169, 173,
  183, 185–7, 192, 198
  mother's, 194–5
  paranoid, 193
  separation, 152, 184
  transference, 185
Anxiety attack, 5
Archetypal forms, 8, 32
  and analyst's behaviour, 96
  and conservation of energy, 23
  genetic factors and, 30
  in interpersonal transference, 67
  personal relationships and, 64
Archetypal ideas, 22n., 35n., 56
Archetypal Images, 2, 7, 11, 17, 20, 22,
  48, 56, 78, 107n., 111, 116, 124, 131,
  166
  in children, 105, 107
  defined, 105n.
  Great Mother, 32
  in individuation, 117,
  numinous quality of, 59, 64
  religious, 8
  representative of instinct, 11, 121
  and symbol, 53, 54
Archetypal motifs, and fixation points, 83
Archetypal stages, 32
  and ontogeny, 29
Archetype(s), 30, 45, 57, 60, 93, 96, 98,
  120ff., 124, 128, 138n., 146, *et
  passim*
  and active imagination, 4
  all or nothing quality of, 167
  and biology, 1ff., 33
  and central nervous system, 105
  changes in, 24, 28
  in childhood, 105ff., 158, 169
  and collective unconscious (psyche),
  2ff., 106
  as compensatory functions, 169
  concept of, and astrological tradition,
  41
  in counter-transference, 186–7
  and ego development, 67
  evolution of, 19, 23
  expressed in bodily experience, 111
  fantasy and, 111, 182

father, 167
giant, 173
heredity of, 8ff., 11
and image, 48, 57, 106, 120
inherited (innate), 120, 166
and initial interview, 186
as inner parents, 177
and instincts, 11ff., 28, 127
and localization, 17
meaningful concidences and, 45, 48
mother, 177
and nervous action, 14ff.
organs of unconscious, 105, 181
origin of, 20
psychoid, 2n., 48, 53
and realization of self, 159
and scientific theory, 56
scintillae and, 118
self as original, 112
source of primordial images, 8
and symbol, 54
and synchronicity, 35ff., 47, 48
theory of, 2, 71
in transference, 50
and transference in childhood, 181ff.
transpersonal, 64
unconscious, concept of, 7
see also Archetypal forms; Archetypal
  Images
Assimilation, 122, 123
Association:
  experiments, 63
  fibres, 16
Astrology, synchronistic basic, 40
Attention, 122
Attis, 152
Attitude:
  affective, 93
  change of, and psychic renewal, 43
  conscious, 42, 47, 58, 106
    reasoning, 46
    and symbol, 57
  of ego, 57
  of mystics, to symbols, 55
  non-symbolic, 54–5
  passive, 190
  rationalistic, 43
  religious, 55
  scientific, 55
  symbolic, and religion, 55
  'that shuns all methods', 65
Automorphism, 156

Baynes, H. G., 62, 63, 102
Behaviour:
  acquired, 21
  analyst's, 63, 96, 97, 102
  archetypes and, 181, 186
  bad, 183
  good, 184

200

INDEX

imitative, 123
infantile patterns, 82
innate, 12
instinctive, *see* Instinctive
patterns of, 181
in standard situations, 181
Biogenetic law, 28ff., 33
Biological concepts, and analysis, 1
Birth, 111
and death, relation, 152
double, 3
Blake, William, 54
Body:
fantasies about, 182
fears of, 185
and mind, dichotomy, 114
relation to psyche, 33–4
Body image, 15
consciousness of, 15
unconscious, 16
whole, 129
Body scheme, 16, 114–15n.
meaning, 115n.
Brain, 13, 14
Brain, W. Russell, 16n., 17n., 52n.
Breast feeding, 182
Brihad-Aranyaka Upanishad, 119
Brother-sister pairing, in marriage, 197
Buddha, 53
Buffon, 19
Buhler, Charlotte, 122

Cahen, R., 156ff., 165, 170, 175
Cardanus, Jerome, 40
Cases:
of scarab, illustrating synchronicity, 43
of synchronicity in owner of two yachts, 44
illustrating imaginary analyst, 73–4
woman using active imagination as defence, 75–6
illustrating acting-out, 77
of 1-year-old boy who scribbled circles, 133–4
of 2½-year-old girl who scribbled circles, 135
of incontinent boy with terrifying parent images, 136
of 2-year-old girl with fits, 136
of 6-year-old boy with hysterical paralysis, 162ff.
of 7-year-old girl with night terrors, 136–7
of delinquent boy who drew swastika, 136
of 8-year-old child who threatened analyst with monster, 144–5
of 4-year-old boy with bedwetting and night fears, 147
of 2-year-old girl with fits, 148ff., 161

of mother with resistance, 170–1
of mother and children, 171
of manic boy aged 6 illustrating value of interpretation, 172
of transformation of neurotic child, 178
of 3-year-old boy illustrating archetypes in the transference, 184
of girl aged 11—a first interview study, 193–5
of boy aged 4— a first interview study, 195–6
Castration fears, 185, 195
Causal:
connections, 36
factors, 46
hypothesis, and Rhine's experiments, 42
Causality, 36, 41, 47, 155, 166
exclusive of chance, 41
relation to space and time, 42
Cause(s):
incredible, 41
individual's belief in, 50
must be considered, 46
see also Causality
Central nervous system, 13
and archetypes, 105
Centroversion, 156
Chance, 36ff., 43
excludes causality, 41
and Rhine's experiments, 42
runs of, 48
and synchronicity, 36
Chaos, 118
Child(ren):
age groups among, 157
analysis of, *see* Child Analysis
delinquent, 178, 179n.
divine, 53, 142, 197
dreams of, 105ff.
of 'early man', 32
growth of consciousness in, 33
individuality of, 161n.
onset of consciousness in, 31
perfect, fantasy of, 197
psychic development, 104
psychic organization, 159
see also Fantasies
Child analysis, ix, 67, 155ff., 181ff.
and adult analysis, 158, 165, 176
individual, 157
of pathological children, 156
and transference, ix, 169
Child guidance, 188ff.
Child images, and wholeness, 61
Childe, V. G. 22n.
Childhood, 157
archetypal images in, 107
ego's origins in, 104ff.
unity in, 197

P

INDEX

Chinese culture, and synchronicity, 49
Christianity, spread of, 22
Circle(s), 113, 120, 133, 144, 150
  and danger situations, 136, 137
  faces as empty, 136
  imagery of, 134, 135
  and integration and disintegration, 148ff.
  protective, 135, 136, 137
  refers to uroboric incest, 135
  represents archetypal non-ego, 134
  and the word 'I', 134, 150
Civilization, 21
Clans, 21
Clementine Homilies, 118
Coincidences:
  meaningful, 43, 44, 45
    and archetypes, 58
    numinosity of, 44
  synchronicity in, 47
Collective elements, amplification of, 8
Collective unconscious, 185
  and archetypes, 2
  distinction from personal unconscious, 2
  and instincts, 2
  theory of, 2
  transpersonal, 2
Combines, 124
Comments, analyst's, 96
Companion, imaginary, 175
Comparative method, 7
Compensation, theory of, 66
Complex, 176
  pathological, 5
  Oedipus, 178
Concept(s):
  abstract scientific, and images, 56
  analytical, and biology, 1
  developmental, 166
  and sense data, bridge between, 22, 56
Concept building, 110–12, 127
  infantile sexuality and, 111
Concern:
  feeling of, 59, 100
  interpretation as expressing, 95
Confession(s), 65
  personal, by analysts, 93–4, 95
Conflict(s), 82, 165, 166, 172, 177, 195, 196
  of analyst, 79, 93
  with analyst, 74
  archetypal, 45
  collective, 158
  with environment, 176
  family, 156, 158
  infantile, 177
  love-hate, in depression, 75
  mother's, 195
  of mother and child, 177

of parents, 161–2
for possession, 27
rationalization of, 173
on subjective plane, 174
unconscious, of children, 161
Confusion, 101
Coniunctio, 145
  see also Conjunction
Conjunction, 142, 144
  in Danaë myth, 147
  of opposites, 139
Conscious, the, 2, 57, 107–8
  centre of, 57
  child's, 106, 115, 125
  development in, 128
  originates in unconscious, 22, 105
  and symbol, 54
  and synchronicity, 47
  and unconscious, 23, 46, 58, 60, 114, 126n., 128
  see also Conscious mind; Consciousness
Conscious mind, 108
  and archetypal images, 11
  integration and, 131
  intellectual resistance of, 7
  union with unconscious, 131
Consciousness, 2, 8, 64, 101, 117, 119, 120, 128, 152, 153, 170
  aim of analysis, 97
  analyst's, 64
  archetypes in, 127
  arises from deintegrates, 99
  centre(s) of, 66, 110, 147
  in child and adult, 33
  in childhood, 106, 182
  contents of, 4
  development (evolution) of, 21, 29, 128, 176
  differences in, 27
  the ego in, 116
  emergence from unconscious, 142
  evolving, 32
  field of, 99
  growth of, 179
  in childhood, 33, 115n.
  heightened, 99
  images of archetypes in, 53
  images, first evidence of, 120
  increased in transference, 64   •
  infant's, 31–2
  in mysticism, 115
  and myth, 23
  neurologists and, 16
  personal, 94
  personal, and ontogeny, 29
  recapitulation of racial, 30, 31
  religion and, 55
  science and evolution of, 23
  in 'scientific age', 22

202

INDEX

social, origins of, 33
and synchronicity, 50
transference and, 99
and the unconscious, 177
whether genetically determined, 30
see also Conscious, the; Conscious mind
Constructive:
impulses, child's, 149
play, 153
Convergence, principle of, 38
Cortex, cerebral, 14, 16, 17n.
Cosmic myths, *see* Myths
Coulton, G. G., 22
Counter-transference, ix, 68, 89ff.
archetypes in, 186–7
illusions, 82
projections, 99
syntonic, 93, 96ff., 99
Credulity, affective, and probability, 39
Culture, 121
development of, 21
and emergence of consciousness, 22
Culture hero, double birth of, 3
see also Hero
Culture pattern:
children and parental, 30
matriarchal myths and, 31
Cupid, 53
Cybernetics, 16

Danaë, 146–7
Darwin, Charles, 19–20
Day-dreaming, 74
Death:
and birth, relation, 152
theories of, 110
Decoy mechanisms, 110
Defence(s), 145
depersonalizing, 75, 102
ego, 161
interpretations as, 100
use of dream and fantasy as, 74,76
Deintegrate(s), 99, 119, 121, 123, 127–8
and instinctive behaviour, 121
and object, 120
of original self, 112, 127
patterns of, 127
Deintegration, 117ff., 120, 125, 129, 132, 146–8, 148ff., 176n., 185
and conscious discrimination, 147
earliest, 119
images of, 148
primitive identity and, 98
progressive, 153
of the self, 127–8
spontaneous property of self, 117
into unconscious archetypes, 128
Delinquency, as heroic act, 179n.

Delusions:
of insane patient, 9
of psychotics, 4
religious, 10
Dependence, in transference, 81–3
Depression, 163
Depressive state, 85
Development, 108
early, 114
ego, *see* Ego development
individual, 67
inner, 179
Devil, 24–5
Diagram, 124, 125
Dialectical procedure, 65
transference and, 103
Dialectical relationship, 97
Dieterich, 9
Differences, individual, 7
Diffusionists, 21–2
Differentiation:
of archetypal contents, 98
of ego, 98
between ego and environment, 129
of inner and outer reality, 111
of psyche and soma, 111
of self and ego, 132–3
of thought and fantasy, 111
Dionysus, 53
Discipline:
in family life, 198
Discovery:
origin of, 21
scientific, process of, 23
Disintegration, 97, 117–18, 146, 147, 150–1, 152, 153
and dismemberment, 151
mandala and, 132
schizoid, 144
Dismemberment, 151
rites of, 152
Divine child, *see* Child(ren)
Doctor(s):
good, fantasy of, 192
as mana personality, 182
Dream(s), 4, 74, 93, 116, 129
big, 105
children's,
archetypal images in, 105
and mythology, 29
and parents' unconscious contents, 105
projected on parents, 106
defensive uses of, 74, 76
and deintegration, 119
about patient, 91
of psychotics, 4
records of, 85, 95
Dream analysis, 73, 174
Dream sequence, shows animus figures, 5

INDEX

Dual mother theme, 3

Eden, Garden of, 177
Education, 65, 127
  conscious, 104
  and diffusionism, 21
  intellectual, 102
  self-, of doctor, 102
  technique of, 67
Educational interpretation, 133
Educative procedure, 98, 102
Ego, 33, 57, 60, 65, 67, 68, 85, 90, 100,
  108, 111, 116–17, 118, 137, 145, 150,
  151, 185, *et passim*
  and archetypes, integrate of, 131
  birth from self, 125
  child's, 162
  danger to, 137
  defence, 80
  differentiation of, 98
  expressed in scribbles, 135
  formation of, 97, 104, 113, 117, 125,
  128
  growing points of, 83
  growth of, 126, 127, 153
  and individuation, 116
  and non-ego,
    dichotomy, 114, 126n.
    synthesis, 126n.
  origins, in childhood, 104ff., 154
  as personal consciousness, 94
  and preconscious, 107
  progression and regression of, 80
  reference of 'I' to, 134
  relation to self, 114n., 116–17, 132,
  135, 147, 150, 159
  and self in childhood, 131ff.
  separation from self, 134, 152
  splitting of, 117
  torn to pieces by self, 153
  two main attitudes of, 57
  and unconscious, mediator, 7
  united with self, circle and, 113
  see also Ego development
Ego boundaries, 108–9, 129, 158
Ego centre (centrum), 113n., 126
  see also Ego nucleus
Ego defences, 161
Ego development, ix, 33, 96, 116, 129,
  134, 144, 159, 169, 176
  archetypes and, 67
  in children, 67, 130, 133, 158
  early, 156
  and integration, 131
  Jung's theory, 104ff.
  and myths, 33
  psycho-biological view, 110
  self and, 83
Ego fragments, 112, 125, 126
  integration of, 126

Ego integration, 125–7
Ego nucleus (-i), 127, 128, 129
  see also Ego centre
Egypt, 21
Elucidation, 65
  of archetypal contents, 98
  psycho-analysis as, 65
Embryology, 28, 29
Emergent viewpoint, 108
Enantiodromia, 137, 149
Endocrine system, 13
Energy, 58, 109
  conservation of, 23
  distributions, 73ff., 76
  psychic, 166
  transference of, 72
Environment, 126, 128, 146, 165
  conflict with, 176
  in delinquency, 179n.
  emotional, 129
  good, 137
  intra-uterine, 11
  parents and, 112
  perfect, 114, 120n.
  and 'self', 114, 129
Eros, 118
E.S.P., 40
Euphorion, 59
Evacuees, 161, 166, 177
Evolution, 19ff.
  of archetypes, *see* Archetypes
  concept of, 23
  hypothetical stages in, 29
  related to concept of archetypes, 19
Excretion, 111, 129
Extrapyramidal function, 17n.
Extra-sensory perception, *see* E.S.P.
Extraversion, 57

Faces, 147
  dangerous, 148
  deintegrates of the self, 148
  fantasies of, 186
Fairbairn, W.R.D. 79
  on libido theory, 83n.
Family conflict, 156
Family problem, approach to, 170, 188
Fantasy(-ies), 5, 73, 74, 78, 119, 129,
  137, 151, 160, 174, 175, 185, 187
  archetypal content, 4n., 167
  and archetypal activity, 3
  of body, 182
  of children, 28, 31, 152
    archetypal images in, 105
  defensive uses of, 74, 76
  at first interview, 186
  of inner cosmos, self as, 75
  Jung's theory of, 167
  about mother, 163–4, 177
  not differentiated from experience, 111

204

INDEX

persecution, 165
pleasure in, 127
and reality, matching, 151
spontaneous, 174
unconscious, 182
Fantasy system(s), 111, 185
in transference, 169
Father(s), 177
as giant, 174
individual, 161n.
primordial image of, 31
sexual role of, 31
Father figure, 149
Father imago, 136
Faust, 59
Feed-back, 16, 16–17n.
Feeling(s), 57, 58, 147, 151
agressive, 91
conscious, transference, 89
erotic, 565
masochistic, 165
maternal, 162
negative, 169
positive, 173
Fenichel, O., 77
Fetish, 8
Filius philosophorum, 142
First half of life, 65
aims of, 116
analysis in, 67
Fixation, mother, 179
Fixation points, 82, 83
Foreknowledge, symbolical, 106
Forms, archetypal, *see* Archetypal forms
Fourfold structure of psyche, 132
Freud, S., 2–3, 64, 82, 113n., 177
on the transference, 66
Friendship, symbolic, 87
Frustration(s), 71, 129, 176
Function(s):
and analogy, 138n.
compensatory, archetypes as, 169
ego, 126
extrapyramidal, 17n.
four, of ego, 57, 58
irrational, 57
nutritive, 109
psychic, 44, 54
and symbol, 57
rational, 57
sexual, 109
Function type, 47

Gabricus and Beya, 142
Gang(s),
child, 159
and individual, 179
Genes, 21, 120n.
theory of, 10

Genetic factors, 11, 30
Genetic psychology, 85
Genetic units, and environment, 120n.
Germ plasm, 10
theory of continuity of, 10
Gessel, A., 113
Giant(s):
dream figure, 173–4
fantasy figure, 185
God, analyst as, 96–7
Good and bad, 173, 174, 176, 177
relation, 145
see also Opposites
Grey matter, 16
Guilt (feelings), 153, 162–3, 171, 174, 177, 192, 194–5
interpretation of, 195
Gull, baby and mother, 12, 121

Hallucination(s), 39
of psychotics, 4
Hans, Strong, 53
Harrison, J. E., 118n.
Hawkey, M., 83n., 156, 160
Henderson, J. L., 62, 68, 71, 87, 88, 103
Heracles, 3
Hereditary units, 120
archetypes as, 9, 10
Heredity:
biogenetic theory and, 30
and environment, 11
theory of, 10, 19, 20
Hermaphrodite(-us), 60
Hermaphroditic figure, projected, 95
Hermes, 53
Hero, 177–80
see also Culture hero
conflict of, 177
motif, 178, 179n.
Hierarchy:
of instinctive patterns, 13
of nervous system, 14
History, consciousness of, 21
Hoghelande, Theodore de, 59–60
Hormones, ovarian and testicular, 13
Horoscopes, 38
of married people, used by Jung, 40
'Human', the term, 94
Hume, R. E. 119
Huxley, Julian, 120n.
Huxley, T. H., 20
Hysteria, 163

I, the word, 113, 125, 134
and circle, 150
as a creation of the self, 119
self united with ego, 126n.
I Ching, 39, 49

205

INDEX

Ideas:
archetypal, *see* Archetypal ideas
flights of, 172
see also Concepts
Identifications, 162
complex of, 198
and primitive identity, 108–9
Identity:
of feeling between parents, 197
of object and mother, 151
primitive, 63, 67, 98, 108, 135, 158, 161; *see also* Participation mystique
of views, 195
Illusion:
counter-transference, 91ff., 95, 187
confessions and, 94
due to projection, 79
Image(s), 4, 22, 80, 117, 120ff., 125, 138, 175, 185
analyst as embodying, 101
archetypes expressed as, 48, 53, 105, 127
bad, 149
circle as, 136
of deintegration process, 148
developmental hypothesis of source of, 9
a distortion, 54
in dreams, 4, 57
eradication by mystics, 115
essential part of symbolic life, 54
evoked in scientific discovery, 23
explanation of, 54
of external object, conscious, 52
fantastic, 98
first evidence of consciousness, 120
functional properties of, 7
how formed, 119, 124
of human being, 124
incarnating, 98, 99
in infant and early man, 32
innate, hypothesis of, 120–1
inner, 23, 52, 56, 57
of inner world, 159
of integrated self, 150
numinous effect of, 127
perception and, 123
perceptual, 51
and personality, 133
photographic, 52
preconscious, 128
projected, 98
and religion, 55
repetitive, 4
of the self, 144–6
in small children, 120
specific, and specific archetypes, 120
and symbol, 51ff.
symbolic, 51, 52, 56, 123

terrifying, 150
see also; Archetypal Image; Body Image; Primordial Images
Image formation, 124–5
Imagery, 2
mythological, 31, 110
psychological, recapitulation and, 30
of the self, 144
Imagination, 51
active, *see* Active Imagination
images of, 33, 57
Imaginative activity, 33, 88, 159n., 175, 181, 187
and active imagination, 33
in children, 4, 174
Imitation, 122, 123, 124, 125
Impulses:
good and bad, 173
instinctual, 175
violent, 173
Incarnation, 98
of image, 99
Incest, 177
uroboric, 135, 156
Incest fantasies, 70n.
Incest taboo, 177
Individual, 109, 180
and archetype, 146
'belief' in, 67, 68
development of, and dreams, 106
and gang, 179
Individual psychology, 65
Individual solution, need for, 85
Individuality, 65, 66, 179
of children, 161n.
emphasis on, 85
Individuation, ix, 66–7, 67–8, 72, 75, 84n., 94n., 96, 128, 134, 138, 143
archetypal images in, 117
cases, Jung's, 87
four stages, 87
goal of, 116
self in, 116–17
transference in, 65, 66
Infancy, 157
self as original archetype of, 112–13
Infant, *see* Child
first year, changes in, 157
Infantilism, in parents, 197
Inflation, 96, 126
negative, 96
Inherited characteristics, 11
Initiation, 8
images of, 107n.
rites, 109
Innate release mechanism, *see* I.R.M.
Inner world, 74, 80, 159, 160, 175
of archetypes, 126n.
images of, 159
and outer world, synthesis, 126n.

INDEX

Insight:
  intellectual, 69
  patient's, 69
Instinct(s), 1, 11, 28, 127–8, 173
  and archetypal images, 11, 24, 121
  in childhood, 109–10
  and collective unconscious, 2
  dynamism of, 28
  and mysticism, 24
  and neurophysiology, 14, 18
  and spirit, 28
  theory of, 18
  of reflex origin of, 13
Instinctive:
  behaviour, 13, 14, 21, 28, 121, 181
    in animals, 121
  nervous system and, 14
  neural pattern of, 13
  psychological mechanisms of, 12
  stimuli needed for, 12
  patterns,
    in animals, 28
    hierarchical nature of, 13
  processes, 90
Instinctual basis of life, 146
Integrate, 151, 153
Integration, 90, 99, 102, 113, 114, 117,
    125, 126, 131, 132, 134, 148ff., 160,
    190
  of the self, 127–8
  two kinds, 131
  see also Ego integration
Integrative processes, 147
Intelligence quotient, 189
Intercourse, dangerous forms of, 186
Interior world, see Inner world
Interpretation(s), 90, 96, 99, 100, 145,
    173, 174, 190, 194, 195
  attitude behind, 96
  as creative act, 100
  as defences, 100
  as expression of concern, 95
  need for, 190
  relieving anxiety, 96
  rules for, 100
  technique of, 67
  transference, 92, 99, 100, 168
  of unconscious process, 65, 174
Interruption in treatment, 84n.
Interview(s):
  analytic, 69
  content of, 190
  dynamics of, 189–90
  first, 172, 181, 188, 190, 193
    analysis of, 190ff.
  framework of, 100
  frequency, 68, 73
  with parents, 169–70
  therapeutic, 190

Introjection, 90
Introversion, 57
Intuition, 39, 47, 57, 58, 59, 138n.
  introverted, 58
I.R.M., 12, 121

'Jack and the Beanstalk', 173
Jackson, Hughlings, 3, 13, 17
Jacobi, J., 62, 72, 114n., 156
Jesus, 3, 53
Jung, C. G.: *passim*
  on analyst's personality, 63–4
  development of his views, 103
  on ego and self, 147
  an empiricist, 4
  individuation cases of, 87
  and interview frequency, 73, 83–4
  on mandala symbolism, 132
  on parents and children, 158, 161n.,
    166
  his patients, 85
  and the preconscious, 107
  on rhythmic activities in infants, 109–
    110
  on *scintillae*, 118–19
  on transference, 65–6, 70
  works by, quoted:
    'The Aims of Psychotherapy', 66,
      85, 101
    Answer to Job, 96
    *Collected Papers on Analytical Psy-
      chology*, 63
    'The Concept of the Collective Un-
      conscious', 2, 3, 4, 9
    *Contributions to Analytical Psycho-
      logy*, 11
    The Development of Personality, 104,
      105, 106, 108, 110, 129, 155,
      161
    'Fundamental Questions of Psycho-
      therapy', 103
    Gestaltungen des Unbewussten, 132n.
    'Instinct and the Unconscious', 11
    *Introduction to a Science of Mytho-
      logy*, 53, 197n.
    Modern Man in Search of a Soul,
      116n.
    The Practice of Psychotherapy, 33n.,
      62, 63, 65, 66, 69, 75, 83, 85, 89,
      99, 101, 102, 103, 138n.
    'Principles of Practical Psycho-
      therapy', 85
    'Problems of Modern Psycho-
      therapy', 69, 102
    'Psychic Conflicts in a Child', 104
    Psychological Types, 52, 54, 132,
      137n.
    Psychology and Alchemy, 59–60,
      132n., 142, 197n.
    Psychology and Religion, 7, 132n.

207

INDEX

Jung, C. G., works by—*contd.*
'The Psychology of the Transference', 62, 66, 79, 88, 99, 101, 138ff.
The Secret of the Golden Flower, 132n.
Seminars on Children's Dreams, 106
'Some Crucial Points in Psycho-Analysis', 63
'The Spirit of Psychology', 118, 119
'The Stages of Life', 116
Symbols of Transformation, 3, 18, 30, 82, 109, 151
'Synchronicity', 35
'The Theory of Psycho-analysis', 82
'Transformation Symbolism in the Mass', 116
Two Essays on Analytical Psychology, 7, 20, 22n., 182
'Über Mandalasymbolik', 132n.

Katha Upanishad, 144
Kellogg, Mrs Rhoda, 124–5, 133
Kepler, J., 23, 56
Kerenyi, C., 53, 54, 60, 118n.
Khunrath, H., 118
King and queen, alchemical, 139
Klein, Melanie, 167n., 177n.
Knowledge, collective and individual, 180
Krishna, 53
Kullervo, 53

Lamarck, 19
Learning:
conscious, 129
transmitted, 21
Leonardo da Vinci, 2–3
Lewis, E., 156, 159
Libidinal:
development, inner, 125
zones, preconscious, 112, 147
Libido, 8, 68, 72, 77, 107, 109, 175, 177
migrations of, 109
object-seeking or pleasure-seeking, 83n.
sexual, 109
theory, Fairbairn on, 83n.
Life:
symbolic, 54
theories of, 110
Linnaeus, 19
Localization:
relative, 17
of sensory stimulus, 15
Logic, 56
infantile, 127
Logos, 142
Lorenz, K, 12, 24, 26–7

Love, 162

Magic, protective, circle as, 137
Magician, 58–9, 60
Magna Mater, 161n.
see also Mother, Great
Man:
early, 20–1
evolution from ape-like ancestors, 20
myth-making, 31
Man of light, 142
Mana personalities, 107n., 117, 182
Mandala, 4, 113, 119, 124, 126, 132–3, 145, 147, 153
in children, 132–3
development of, 137–44
Marriage, 188ff., 198
brother-sister pairing in, 197
Masochistic feeling, 165
Massa confusa, 60
Masturbation, 109, 195
Mathematical thinking, 36
Mating:
behaviour, 12, 13
impulses, 12
Matriarchy, 31
Maturation, 81, 149
psychic, dreams and, 106
Mayer, Robert, 22n.
Mechthild of Magdeburg, 24–7, 54
Memory(-ies), 17n., 116
in children, 113n., 123, 196
repression of, 92
of whole self image, 150
Memory images, 92, 98
Memory traces, image and, 54
Mendel, Gregor, 10
Menstruation, and disease, 195
Mercurius, 60, 101
Metabole, 54–5
Metaphor, 56
Metman, Philip, 40n.
Meyer, Prof., 16n.
Middle age group, in children, 157, 159, 166
Mind, and body, dichotomy, 114
Mind pictures, 133
'Modern man', 65
Money-Kyrle, R. G., 90n., 98n.
Monster, 144
Mood, 59
Moody, R., 62, 84, 88, 89–90, 97
Morality, good and bad, 173
Moroney, M. J., 38n.
Mother:
analysis, of, 170, 172
archetypal, 174
bad, 179
dark aspect of, 145
disintegrating, fantasy of, 152

INDEX

fantasies about, 163
good and bad, 165
Great, 32, 33
as giant, 174n.
neurosis of, 170
personal, 161n.
projections of, 172
resistance to, 178
terrible, 151
Mother fixation, 179
Mother imago, 32
whole, 33
Mothers, two, delusion of, 3
Motor:
area, 15
system, 15
units, of nervous system, 14
Multiplication law, 37
Mutations, 10
Mystical experiences,
of Mechthild of Magdeburg, 24-5
quasi-, 22
validity of, 55
Mysticism:
and archetypal images, 24
consciousness in, 115
and instinct, 24
Myth(s), 4, 23, 54, 56, 102, 111, 115n.,
118, 119
analyst's, 102
comparative study of, 52
consciousness of meaning, 53
cosmic, 31, 118
a cultural form, 30-1
as expression of inner process, 54
and guilt feeling, 177
and infantile life of race, 30
matriarchal, 31-2
part of social structure, 31
requisite of primitive life, 31
and transference, 101
Myth-making, 30, 31
Mythologem, 53, 57, 60
definition, 53
Mythological:
forms, 33
images, 110
motives (themes), 4
analogy with children's dreams, 29
theme, of the impossible, 40
Mythology, 53, 101

Natural scientists, and theories, 35
Natural selection, 19-20, 21
Nervous system:
autonomic, 13
central, 13
hierarchy of, 14
Neumann, Erich, 22n., 23, 28, 32, 115n.
134n., 135, 150n., 151, 154, 156

Neuro-endocrine system, innate, 13
Neurology, ix
Neurophysiology, 18
electronic principles in, 16n.
Neurosis:
causal elements, 82
child's, 164
collective manifestation, 3
genesis of, 82
of mothers, 170
and two mothers theme, 3
Non-ego:
and ego, dichotomy, 114
sphere, 126n.
Normality or individual development,
65, 66
Null hypothesis, 37, 41
Rhine and, 42
synchronicity alternative to, 41
Numinosity:
of archetypal image, 59
of meaningful coincidence, 44
of unconscious images, 108
Numinosum, 2
Numinous:
experience, 8
images, 112, 127
Nurture:
and archetypal change, 28
cannot be source of archetypes, 9
culture and, 121
and nature, 3, 121
Nutrition, 109
Nutritional phase, 109, 110, 164
Nutritional zone, 109

Object(s):
aggressive, 176
archetypes and images as, 60
bad, 176, 182-3
and deintegrate, 120
external, 183
good, 183
and image, 52, 124
inner, 183
dangerous, 186
of ego, 131
and inner images, 56
part and whole, images and, 32
and subject, 120
and symbol, 55, 61
Object relations, in infancy, 123
Object seeking, 120, 121
Oedipus complex, 178
Old Wise Man, 76
Omnipotence:
feeling of, 145, 192
mother's sense of, 170
of thought, 144, 146
Ontogeny, 28-9, 32, 115n.

209

INDEX

Opposites, 147, 176, 177
  conjunction of, *see* union of
  thinking in, 144
  union of, 52, 60, 139, 145
  and formation of self, 138
Opus, alchemical, 138
Oral phase, 164
Order, 131
Organism, whole, 114
Original self, deintegrates and deintegration, 112, 127
Orpheus, Orphic cult, 118
Osiris, 152
Outer world, 160
  adaptation to, 126n.

Pain and pleasure, 176
Palaeontology, 19
Paracelsus, 120
Parakinesis, 40
Paralysis, hysterical, 162
Parapsychology, 35, 40
Parent(s):
  analysis of, 162
  analyst as, 81
  conflicts of, 161–2
  co-operation between, 196
  dreams projected on, 106
  and environment, 112
  external, 177
  fantasy of persecution by, 170
  identity of feeling between, 197
  image and concept of, 112
  infantilism in, 197
  inner, 177
  interviews with, 169
  real and fantasy relationship to, 182
  relationship between, 198
  responsibility of, 198
  treatment of, 156
  unconsciousness of, 108, 155–6, 171
  unconscious contents of, and children's dreams, 105
Parent imagos, 81, 182
  dramatization of, 85
  projected, 81, 102, 136
Participation mystique, 90, 108, 135, 150
  see also Identity, primitive
Passive therapy, 165
Patient-analyst relationship, *see* Analytic relationship
Patriarchal society, 31
Pauli, W., 22–3, 35n., 56
Perception(s), 12, 15, 42, 121–5
  and image, 54, 123
  inner, 52
  localization of, 15
  myth as, 53
  patient's, 79, 88–9
  symbolism and, 51

Persecution fantasy, 165, 170
Perseus, 147
Persona, analyst's, 63
Personal and collective experiences, distinction, 3
Personal Unconscious, *see* Unconscious
Personality(-ies):
  analyst's, *see* Analyst
  fragmentary, 168
  and image, 133
  integration of, 99
  patient's, distortion of, 71
  superordinate, 159
Persuasion, 192
Phallus, 139
Pharaohs, the, 3
Philo Judaeus, 10
Philosophy:
  of life, 72
  scientific, 3
Phylogeny, 28, 29, 32, 115n.
Physiology, ix
Piaget, J., 18, 122–3, 125, 165n.
P.K., 40
Plaut, A., 62, 98
Play, 122, 123, 129, 152, 166
  analogy with mythology, 29
  archetypes in, 4n., 187
  constructive, 153
  and deintegration, 119
  sex, 146
Pleasure, 109
  and pain, 176
Plutarch, 118n.
Pneuma, 2
Post-analysis period, 71, 87
Postural mechanism, tonic, 122
Preconscious, 98, 107–8, 111, 120
  centres, 112
  state, 125, 127, 129
Prediction, 36
  in Rhine's experiments, 42
Predisposition(s):
  innate, 128
  organized, 17
Pre-ego stage, 135
Presexual stage, 110
Prima materia, 59–60
Primal scene, fantasy of, 145
Primitive societies, 110
Primordial images, 8, 48, 181, 185
  of father, 161n.
  see also Archetypes
Probability, 37ff.
  empirical, 38
  mathematical, 39
  numerical definition, 38n.
  theory, 38
  true, 38
  see also Chance

INDEX

Progression, 108, 153, 159
and regression, 30
Projection(s), 67, 80, 88, 90, 91, 94, 97, 98, 100, 136, 148, 161n., 168, 172, 182
on analyst, unrealized, 73
basis of acting out, 78
archetypal, 98, 101
from child's unconscious, 160
counter-transference, 99
and counter-transference illusion, 91
dominates perception, 81
dramatizing transference, 81
fantastic, 94
of mother, 172
of parent images, 136
reintegration into individual, 102
of terrifying image, 150
true, 79
of unconscious contents, 102
Projection-perception scale, 79–80, 89
Projection screen, analyst as, 70, 103
Prometheus, 177
Psyche:
and body, 14
relation, 33–4
child's, 157, 161
and parents' unconscious, 108
collective, 106
fourfold structure, 132
Jung's model of, 57
mother's, 171
objective, 159
and Rhine's experiments, 42
and soma, 114
differentiation, 111, 114
and environment, 115
transpersonal objective, 84
unconscious, 8, 49
see also Archetypes
Psychiatry, ix
Psycho-analysis, 65, 77, 176
and frequency of treatment, 84
Jung's criticism of, 82
transference in, 66
Psychotherapy:
individual, 157
Jung and, 103
Ptolemy (astrologer), 40
Punishment, 167
Purpose, 17

Rain, 139
Rapport, 178, 196
Rationalism, 56
Read, Sir Herbert, 133
Reality:
adult, 111
and fantasy, matching, 151
inner and outer, 111
Reassurance, 151, 184

Rebirth:
motif of, 3
theories of, 110
Rebirth ritual, 3
Rebirth symbol, scarab as, 43
Recapitulation, 30, 31, 33
see Ontogeny; Phylogeny
Receptors, 14
Recognition, 125
Reflex(es), 123n.
conditioned, 13
innate, 13
Reflex:
apparatus, sensory motor, 14
arc, 14
mechanism(s), 12, 13, 18
Regression, 82, 116, 118, 136, 148, 151, 153, 164
artificial, 83
Regressive trends, bringing into consciousness, 100
Reincarnation, 111
Relationship:
analytical, see Analytical relationship
between parents, 198
child-parent, 111, 164, 166
dialectical, 97
human, transference, as, 88
interpersonal, 188
patient's personal, 65
personal, child's, 169
primitive form of, 99
Release mechanism, innate, 13, 124
Religion:
comparative, 101
and science, 56
and symbolic attitude, 55
Repetition compulsion, 82
Replacement activity, 78
Reporting, 74, 189
Repression, 50
Freud's theory of, 3
of memories, 92
Reproductive behaviour, 13
Resistance(s), 71, 74, 145, 163, 164, 165, 170
in analysts, 96
to imposed control, 196
to mother, 178
Reticular formation, 16n.
Reverberating circuits, 16
Rhine, J. B., 41–2
Rhythm, 18, 109–10
of integration-deintegration, 128
Rhythmic:
act, of suckling, 109
activity of brain cells, 'spontaneous', 18
movements, 13
in children, 109–10, 124

INDEX

Right-of-possession ceremony, 27
Rôles, playing, 187
Rosarium philosophorum, 138ff.
Russell, Bertrand, 38n., 55

Sampling, random, 40
Sandford, Mrs, 157n.
Scansion, 16, 16–17n.
Scarab, dream of, 43
Scepticism, scientific, 40
Schema(ta), 120ff.
  assimilatory, 122
  body, *see* Body Schema
  grasping, 122
  hearing, 122
  organized, 17
  represent reflex action, 123
  sucking, 123
  visual, 122
Schizophrenia, 118
  case of paranoid, 9
Science:
  and evolution of consciousness, 23
  and religion, 56
Scientific:
  knowledge, theory of, and synchro-
    nicity, 35
  theories,
    and mystical experiences, 22
    relation with facts, 35
Scintillae, 118, 120
Scott, R. D. C., 115n.
Scribbles, 124–5, 133, 135
  agressive, 135
Second Half of Life, 67, 116
Self, 60, 68, 97, 102, 107n., 115, 116–17,
  119, 128 *et passim*
  and analyst's syntonic reactions, 96
  archetypal experience of, 159
  boundaries of, 109
  in childhood, 112ff.
    and in individuation, 117
  and conscious discrimination, 147
  deintegrates and, 83, 119
  deintegration of, 137, 152
  and ego,
    in childhood, 131ff., 159
    united, 113, 150
  emergence of, 81
  formed by conjunction of opposites,
    138
  image(s) of, 137, 144–6
  in individuation and childhood, 116–17
  integrated, 152
  integrates and deintegrates, 97, 98,
    126, 128, 137
  integrates ego fragments, 126
  integration and disintegration of,
    127–8
  intelligible field of study, 131–2

Jung on the, 116–17
  as origin of ego, 116
  original, 115, 116, 120
  as original archetype, 112, 114
  prime mover in analytic process, 97
  relation to ego development, 83
  as source of danger to ego, 137
  symbolism of the, 116
  symbols, 87
  unconscious prefiguration of ego, 117
    147
'Self', 114
  bad, 169
  and environment, 128–9
    dichotomy, 114
Self-analysis, 87
Self-ego axis, 134, 154, 156
Sensation, 57, 59
Sense perception, *see* Perception
Sensory system, 14, 15
Sex:
  instincts, infantile, 127
  play, 146, 186
Sexual:
  activity, 109
  interest, 127
    interpretation of, 194
  zone, 109
Sexuality, 109, 110
  adult, 111
  and concept building, 111
  infantile, 82, 111
  and spiritual life, 111
Shadow, 107n., 117, 160
  figure, 175
  side, 168
'Shadow, living the', 77, 78
Shame, 183
Sherrington, Sir Charles, 13, 17n., 18n.
Silberer, H., 142
Similarities, recognition of, 127
Situation, actual, 82–3, 189
  found in transference, 100
Smith, Elliot, 21
Soma, and psyche, dichotomy, 114
  see also Body
Soul, 25, 27, 106, 119
  child's preconscious, 106, 161n.
  'Perils of the', 132, 135, 137
  projection of, 136
Space:
  and causality, 42
  unconscious and, 57
Species, organic development of, 29
Speech disorders, 16
Spencer, Herbert, 17
Spirit, 2
Spontaneity, 187
Statistics, 36, 38, 41
  logic of, 41

212

INDEX

Stein, L., 51, 52, 54, 62, 63, 78, 79, 134
  on counter-transference, 93
Stimuli, 12
  sensory, 13
  localization of, 15
  sign, 12, 13
Subject and object, distinction, 120
Subjective:
  and objective experiences, distinction, 3
  plane, 174
Sucking, pleasure in, 122
Suckling, 109
Suggestion, 9, 65
Suzuki, D. T., 144n.
Symbol(s), 53, 60
  and archetypal image, 53-4
  combines two opposites, 52
  conscious attitude and, 57
  derivation and definition, 51
  general significance, 7
  and image, 51ff.
  Jung's definition, 52, 58
  living, 55
  nature, 32
  tally as, 52
  transcendent function of, 60
  wholeness as a, 61
Symbolic image, natural history of, 7
Symbolism, 51, 131
  archetypal, 87
  of the self, 116
Synchronicity, 34, 35ff., 127n.
  acausal connecting principle, 36
  alternative to null hypothesis, 41
  and archetypes, 41, 47
  and chance, 36
  and Chinese culture, 49
  and consciousness, 47, 50
  defined, 35, 36
  incredibility of, 39
  Jung's experiment, 40
  meaningful coincidence, 35
  phenomena of, 40
Synthetic treatment, processes, 84, 87, 88, 131
Syntony, counter-transference, 91, 187

Team method, 189, 191
Technique(s), 90
  abandonment of, 65
  analyst's, 69
  archetypal reactions and, 64
  as defence, 76
  as inducing transference, 70
  patient's, 69
Temenos, 134
Teresa of Avila, St, 54
Testing:
  of analyst, 76
  of images, 110

Theories:
  of life, death, and rebirth, 110
  in psychology, 104
  scientific, 56
  abstract equivalent of archetypes, 56
Therapy, passive, 165
Thinking, 44, 57, 59
  defensive, 43
  see also Thought
Thought(s):
  abstract, and religion, 55-6
  and fantasy, differentiation, 111
  omnipotence of, 144, 146
  secret, 92-3
Threshold, conscious, lowering of, 98
Time:
  association in, 127
  and causality, 42
  unconscious and, 57
Tinbergen, N., 12, 13
Tom Thumb, 53
Totality, image of, 144
Toynbee, A. J., 132
Tradition, 21
  astrological, 40, 41
Transference, vii, 44, 50, 62ff., 101, 167
  and active imagination, 80
  ambivalent, 47
  analysis of, and distortion, 71
  archetypal, 75, 82, 182
  autonomous, 88
  bringing into consciousness, 99
  central place in analysis, 66
  in child analysis, 169
  in childhood, archetypes and, 181ff.
  collective, 68
  as container, 75
  conscious, situation in, 95
  dependent, 81-3, 85
  infantile, 87
  in individuation process, 65, 66
  interpreting, 99, 100, 168
  Jung and, 70, 103
  naturalness v. artificiality of, 70
  negative, 163
  objective, see transpersonal below
  personal and archetypal, 75
  personal aspect of, 88
  positive, 149, 185
  as projection, 79-80, 96
  projection theory of, 79
  reducing, 94-5
  sexual, 90
  social, 68
  technique induces, 70
  theory of archetypes and, 71
  transpersonal, 65, 68, 88, 89, 95
  and transpersonal objective psyche, 84
  and typology, 87
  in younger people, 68

213

INDEX

Transference analysis, and psycho-therapy, 65
Transference neurosis, 82
Transference situations, integrative action of self in, 126
Transformation, 178
  process of, 43, 77
  stage of, 192
Transition, images of, 107n.
Transpersonal, *see* Collective
Treatment, breaking off, 85
'Truth', and unconscious knowledge, 111
Type(s), 159

Unconscious, 57, 107–8, 116–17
  activity of archetypes in, 20
  analyst's relation to, 64, 89. 90
  archetypes organs of, 181
  child's, 182
  and conscious, 23, 46, 114, 177
  as dynamic unit, 17
  expression in images and myths, 4
  in family group, 172
  image of, 59
  investigation in analysis, 70
  mother's, 171
  origin of conscious ego, 104, 106
  personal and transpersonal (collective), 2, 64
  'personates', 168
  process, in transference, 96
  projected on to children, 172
  psychic activity, neurologists and, 16
  repressed personal, 2
  and repression, 3
  and symbol, 54
  and synchronicity, 50n.
  and transference, 64
  transpersonal, 2, 85
  see also Collective unconscious
Unconscious:
  functioning, 104
  knowledge, 152
  process, in alchemy and individuation, 143

Unconsciousness:
  of archetypes, 181
  mutual, 101
  as non-differentiation, 108
  of small child, 108
Unintegrated state, primary, in infancy, 114, 117, 118, 131
Unity, dissolving sense of, with universe, 45
Uroboros, 135
  see also Incest, uroboric

Value(s):
  conscious, good and bad as, 145
  feeling of, 138n.
Variations, structural, in species, 20
Vas hermeticum, 139
Visual images, 122
Vocational aims, *see* Aims

Water, of heaven and earth, 139ff.
Weismann, 10
Whitening process, 142
Whitmont, E., 83
Wholeness, 61, 115, 116, 131
  archetype of, 112
  image of, 114
  original, 120
  potential, 126n.
  transcending consciousness, 97
Wickes, Frances G., 62, 107n., 108, 129n., 155, 156
Wiener, 16n.
Winnicott, D. W., 114, 117, 120n.
Word association test, 63
Wolves, 26–8
Words, power, 180

Zen Buddhism, 115
Zeus, 147
Zone(s):
  anal, 83
  and analogic linkage, 112
  of body, 110
  nutritional, 109
  preconscious libidinal, 112, 147
  sexual, 109
Zueblin, J., 156, 159n.